JavaScript Mobile Application Development

Create neat cross-platform mobile apps using Apache
Cordova and jQuery Mobile

Hazem Saleh

BIRMINGHAM - MUMBAI

JavaScript Mobile Application Development

First published: October 2014

Production reference: 1161014

Published by Packt Publishing Ltd.
Livery Place
35 Livery Street
Birmingham B3 2PB, UK.

ISBN 978-1-78355-417-1

www.packtpub.com

Cover image by Neha Rajappan (neha.rajappan1@gmail.com)

Credits

Author
Hazem Saleh

Reviewers
Raymond, Xie Liming

Ranganadh Paramkusam

Juris Vecvanags

Commissioning Editor
Akram Hussain

Acquisition Editor
Richard Harvey

Content Development Editor
Madhuja Chaudhari

Technical Editor
Shashank Desai

Copy Editors
Sayanee Mukherjee

Karuna Narayanan

Project Coordinator
Rashi Khivansara

Proofreaders
Simran Bhogal

Maria Gould

Ameesha Green

Paul Hindle

Indexer
Hemangini Bari

Graphics
Abhinash Sahu

Production Coordinator
Adonia Jones

Cover Work
Adonia Jones

About the Author

Hazem Saleh has 10 years of experience in Java EE, mobile, and open source technologies. He has worked as a technical consultant for many clients in Europe (Sweden), North America (USA and Canada), South America (Peru), Africa (Egypt, Morocco, and Zambia), and Asia (Qatar, Kuwait, and KSA). He is an Apache committer and a person who has spent many years of his life writing open source software. Besides being the author of *JavaScript Unit Testing*, *Packt Publishing*, and *Pro JSF and HTML5: Building Rich Internet Components*, *Apress*, and the co-author of *The Definitive Guide to Apache MyFaces and Facelets*, *Apress*, he has also authored many technical articles. He is also a contributing author recognized by *developerWorks* and a technical speaker at both local and international conferences such as ApacheCon in North America, GeeCon, JSFDays, CONFESS in Vienna, and JavaOne in San Francisco, Moscow, and Shanghai. Hazem is now working for IBM Egypt as an advisory software engineer. He is a member of the IBM Mobile Global Center of Competency (CoC) and an IBM Certified Expert IT specialist (L2).

I would like to thank my wife, Naglaa, for supporting me while writing this book. She has always motivated me to continue this long journey until its end. I definitely dedicate this book to her with love and pleasure. I would also like to thank my wonderful kids, Nada (4-year-old girl) and Ali (1-year-old boy), for always making me happy. I would like to thank my mother, father, brother, and sister for understanding why I was not available during many weekends as I was writing this book. A special thanks to everyone in the Apache Cordova community for making the development of cross-platform mobile apps much less painful than it could be. Finally, I would like to thank all the technical reviewers and editors for improving the content of this book.

About the Reviewers

Raymond, Xie Liming is a software R&D expert with experience of over 16 years working in multiple IT domains, including networking, multimedia IP communication, insurance, telecom, and mobile apps/games.

Raymond holds a Master's degree in Science from Fudan University. He is also a PMI-certified Project Management Professional.

He has worked as a senior manager for Softfoundry Singapore, eBaoTech, and the Ericsson Shanghai R&D center, leading an R&D team working on enterprise- and carrier-class software. In December 2013, Raymond founded his own company, RjFun Technologies, that focuses on mobile apps/games and also produces reusable components for them.

He has rich experience in R&D management and is also a software expert with hands-on architecting and development skills. He is very active on GitHub and the Cordova/PhoneGap community, where his nickname is "floatinghotpot".

He now lives with his wife, Jenny, in Shanghai, China.

Ranganadh Paramkusam holds a degree in Computer Science and Engineering. He began his career developing cross-platform applications for iOS, Android, and BlackBerry using PhoneGap, Sencha, and AngularJS. He has developed more than 30 mobile applications. He later started working with native code such as iOS and Java to create PhoneGap plugins to bring the native UI/UX in hybrid mobile applications.

Ranganadh developed plugins using Google's Native Client (NaCl) and Portable Native Client (PNaCl) to give a desktop application performance to web applications and created browser extensions using Google APIs for Google Chrome and Firefox. His works include a web-based image editor, text editor (a replica of Adobe's Brackets application), web-based image editor using the HTML5 Canvas element to apply the enhance, filter, resize, and various other effects, and chat application using Node.js and MongoDB. He also created an algorithm that synthesizes words and gives responses made by string patterns, which match and are developed using Python.

Ranganadh acquired the Oracle Certified Associate (OCA) certificate in 2010 and also certified for the Python language from MIT in 2013. He was awarded with Techno Geek for the year 2012-13 and Emerging Performer of the year 2013-14 for his works.

He aims at linking JavaScript to low- and medium-level languages, and he works with the C++, Python, Objective-C, and Java languages. He is currently working as a senior programmer in the Center Of Excellence (COE) department in Hidden Brains Infotech Pvt. Ltd., India. He is active on GitHub, the PhoneGap community, and stack overflow.

I would like to thank my family and friends for their support while working on all this stuff.

Juris Vecvanags started his career in the IT field in the early '90s. During this time, he had a chance to work with a broad range of technologies and share his knowledge with Fortune 500 companies as well as private and government customers.

Before moving to Silicon Valley, he had a well-established web design company in Europe. He is currently working as a senior solutions engineer for Sencha Inc., helping customers write better apps both for desktop and emerging mobile platforms. When it comes to web technologies, his invaluable experience makes him a trusted advisor and competent reviewer.

Away from the office, you will find him speaking at Meetups in the San Francisco Bay area and Chicago. The topics include Node.js, ExtJs, and Sencha Touch. He is passionate about bleeding-edge technologies and everything related to JavaScript.

I would like to thank my family for their constant support while working on this book.

www.PacktPub.com

Support files, eBooks, discount offers, and more

For support files and downloads related to your book, please visit www.PacktPub.com.

Did you know that Packt offers eBook versions of every book published, with PDF and ePub files available? You can upgrade to the eBook version at www.PacktPub.com and as a print book customer, you are entitled to a discount on the eBook copy. Get in touch with us at service@packtpub.com for more details.

At www.PacktPub.com, you can also read a collection of free technical articles, sign up for a range of free newsletters and receive exclusive discounts and offers on Packt books and eBooks.

http://PacktLib.PacktPub.com

Do you need instant solutions to your IT questions? PacktLib is Packt's online digital book library. Here, you can search, access, and read Packt's entire library of books.

Why subscribe?

- Fully searchable across every book published by Packt
- Copy and paste, print, and bookmark content
- On demand and accessible via a web browser

Free access for Packt account holders

If you have an account with Packt at www.PacktPub.com, you can use this to access PacktLib today and view 9 entirely free books. Simply use your login credentials for immediate access.

Table of Contents

Preface

Mobile development is one of the hottest trends and an essentiality in today's software industry. As you might have noticed, almost every popular website today has its own equivalent mobile application version to allow its current users to access the website's functions from their mobiles and cater to a large number of users who don't have personal computers. Adding to this, with the powerful hardware specification and computing capability of today's smart phones, they have become real competitors to personal computers, and many people now prefer to use their smart phones for their daily activities (such as checking the current news, capturing videos and posting them on Facebook and YouTube, and checking e-mails), instead of using their personal computers.

Although developing mobile applications is a really interesting thing, it is worth mentioning that developing them on mobile platforms requires mobile developers to put in a lot of effort and have a wide skill set. For example, in order to develop a native mobile application on Android phones and tablets, the developer should be familiar with the Android SDK and Java programming language. In contrast, if there is a need to develop the same mobile application on iPhone and iPad devices, the mobile developer has to be familiar with Xcode and the Objective-C language. A developer on a Windows Phone, however, will require skills in .NET programming in order to develop an app.

Adding to the previous challenges, and as each mobile platform has its own philosophy of mobile application development, you will need to handle the different types of problems that you will face on every platform using different programming languages. For example, you might face a common problem when reimplementing your Android application logic (which is written using Java) on the Windows Phone 8 platform. The problem will most likely be that your code logic, which was sending an SMS directly from your application code without any interruptions, is not valid anymore, as in the Windows Phone platform, it is not allowed to send SMS messages from the application code without launching the default platform SMS application. This means that you will need to do this logic change in your new code, which is implemented using a different programming language (a .NET programming language in this case).

All of these challenges will cost you a huge amount of development and testing effort in order to develop an important mobile application that can work on many mobile platforms.

All of these previous facts and challenges offered me a great motive to write this book. This book is about how to efficiently develop mobile applications using common web technologies, such as HTML, CSS, and JavaScript. After finishing this book, you should be able to develop your mobile application on different mobile platforms using only JavaScript, without having to learn the native programming languages of every mobile platform. This will definitely reduce the development cost and effort of your cross-platform mobile application, as you will use only one popular programming language, which is JavaScript. Adding to this, using a single popular programming language to handle the different problem types of every mobile platform will allow handling these problems to be in a centralized place in the code. This increases the readability and maintainability of your mobile application code across mobile platforms.

In order to achieve this mission, this book focuses on Apache Cordova, a platform that uses HTML, CSS, and JavaScript to build mobile applications. Apache Cordova offers a set of APIs that allow the mobile application developer to access native mobile functions, which will be covered in more detail in *Chapter 1, An Introduction to Apache Cordova*.

The Apache Cordova project was originally known as PhoneGap. The PhoneGap project was started in 2008 by a company called Nitobi, with the goal to simplify cross-platform mobile development using a team of mobile developers. However, this framework supported only one platform: Apple iPhone. Fortunately, it then added Android and BlackBerry support.

In 2009, this project won the People's Choice Award at O'Reilly Media's 2009 Web 2.0 Conference, with the framework being used to develop many applications since then. The PhoneGap team continued working hard on the project to support more mobile platforms and enhance the project APIs.

In 2011, Adobe announced the acquisition of Nitobi, and the project contributed to Apache Software Foundation, first called Apache Callback and later renamed to Apache Cordova. Interestingly enough, Cordova was the name of the street where the Nitobi offices were located. In this book, Apache Cordova is the project that will be discussed.

In order to develop neat-looking mobile applications, this book also utilizes jQuery Mobile. jQuery Mobile is one of the best mobile web application frameworks, and it allows the web developer to develop web applications that are mobile friendly.

Finally, this book is a practical guide for web developers who need to develop interactive mobile applications using their current skill set. If you are a native mobile application developer who wants to develop your mobile applications in much less time and effort using JavaScript and Apache Cordova, you will also find this book to be incredibly useful.

What this book covers

Chapter 1, An Introduction to Apache Cordova, teaches you what Apache Cordova is and the differences between mobile web, mobile hybrid, and mobile native applications. You will also know why we should use Apache Cordova, along with the current Apache Cordova architecture, and finally, the chapter offers an overview of the Apache Cordova APIs.

Chapter 2, Developing Your First Cordova Application, explains how to develop, build, and deploy your first Sound Recorder mobile application on the Android platform.

Chapter 3, Apache Cordova Development Tools, explains how to configure your Android, iOS, and Windows Phone development environments. You will also learn how to support and run your Sound Recorder mobile application on both iOS and Windows Phone 8 platforms.

Chapter 4, Cordova API in Action, dives deep into the Apache Cordova API, and you will see it in action. You will learn how to work with the Cordova accelerometer, camera, compass, connection, contacts, device, geolocation, globalization, and InAppBrowser APIs by exploring the code of the Cordova Exhibition app. The Cordova Exhibition app is designed and developed to show complete usage examples of the Apache Cordova core plugins. The Cordova Exhibition app supports Android, iOS, and Windows Phone 8.

Chapter 5, Diving Deeper into the Cordova API, continues to dive into the Apache Cordova API by exploring the remaining main features of the Cordova Exhibition app. You will learn how to work with the Cordova media, file, capture, notification, and storage APIs. You will also learn how to utilize the Apache Cordova events in your Cordova mobile app.

Chapter 6, Developing Custom Cordova Plugins, dives deep into Apache Cordova and lets you create your own custom Apache Cordova plugin on the three most popular mobile platforms: Android, which uses the Java programming language, iOS, which uses the Objective-C programming language, and Windows Phone 8, which uses the C# programming language.

Chapter 7, Unit Testing the Cordova App's Logic, explains how to develop JavaScript unit tests for your Cordova app logic. You will learn the basics of the Jasmine JavaScript unit testing framework and understand how to use Jasmine in order to test both the synchronous and asynchronous JavaScript code. You will learn how to utilize Karma as a powerful JavaScript test runner in order to automate the running of your developed Jasmine tests. You will also learn how to generate the test and code coverage reports from your developed tests. Finally, you will learn how to fully automate your JavaScript tests by integrating your developed tests with Continuous Integration tools.

Chapter 8, Applying it All – the Mega App, explores how to design and develop a complete app (Mega App) using the Apache Cordova and jQuery Mobile APIs. Mega App is a memo utility that allows users to create, save, and view audible and visual memos on the three most popular mobile platforms (Android, iOS, and Windows Phone 8). In order to create this utility, Mega App uses jQuery Mobile to build the user interface and Apache Cordova to access the device information, camera, audio (microphone and speaker), and filesystem. In this chapter, you will learn how to create a portable app that respects the differences between Android, iOS, and Windows Phone 8.

What you need for this book

You should have basic knowledge of the common web technologies (HTML, CSS, and JavaScript). It is also highly recommended that you learn the basics of jQuery and jQuery Mobile in order to be familiar with the code examples. A quick introduction to jQuery and jQuery Mobile can be found at http://www.w3schools.com/jquery/ and http://www.w3schools.com/jquerymobile/, respectively.

Who this book is for

If you are a web developer, then reading this book to learn how to develop mobile applications using Apache Cordova is a great option for you, as you don't have to spend extra time learning JavaScript, CSS, and HTML before reading this book.

If you are a native mobile developer, then spending some time learning about the common web technologies, namely JavaScript, CSS, and HTML, will add great value and impact to your work. After acquiring these skills, along with reading this book to learn about Apache Cordova, you will be able to develop cross-platform mobile application(s) in much less time and effort as compared to the time and effort you will need to spend in order to develop the same application(s) on every platform using the native programming languages.

Conventions

In this book, you will find a number of styles of text that distinguish between different kinds of information. Here are some examples of these styles and an explanation of their meaning.

Code words in text, database table names, folder names, filenames, file extensions, pathnames, dummy URLs, user input, and Twitter handles are shown as follows: "This js directory also includes the common.js file that includes the common app utilities."

A block of code is set as follows:

```xml
<?xml version='1.0' encoding='utf-8'?>
<widget id="com.jsmobile.soundrecorder" version="0.0.1"
xmlns="http://www.w3.org/ns/widgets" xmlns:cdv="http://cordova.apache.
org/ns/1.0">
```

```
<name>SoundRecorder</name>
<description>
        A sample Apache Cordova application that responds
to the deviceready event.
</description>
<author email="dev@cordova.apache.org" href="http://cordova.io">
        Apache Cordova Team
</author>
<content src="index.html" />
<access origin="*" />
</widget>
```

When we wish to draw your attention to a particular part of a code block, the relevant lines or items are set in bold:

```
(function() {

    var memoManager = MemoManager.getInstance();
    var recInterval;

    $(document).on("pageinit", "#memoCapture", function(e) {
        $("#saveMemo").on("tap", function(e) {
            e.preventDefault();

            var memoItem = new MemoItem({
                "type": $("#mtype").val(),
                "title": $("#title").val() || "Untitled",
                "desc": $("#desc").val() || "",
                "location": $("#location").val() || "",
                "mtime":  $("#mtime").html() || new Date().
toLocaleString(),
                "id": $("#mid").val() || null
            });

            memoManager.saveMemo(memoItem);

            $.mobile.changePage("#memoList");
        });

        // ...
    });
})();
```

Any command-line input or output is written as follows:

```
> sudo npm install -g cordova
```

New terms and **important words** are shown in bold. Words that you see on the screen, in menus or dialog boxes for example, appear in the text like this: "Once you are done, click on the **Stop Recording** button to finish recording."

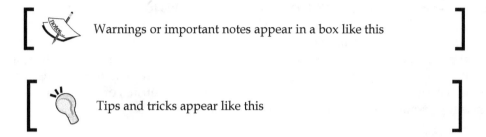

Warnings or important notes appear in a box like this

Tips and tricks appear like this

Reader feedback

Feedback from our readers is always welcome. Let us know what you think about this book—what you liked or may have disliked. Reader feedback is important for us to develop titles that you really get the most out of.

To send us general feedback, simply send an e-mail to feedback@packtpub.com, and mention the book title through the subject of your message.

If there is a topic that you have expertise in and you are interested in either writing or contributing to a book, see our author guide on www.packtpub.com/authors.

Customer support

Now that you are the proud owner of a Packt book, we have a number of things to help you to get the most from your purchase.

Downloading the example code

You can download the example code files for all Packt books you have purchased from your account at http://www.packtpub.com. If you purchased this book elsewhere, you can visit http://www.packtpub.com/support and register to have the files e-mailed directly to you.

Errata

Although we have taken every care to ensure the accuracy of our content, mistakes do happen. If you find a mistake in one of our books—maybe a mistake in the text or the code—we would be grateful if you would report this to us. By doing so, you can save other readers from frustration and help us improve subsequent versions of this book. If you find any errata, please report them by visiting http://www.packtpub. com/support, selecting your book, clicking on the **errata submission form** link, and entering the details of your errata. Once your errata are verified, your submission will be accepted and the errata will be uploaded to our website, or added to any list of existing errata, under the Errata section of that title.

Piracy

Piracy of copyright material on the Internet is an ongoing problem across all media. At Packt, we take the protection of our copyright and licenses very seriously. If you come across any illegal copies of our works, in any form, on the Internet, please provide us with the location address or website name immediately so that we can pursue a remedy.

Please contact us at copyright@packtpub.com with a link to the suspected pirated material.

We appreciate your help in protecting our authors, and our ability to bring you valuable content.

Questions

You can contact us at questions@packtpub.com if you are having a problem with any aspect of the book, and we will do our best to address it.

1
An Introduction to Apache Cordova

In this chapter, we will discover the world of Apache Cordova and cover the following topics:

- What Apache Cordova is
- The differences between the different mobile development approaches (mobile web, hybrid mobile, and native mobile applications)
- Why you should use Apache Cordova to develop your mobile applications
- The basics of Apache Cordova architecture

Finally, we will have a quick overview of the current APIs of Apache Cordova 3.

What is Apache Cordova?

The Apache Cordova project is an Apache open source project that targets the creation of native mobile applications using common web technologies such as **HyperText Markup Language (HTML)**, **Cascading Style Sheets (CSS)**, and JavaScript. It offers a set of JavaScript APIs, which provide access to a number of natively built core plugins. Cordova offers many core APIs, some of which grant the ability to perform the following:

- Process the device contact lists
- Process files on the device storage
- Capture a photo using the device camera
- Get a photo from the device gallery
- Record voice using the device microphone

- Get device direction using the device compass
- Retrieve the device locale
- Find out the device location
- Get the device motion
- Get the device connection information

Cordova supports a wide variety of different mobile platforms such as:

- Android
- iOS
- Windows platform:
    - Windows Phone 7 (this support will be removed soon in Cordova Version 3.7)
    - Windows Phone 8
    - Windows 8
- BlackBerry
- Tizen
- Web OS
- Firefox OS
- Bada
- Ubuntu

The Apache Cordova official API documentation is at `http://docs.cordova.io`.

You can also refer to the following GitHub repositories to find the source code of Apache Cordova implementations on the different platforms:

- Cordova for Android (`https://github.com/apache/cordova-android`)
- Cordova for iOS (`https://github.com/apache/cordova-ios`)
- Cordova for Windows 8 (`https://github.com/apache/cordova-wp8`)
- Cordova for BlackBerry (`https://github.com/apache/cordova-blackberry`)
- Cordova for Tizen (`https://github.com/apache/cordova-tizen`)
- Cordova for Web OS (`https://github.com/apache/cordova-webos`)

- Cordova for Firefox OS (`https://github.com/apache/cordova-firefoxos`)
- Cordova for Bada (`https://github.com/apache/cordova-bada`)
- Cordova for Ubuntu (`https://github.com/apache/cordova-ubuntu`)

You will find it very useful to know about GitHub, which is a web-based hosting service for software development projects that use the Git revision control system. GitHub offers both paid plans for private repositories and free accounts for open source projects. The site was launched in 2008 by Tom Preston-Werner, Chris Wanstrath, and PJ Hyett.

The differences between mobile web, hybrid mobile, and native mobile applications

It is very important to understand the differences between mobile web, hybrid mobile, and native mobile applications. Mobile web application(s) can be accessed using the web browser and are designed to be responsive. Responsive means that they can adapt their views in order to be displayed properly on different resolutions of mobile and tablet devices. Mobile web applications usually require you to be online in order to use them. They are not real mobile native applications, although they might have the same look and feel as mobile native applications that use the CSS technology. Mobile web applications are, in fact, not uploaded to app stores and do not have the same physical formats of the platform native mobile applications. They use limited native features of the mobile device, such as geolocation and storage features.

Although hybrid and native mobile applications have the same physical formats, they are developed using totally different technologies. Hybrid mobile applications are developed using common web technologies (HTML, CSS, and JavaScript), while native mobile applications are developed using the mobile platform programming language (for example, Java for Android, Objective-C for iOS, and .NET programming language(s) for Windows Phone).

If you are a native mobile application developer, then in order to develop a single native application that can work on the different mobile platforms, you will need to develop your application on one platform and then reimplement its logic on other platforms. Reimplementing the same logic on every platform that you have to support is a pain. This is because you will need to use the mobile platform programming language and handle different types of problems, which you will face on every platform.

Hybrid applications have the great advantage of allowing you to use the same code base (which consists of your HTML, CSS, and JavaScript code) for the different platforms of your application. This means that you write your application code once, and then, you can run it everywhere. Of course, you might need to do specific changes on every platform, but in the end, these changes are mostly minimal. Adding to this advantage, all of your application logic is implemented using a single and neat programming language, which is JavaScript.

The time taken to develop hybrid mobile applications, which run across many mobile platforms, will definitely be shorter. Furthermore, the required resources to implement a hybrid mobile project will be minimized compared to developing native mobile applications. This is because hybrid applications use a unified programming language (JavaScript), while native mobile applications use many non-unified programming languages (such as Objective-C, Java, and C#), which, by definition, require a larger team of developers with different skill sets.

Finally, it is worth mentioning that native mobile applications might be a little bit faster than hybrid applications (assuming that they are implementing the same set of requirements), because native applications are compiled and native code is optimized. However, applying the common best practices in your hybrid applications can definitely increase your application's performance to be as close as the native application. In this book, you will learn how to boost the performance of your hybrid mobile application using Apache Cordova and jQuery Mobile.

If you take a look at the following table, you will find that it summarizes the differences between the three types of mobile applications:

	Mobile web	Hybrid application	Native application
Uploaded to app store	No	Yes	Yes
Used technologies	JavaScript, CSS, and HTML		The native programming language of the platform
Complexity	Normal	Normal	High
Cross-platform mobiles support	Yes	Yes	No
Device native features	Partial	Full (thanks to Hybrid application frameworks such as Apache Cordova).	Full
Performance (assuming following best practices)	Very good		Excellent

This table summarizes the key differences between mobile web, hybrid mobile, and native mobile applications.

 Apache Cordova is currently one of the most popular frameworks for building Hybrid applications.

From the developers' perspective, if you are a web developer, then creating hybrid applications using Apache Cordova is a great option for you as you will not have to spend time learning JavaScript, CSS, and HTML. Using your existing skill set with Apache Cordova allows you to develop cross-platform mobile applications in less time.

If you are a native developer, then spending some time learning the common web technologies will add great value and have an impact on your work. This is because after acquiring these skills along with Apache Cordova, you will be able to develop cross-platform mobile application(s) in less time and effort compared to the time and effort you would spend in order to develop the same application(s) on every platform using native programming languages.

Why you should use Cordova

In order to understand the importance of using Apache Cordova, you first need to understand the current challenges of mobile development, which are summarized as follows:

- Every mobile platform has its own programming philosophy
- Every mobile platform has its own set of unique problems
- Developing, testing, and maintaining native application(s) on different mobile platforms is expensive

One of the biggest challenges of current mobile development is that every mobile platform has its own programming philosophy. There are various programming languages and tools that are required in order to develop mobile applications on the different platforms. For example, if you want to develop a native mobile application on Android, you will need to use Java as the programming language and Eclipse or IntelliJ (or another equivalent Java IDE) as an **Integrated Development Environment (IDE)**. On the other hand, if you want to develop a native mobile application in iOS, you will need to use Objective-C as the programming language and Xcode or JetBrains AppCode as the programming IDE. Finally, if you want to develop a Windows platform mobile application, you will need to use a .NET programming language and Visual Studio as the IDE.

As a result of this previous challenge, developing, testing and maintaining a single application that has different implementations on mobile platforms is really hard and costly. You will have many code bases that are usually inconsistent, because every code base will be written in a different language by developers from different backgrounds. This is because it is really hard to find a single developer who is aware of all of these programming languages and tools.

 Using an IDE to develop mobile applications is not mandatory. However, it is recommended as it speeds up the process of application development and testing.

Adding to these challenges, handling the incompatible behaviors of mobile platforms is a challenge that cannot be ignored. One of the problems that you might face when you develop your native Android application on iOS is that you cannot send SMS messages directly using the platform API without launching the native platform SMS application to the user. On the other hand, in Android, you can send SMS messages using the platform API directly from your application code. This means that you will have the burden of not only implementing your application logic on the different platforms, but you might also need to implement different workarounds using different programming languages in order to have a consistent behavior of your application as much as you can across the mobile platforms.

Using Apache Cordova will reduce the complexity of these challenges. It will give you the ability to use a single programming language (JavaScript) to write your application on the different mobile platforms; you won't need to have a big set of programming languages anymore after using Apache Cordova. Apache Cordova gives you the ability to have a common code base for all of the implementations of your application on the different mobile platforms. This means that the complexity of developing, testing, and maintaining your mobile application will be greatly reduced.

Having a single code base that is developed using JavaScript gives a great flexibility for mobile developers to handle the unique problems of every mobile platform. This puts everything neatly in a centralized place in the code. This makes your application code more readable and maintainable.

Cordova architecture

The following diagram includes the main components of an Apache Cordova application (HTML, CSS, and JavaScript files). It can also contain helper files (such as application's JSON resource bundle files). Here, HTML files include JavaScript and CSS files. In order to access a device's native feature, JavaScript application objects (or functions) call Apache Cordova APIs.

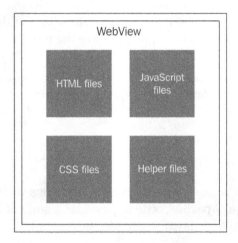

Apache Cordova creates a single screen in the native application; this screen contains only a single WebView that consumes the available space on the device screen. Apache Cordova uses the native application's WebView in order to load the application's HTML and its related JavaScript and CSS files.

It is important to note that WebView is a component that is used to display a web page or content (basically HTML) in the application window. We can simply say that it is an embedded mobile web browser inside your native application that allows you to display the web content.

When the application launches, Apache Cordova loads the application's default startup page (usually `index.html`) in the application's WebView and then passes the control to the WebView, allowing the user to interact with the application. Application users can interact with the application by doing many things such as entering data in input fields, clicking on action buttons, and viewing results in the application's WebView.

Thanks to this technique and because WebView is a native component that provides web content rendering, users feel that they are interacting with a native application screen if the application's CSS is designed to have the mobile platform look and feel.

WebView has an implementation in all the major mobile platforms. For example, in Android, WebView refers to the `android.webkit.WebView` class. In iOS, however, it refers to the `UIWebView` class that belongs to the `System/Library/Frameworks/UIKit` framework. In the Windows Phone platform, meanwhile, it refers to the `WebView` class that belongs to the `Windows.UI.Xaml.Controls` classes.

In order to allow you to access a mobile's native functions such as audio recording or camera photo capture, Apache Cordova provides a suite of JavaScript APIs that developers can use from their JavaScript code, as shown in the following diagram:

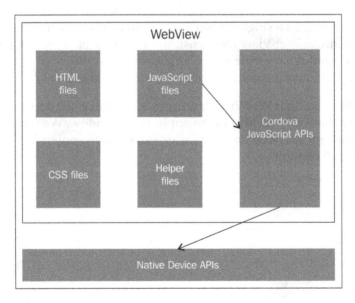

The calls to Apache Cordova JavaScript APIs are translated to the native device API calls using a special bridge layer. In Apache Cordova, the device native APIs are accessed from Apache Cordova plugins.

 You will learn how to develop your own custom Cordova plugin in *Chapter 6, Developing Custom Cordova Plugins.*

The beautiful thing behind this approach is that you can use a unified API interface in order to perform a specific native function (such as camera photo capturing or audio recording) transparently across the various mobile platforms. It is important to note that in order to perform these native functions as a native developer, you will need to call completely different native APIs that are usually implemented using different native programming languages. All of the Cordova JavaScript-unified APIs and their corresponding native code implementations are implemented using plugins. We will illustrate Cordova plugins in much more detail in *Chapter 6, Developing Custom Cordova Plugins.*

If you are interested to know what will happen when a call is performed to a Cordova JavaScript API, then we can take a look at a complete example for a Cordova API call under Android and Windows Phone platforms. In order to get a complete picture, you simply call the following Cordova JavaScript API:

```
navigator.camera.getPicture(onSuccess, onFail, { quality: 50,
    destinationType: Camera.DestinationType.DATA_URL
});

function onSuccess(imageData) {
    var image = document.getElementById('myImage');
    image.src = "data:image/jpeg;base64," + imageData;
}

function onFail(message) {
    alert('Failed because: ' + message);
}
```

As shown in preceding code snippet, a simple call to the getPicture() method of the camera object is performed with the following three parameters:

- onSuccesscallback: This parameter is called if the getPicture operation succeeds.

- onFailcallback: This parameter is called if the getPicture operation fails.

- { quality: 50, destinationType: Camera.DestinationType. DATA_URL }: This is a JavaScript object that contains the configuration parameters. In our example, only the two parameters, quality, which refers to the quality of the output picture (it should be a value from 0 to 100), and destinationType, which refers to the format of the return value, are specified. It can have one of the three values: DATA_URL, which means that the format of the returned image will be Base64-encoded string, FILE_URI, which means that the image file URI will be returned, or NATIVE_URI, which refers to the image native URI.

As we set destinationType to Camera.DestinationType.DATA_URL, the parameter of onSuccess will represent the Base-64 encoded string of the captured image.

This simple call to the getPicture() method of the camera object calls the following Android Java native code. Please note that this code is the actual code for the Apache Cordova Camera plugin Version 3. If you are a native Android developer, then the following two code snippets will look very familiar to you:

```
public void takePicture(int returnType, int encodingType) {
    // Code is omitted for simplicity ...

    // Display camera
    Intent intent = new Intent("android.media.action.IMAGE_CAPTURE");

    // Specify file so that large image is captured and returned
    File photo = createCaptureFile(encodingType);

    intent.putExtra(android.provider.MediaStore.EXTRA_OUTPUT, Uri.
fromFile(photo));
    this.imageUri = Uri.fromFile(photo);

    if (this.cordova != null) {
        this.cordova.startActivityForResult((CordovaPlugin) this,
intent, (CAMERA + 1) * 16 + returnType + 1);
    }
}
```

As shown in the previous code, in order to open a camera in an Android device, you need to start the `"android.media.action.IMAGE_CAPTURE"` intent and receive the result back using the `startActivityForResult()` API of the Android `Activity` class. In order to receive the image capture intent result in Android, your Android `Activity` class needs to implement the `onActivityResult()` callback, as shown in the following Apache Cordova Android Camera plugin code:

```
public void onActivityResult(int requestCode, int resultCode, Intent
intent) {
    // Get src and dest types from request code
    int srcType = (requestCode / 16) - 1;
    int destType = (requestCode % 16) - 1;
    int rotate = 0;

    // If CAMERA
    if (srcType == CAMERA) {

        // If image available
        if (resultCode == Activity.RESULT_OK) {
            // ... Code is omitted for simplicity ...

            Bitmap bitmap = null;
            Uri uri = null;

            // If sending base64 image back
            if (destType == DATA_URL) {
                bitmap = getScaledBitmap(FileHelper.
stripFileProtocol(imageUri.toString()));

                // ... Code is omitted for simplicity ...

                this.processPicture(bitmap);
            }

            // If sending filename back
            else if (destType == FILE_URI || destType == NATIVE_
URI) {
                if (this.saveToPhotoAlbum) {
                    Uri inputUri = getUriFromMediaStore();
```

```
                    //Just because we have a media URI doesn't
    mean we have a real file, we need to make it
                    uri = Uri.fromFile(new File(FileHelper.
    getRealPath(inputUri, this.cordova)));
                } else {
                    uri = Uri.fromFile(new File(DirectoryManager.
    getTempDirectoryPath(this.cordova.getActivity()), System.
    currentTimeMillis() + ".jpg"));
                }

                if (uri == null) {
                    this.failPicture("Error capturing image - no
    media storage found.");
                }

                // ... Code is omitted for simplicity ...
                // Send Uri back to JavaScript for viewing image
                this.callbackContext.success(uri.toString());
            }

            // ... Code is omitted for simplicity ...
        } catch (IOException e) {
            e.printStackTrace();
            this.failPicture("Error capturing image.");
        }
    }

    // If cancelled
    else if (resultCode == Activity.RESULT_CANCELED) {
        this.failPicture("Camera cancelled.");
    }

    // If something else
    else {
        this.failPicture("Did not complete!");
    }
    }
}
```

If the camera capture operation succeeds, then resultCode == Activity.RESULT_
OK will be true, and if the user requires the result of the captured image as a Base-
64 encoded string, then the captured bitmap image is retrieved and processed in
the processPicture(bitmap) method. As shown in the following code snippet,
processPicture(bitmap) compresses the bitmap image and then converts it to a byte
array, which is encoded to Base-64 array. This is then finally converted to a string that
is returned to the JavaScript Cordova client using this.callbackContext.success().
We will illustrate Android CallbackContext in more detail later in this book.

If the user requires the result of the captured image as a file or native URI string, then the file URI of the image file is retrieved and sent to the JavaScript Cordova client using `this.callbackContext.success()`.

```
public void processPicture(Bitmap bitmap) {
    ByteArrayOutputStream jpeg_data = new ByteArrayOutputStream();
    try {
        if (bitmap.compress(CompressFormat.JPEG, mQuality, jpeg_data))
{
            byte[] code = jpeg_data.toByteArray();
            byte[] output = Base64.encode(code, Base64.DEFAULT);
            String js_out = new String(output);
            this.callbackContext.success(js_out);
            js_out = null;
            output = null;
            code = null;
        }
    } catch (Exception e) {
        this.failPicture("Error compressing image.");
    }
    jpeg_data = null;
}
```

> In Android native development, an Android `Activity` class is generally a thing that the user can do. The `Activity` class is also responsible for the creation of a window for you in which you can place your **User Interface (UI)** while using the `setContentView()` API. An Android `Intent` is an abstract description of an operation to be performed so that it can be used with `startActivity` or `startActivityForResult` to launch an activity, as shown in the previous example of Camera photo capturing.

If you are using Microsoft Windows Platform 7 or 8, for example, the call to the `getPicture()` method of the `camera` object will call the following Windows Phone C# native code. Please note that this code is the actual code for Apache Cordova Camera Windows Phone plugin. If you are a native Windows Phone developer, the next two code snippets will look very familiar to you:

```
CameraCaptureTask cameraTask;

public void takePicture(string options)
{
    // ... Code is omitted for simplifying things ...

    if (cameraOptions.PictureSourceType == CAMERA)
    {
```

```
        cameraTask = new CameraCaptureTask();
        cameraTask.Completed += onCameraTaskCompleted;
        cameraTask.Show();
    }

    // ... Code is omitted for simplifying things ...
}
```

As shown in the preceding code, in order to open a camera in a Windows Phone device, you need to create an instance of `CameraCaptureTask` and call the `Show()` method. In order to receive the image capture result on the Windows Phone platform, you need to define an event handler that will be executed once the camera task completes. In the previous code, `onCameraTaskCompleted` is the event handler that will be executed once the camera task completes. The following code snippet shows the `onCameraTaskCompleted` handler code with its helper methods:

```
public void onCameraTaskCompleted(object sender, PhotoResult e)
{
    // ... Code is omitted for simplifying things ...
    switch (e.TaskResult)
    {
        case TaskResult.OK:
            try
            {
                string imagePathOrContent = string.Empty;

                if (cameraOptions.DestinationType == FILE_URI)
                {
                    // Save image in media library
                    if (cameraOptions.SaveToPhotoAlbum)
                    {
                        MediaLibrary library = new MediaLibrary();
                        Picture pict = library.SavePicture(e.
OriginalFileName, e.ChosenPhoto); // to save to photo-roll ...
                    }

                    int orient = ImageExifHelper.
getImageOrientationFromStream(e.ChosenPhoto);
                    int newAngle = 0;

                    // ... Code is omitted for simplifying things ...
```

```
                    Stream rotImageStream = ImageExifHelper.
RotateStream(e.ChosenPhoto, newAngle);

                    // we should return stream position back after
saving stream to media library
                    rotImageStream.Seek(0, SeekOrigin.Begin);

                    WriteableBitmap image = PictureDecoder.
DecodeJpeg(rotImageStream);

                    imagePathOrContent = this.
SaveImageToLocalStorage(image, Path.GetFileName(e.OriginalFileName));
                }
                else if (cameraOptions.DestinationType == DATA_URL)
                {
                    imagePathOrContent = this.GetImageContent(e.
ChosenPhoto);
                }
                else
                {
                    // TODO: shouldn't this happen before we launch
the camera-picker?
                    DispatchCommandResult(new
PluginResult(PluginResult.Status.ERROR, "Incorrect option:
destinationType"));
                    return;
                }

                DispatchCommandResult(new PluginResult(PluginResult.
Status.OK, imagePathOrContent));

            }
            catch (Exception)
            {
                DispatchCommandResult(new PluginResult(PluginResult.
Status.ERROR, "Error retrieving image."));
            }
            break;

        // ... Code is omitted for simplifying things ...
    }
}
```

If the camera capture operation succeeds, then e.TaskResult == TaskResult. OK will be true, and if the user requires the result of the captured image as a Base-64 encoded string, then the captured image is retrieved and processed in the GetImageContent(stream) method. The GetImageContent(stream) function, which is shown in the following code snippet, converts the image to a Base-64 encoded string that is returned to the JavaScript Cordova client using the DispatchCommandResult() method. We will illustrate the DispatchCommandResult() method in more detail later on in this book.

If the user requires the result of the captured image as a file URI string, then the file URI of the image file is retrieved using the SaveImageToLocalStorage() method (whose implementation is shown in the following code snippet) and is then sent to the JavaScript Cordova client using DispatchCommandResult():

```
private string GetImageContent(Stream stream)
{
    int streamLength = (int)stream.Length;
    byte[] fileData = new byte[streamLength + 1];
    stream.Read(fileData, 0, streamLength);

    //use photo's actual width & height if user doesn't provide
width & height
    if (cameraOptions.TargetWidth < 0 &&
cameraOptions.TargetHeight < 0)
    {
        stream.Close();
        return Convert.ToBase64String(fileData);
    }
    else
    {
        // resize photo
        byte[] resizedFile = ResizePhoto(stream, fileData);
        stream.Close();
        return Convert.ToBase64String(resizedFile);
    }
}

private string SaveImageToLocalStorage(WriteableBitmap image,
string imageFileName)
{
    // ... Code is omitted for simplifying things ...
```

```
    var isoFile =
IsolatedStorageFile.GetUserStoreForApplication();
    if (!isoFile.DirectoryExists(isoFolder))
    {
        isoFile.CreateDirectory(isoFolder);
    }


    string filePath = System.IO.Path.Combine("///" + isoFolder +
"/", imageFileName);

    using (var stream = isoFile.CreateFile(filePath))
    {
        // resize image if Height and Width defined via options
        if (cameraOptions.TargetHeight > 0 && cameraOptions.
TargetWidth > 0)
        {
            image.SaveJpeg(stream, cameraOptions.TargetWidth,
cameraOptions.TargetHeight, 0, cameraOptions.Quality);
        }
        else
        {
            image.SaveJpeg(stream, image.PixelWidth,
image.PixelHeight, 0, cameraOptions.Quality);
        }
    }

    return new Uri(filePath, UriKind.Relative).ToString();
}
```

As you can see from the examples of Android and Windows Phone Platforms, in order to implement a photo capture using the device camera on two mobile platforms, we had to use two different programming languages and deal with totally different APIs. Thanks to Apache Cordova unified programming JavaScript interface, you don't even need to know how every mobile platform is handling the native stuff behind the scene, and you can only focus on implementing your cross-platform mobile application's business logic with a neat unified code base.

By now, you should have been comfortable with knowing and understanding the Apache Cordova architecture. In the upcoming chapters of this book, however, we will explain the bits of Apache Cordova in more detail, and you will acquire a deeper understanding of the Apache Cordova architecture by creating your own custom Cordova plugin in *Chapter 6, Developing Custom Cordova Plugins*.

Overview of Cordova APIs

Currently, Apache Cordova supports the following mobile native functions APIs:

- `Accelerometer`: This allows you to capture the device motion in all directions (x, y, and z)

- `Camera`: This allows you to use the default camera application in order to capture photos

- `Capture`: This allows you to capture audio using the device's audio recording application, capture images using the device's camera application, and capture video using the device's video recording application

- `Compass`: This allows you to get the direction that the device is pointing to

- `Connection`: This provides you with the information about the device's cellular and Wi-Fi connection

- `Contacts`: This allows you to access the device's contacts database, create new contacts in the contacts list, and query the existing device contacts list

- `Device`: This allows you to get the hardware and software information of the device; for example, it allows you to get the device model, receive the platform and its version, and finally, receive the device name

- `Events`: This allows you to listen and create handlers for Apache Cordova life cycle events. These life cycle events are as follows:
    - `deviceready`: This event fires once Apache Cordova is fully loaded
    - `pause`: This event fires if the application is put into the background
    - `resume`: This event fires if the application is resumed from the background
    - `online`: This event fires if the application becomes connected to the Internet
    - `offline`: This event fires if the application becomes disconnected from the Internet
    - `backbutton`: This event fires if the user clicks the device's back button (some mobile devices have a back button, such as Android and Windows Phone devices)
    - `batterycritical`: This event fires if the device's battery power reaches a critical state (that is, reaches the critical-level threshold)

- ° `batterylow`: This event fires if the device battery power reaches the low-level threshold

- ° `batterystatus`: This event fires if there is a change in the battery status

- ° `menubutton`: This event fires if the user presses the device's menu button (the menu button is popular for Android and BlackBerry devices)

- ° `searchbutton`: This event fires if the user presses the device's search button (the search button can be found in Android devices)

- ° `startcallbutton`: This event fires when the user presses the start and end call buttons of the device

- ° `endcallbutton`: This event fires when the user presses the start and end call buttons of the device

- ° `volumeupbutton`: This event fires when the user presses the volume up and down buttons of the device

- ° `volumedownbutton`: This event fires when the user presses the volume up and down buttons of the device

- `File`: This allows you to process files (which is to read, write, and navigate filesystem directories), and it is based on the W3C file APIs

- `Geolocation`: This allows you to receive the device's location using GPS or using network signals, and it is based on W3C geolocation APIs

- `Globalization`: This allows you to get the user's locale and perform locale-specific operations

- `InAppBrowser`: This represents a web browser view that is displayed when any call to `window.open()` or a link whose target is set to `"_blank"` is clicked

- `Media`: This allows for the recording of audio files programmatically, without using the device default recording application, as well as playing audio files

- `Notification`: This allows the display of audible notifications such as beeps, the display of tactile notifications such as vibrations, and displaying visual notifications such as the normal device visual messages to the user

- `Splashscreen`: This allows you to display application splash screen

- `Storage`: Apache Cordova provides the following storage capabilities:

  ○ Using the W3C web storage interface which is about `LocalStorage` and `SessionStorage`. It is important to know that local storage is a permanent storage that exists on your device even if your application is closed, while session storage is a temporary storage that is erased when the user session ends, which is when the application is closed.

  ○ Using the full features of relational databases by supporting Web SQL on almost all the platforms. For Windows Phone and Windows Platform, it supports `IndexedDB`, which is currently a W3C standard.

 Although Web SQL is deprecated, it was and still is a powerful specification for creating and working with relational data.

All of these APIs will be illustrated in far more detail, along with examples, as you read this book. It is important to note that not all of these APIs are supported in all the platforms. You will be able to specifically check which ones are not supported in the following list. Also note that this list applies to Apache Cordova Version 3.4, and it might be changed later. The following table shows the unsupported APIs on the different platforms. Please note that X here means unsupported:

	Firefox OS	Tizen	Windows 8	Blackberry 10
Capture API	X	X	X	
Compass	X			
Connection	X			
Contacts		X	X	
Events	X			
File	X	X		
Globalization	X	X	X	X
InAppBrowser	X	X		
Media	X			
Notification	X			
Splashscreen	X	X		
Storage	X			

Summary

In this chapter, you have been given a powerful introduction to Apache Cordova. You now know what Apache Cordova is, and understand the current challenges of today's mobile development and how it can reduce the complexities of these challenges. You should now understand the differences between mobile web, hybrid mobile, and native mobile applications. You should also know the architecture of Cordova and how it works behind the scenes with an example of a photo capture using a camera. Finally, you have an overview of Apache Cordova APIs and what every API does from a high-level point of view.

In the next chapter, you will start the real work with Apache Cordova by developing your first Apache Cordova application from scratch.

2
Developing Your First Cordova Application

In the previous chapter, you had a powerful introduction to Apache Cordova. In this chapter, you will develop, build, and deploy your first Apache Cordova application from scratch. The application you will develop is a Sound Recorder utility that you can use to record your voice or any sound and play it back. In this chapter, you will learn about the following topics:

- Generating your initial Apache Cordova project artifacts by utilizing the Apache Cordova **Command-line Interface (CLI)**

- Developing and building your mobile application from the initial Cordova generated code

- Deploying your developed mobile application to a real Android mobile device to see your application in action

An introduction to Cordova CLI

In order to create, develop, build, and test a Cordova application, you first need to use the Cordova CLI. Using this, you can create new Apache Cordova project(s), build them on mobile platforms such as iOS, Android, Windows Phone, and so on, and run them on real devices or within emulators. Note that in this chapter, we will focus on deploying our Sound Recorder application in Android devices only.

 In the next chapter, we will learn how to deploy our Sound Recorder application in iOS and Windows Phone devices.

Installing Apache Cordova

Before installing Apache Cordova CLI, you need to make sure that you install the following software:

- **Target platform SDK**: For Android, you can download its SDK from `http://developer.android.com/sdk/index.html` (for other platforms, you need to download and install their corresponding SDKs)

- **Node.js**: This is accessible at `http://nodejs.org` and can be downloaded and installed from `http://nodejs.org/download/`

 If you want to know more about the details of configuring Android, iOS, and Windows Phone environments in your development machine, refer to *Chapter 3, Apache Cordova Development Tools*.

After installing Node.js, you should be able to run Node.js or **node package manager** (**npm**) from the command line. In order to install Apache Cordova using npm, run the following command (you can omit `sudo` if you are working in a Windows environment):

```
> sudo npm install -g cordova
```

It's worth mentioning that npm is the official package manager for Node.js and it is written completely in JavaScript. npm is a tool that allows users to install Node.js modules, which are available in the npm registry.

 The sudo command allows a privileged Unix user to execute a command as the super user, or as any other user, according to the sudoers file. The sudo command, by default, requires you to authenticate with a password. Once you are authenticated, you can use the command without a password, by default, for 5 minutes.

After successfully installing Apache Cordova (Version 3.4.0), you should be able to execute Apache Cordova commands from the command line, for example, the following command will show you the current installed version of Apache Cordova:

```
> cordova -version
```

In order to execute the Cordova commands without any problem, you also need to have Apache Ant installed and configured in your operating system.

You can download Apache Ant from `http://ant.apache.org`. The complete instructions on how to install Ant are mentioned at `https://ant.apache.org/manual/install.html`.

Generating our Sound Recorder's initial code

After installing Apache Cordova, we can start creating our Sound Recorder project by executing the following command:

```
> cordova create soundRecorder com.jsmobile.soundrecorder SoundRecorder
```

After successfully executing this command, you will find a message similar to the following one (note that the location path will be different on your machine):

```
Creating a new cordova project with name "SoundRecorder" and id
"com.jsmobile.soundrecorder" at location "/Users/xyz/projects/
soundRecorder"
```

If we analyze the `cordova create` command, we will find that its first parameter represents the path of your project. In this command, a `soundRecorder` directory will be generated for your project under the directory from which the `cordova create` command is executed. The second and third parameters are optional. The second parameter, `com.jsmobile.soundrecorder`, provides your project's namespace (it should be noted that in Android projects, this namespace will be translated to a Java package with this name), and the last parameter, `SoundRecorder`, provides the application's display text. You can edit both these values in the `config.xml` configuration file later, which will be illustrated soon.

The following screenshot shows our `SoundRecorder` project's generated artifacts:

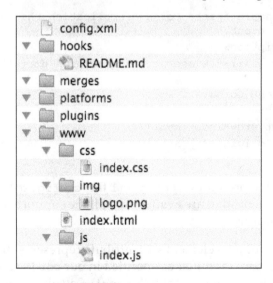

The Sound Recorder's initial structure

As shown in the preceding screenshot, the generated Apache Cordova project contains the following main directories and files:

- www: This directory includes your application's HTML, JavaScript, and CSS code. You will also find the application's starting page (index.html), along with various subdirectories, which are as follows:

  - css: This directory includes the default Apache Cordova application's CSS file (index.css)

  - js: This directory includes the default Apache Cordova application's JavaScript file (index.js)

  - img: This directory includes the default Apache Cordova application's logo file (logo.png)

- config.xml: This file contains the application configuration. The following code snippet shows the initial code of the config.xml file:

```xml
<?xml version='1.0' encoding='utf-8'?>
<widget id="com.jsmobile.soundrecorder" version="0.0.1"
        xmlns="http://www.w3.org/ns/widgets"
        xmlns:cdv="http://cordova.apache.org/ns/1.0">
    <name>SoundRecorder</name>
    <description>
        A sample Apache Cordova application that responds to the
deviceready event.
    </description>
    <author email="dev@cordova.apache.org" href="http://cordova.
io">
        Apache Cordova Team
    </author>
    <content src="index.html" />
    <access origin="*" />
</widget>
```

As shown in the preceding config.xml file, config.xml contains the following elements that are available on all the supported Apache Cordova platforms:

  - The <widget> element's id attribute represents the application's namespace identifier as specified in our cordova create command, and the <widget> element's version attribute represents its full version number in the form of major.minor.patch.

- ○ The `<name>` element specifies the application's name.

- ○ The `<description>` and `<author>` elements specify the application's description and author, respectively.

- ○ The `<content>` element (which is optional) specifies the application's starting page that is placed directly under the www directory. The default value is `index.html`.

- ○ The `<access>` element(s) defines the set of external domains that the application is allowed to access. The default value is `*`, which means that the application is allowed to access any external server(s).

Specifying the `<access>` element's origin to `*` is fine during application development, but it is considered a bad practice in production due to security concerns. Note that before moving your application to production, you should review its whitelist and declare its access to specific network domains and subdomains.

There is another element that is not included in the default `config.xml`, and this is the `<preference>` element. The `<preference>` element(s) can be used to set the different preferences of the Cordova application and can work on all or a subset of the Apache Cordova-supported platforms. Take the example of the following code:

```
<preference name="Fullscreen" value="true" />
```

If the `Fullscreen` preference is set to `true`, it means that the application will be in fullscreen mode on all Cordova-supported platforms (by default, this option is set to `false`). It is important to note that not all preferences work on all Cordova-supported platforms. Consider the following example:

```
<preference name="HideKeyboardFormAccessoryBar" value="true"/>
```

If the `HideKeyboardFormAccessoryBar` preference is set to `true`, then the additional helper toolbar, which appears above the device keyboard, will be hidden. This preference works only on iOS and BlackBerry platforms.

- `platforms`: This directory includes the application's supported platforms. After adding a new platform using Apache Cordova CLI, you will find a newly created directory that contains the platform-specific generated code under the `platforms` directory. The `platforms` directory is initially empty because we have not added any platforms yet. We will add support to the Android platform in the next step.

- `plugins`: This directory includes your application's used plugins. If you aren't already aware, a plugin is the mechanism to access the device's native functions in Apache Cordova. After adding a plugin (such as the `Media` plugin) to the project, you will find a newly created directory under the `plugins` directory, which contains the plugin code. Note that we will add three plugins in our Sound Recorder application example.

- `merges`: This directory can be used to override the common resources under the `www` directory. The files placed under the `merges/[platform]` directory will override the matching files (or add new files) under the `www` directory for the specified platform (the `[platform]` value can be iOS, Android, or any other valid supported platform).

- `hooks`: This directory contains scripts that can be used to customize Apache Cordova commands. A hook is a piece of code that executes before and/or after the Apache Cordova command runs.

An insight into the www files

If we look in the `www` directory, we will find that it contains the following three files:

- `index.html`: This file is placed under the application's `www` directory, and it contains the HTML content of the application page

- `index.js`: This file is placed under the `www/js` directory, and it contains a simple JavaScript logic that we will illustrate soon

- `index.css`: This file is placed under the `www/css` directory, and it contains the style classes of the HTML elements

The following code snippet includes the most important part of the `index.html` page:

```
<div class="app">
    <h1>Apache Cordova</h1>
    <div id="deviceready" class="blink">
        <p class="event listening">Connecting to Device</p>
        <p class="event received">Device is Ready</p>
    </div>
</div>
<script type="text/javascript" src="cordova.js"></script>
<script type="text/javascript" src="js/index.js"></script>
<script type="text/javascript">
    app.initialize();
</script>
```

The index.html page has a single div "app", which contains a child div "deviceready". The "deviceready" div has two paragraph elements, the "event listening" and "event received" paragraphs. The "event received" paragraph is initially hidden as indicated by index.css:

```css
.event.received {
    background-color:#4B946A;
    display:none;
}
```

In the index.html page, there are two main JavaScript-included files, as follows:

- cordova.js: This file contains Apache Cordova JavaScript APIs
- index.js: This file contains the application's simple logic

Finally, the index.html page calls the initialize() method of the app object. Let's see the details of the app object in index.js:

```javascript
var app = {
    initialize: function() {
        this.bindEvents();
    },
    bindEvents: function() {
        document.addEventListener('deviceready', this.onDeviceReady,
false);
    },
    onDeviceReady: function() {
        app.receivedEvent('deviceready');
    },
    receivedEvent: function(id) {
        var parentElement = document.getElementById(id);
        var listeningElement = parentElement.querySelector('.
listening');
        var receivedElement =
parentElement.querySelector('.received');

        listeningElement.setAttribute('style', 'display:none;');
        receivedElement.setAttribute('style', 'display:block;');

        console.log('Received Event: ' + id);
    }
};
```

The initialize() method calls the bindEvents() method, which adds an event listener for the 'deviceready' event. When the device is ready, the onDeviceReady() method is called, and this in turn calls the receivedEvent() method of the app object.

In the receivedEvent() method, the "event listening" paragraph is hidden and the "event received" paragraph is shown to the user. This is to display the **Device is Ready** message to the user once Apache Cordova is fully loaded.

 It is important to note that you must not call any Apache Cordova API before the 'deviceready' event fires. This is because the 'deviceready' event fires only once Apache Cordova is fully loaded.

Now you have an Apache Cordova project that has common cross-platform code, so we need to generate a platform-specific code in order to deploy our code on a real device. To generate Android platform code, you need to add the Android platform as follows:

```
> cd soundRecorder
> cordova platform add android
```

In order to add any platform, you need to execute the cordova platform command from the application directory. Note that in order to execute the cordova platform command without problems, you need to perform the following instructions:

- Have Apache Ant installed and configured in your operating system as described in the *Installing Apache Cordova* section
- Make sure that the path to your Android SDK platform tools and the tools directory are added to your operating system's PATH environment variable

After executing the cordova platform add command, you will find a new subdirectory Android added under the soundRecorder/platforms directory. In order to build the project, use the following command:

```
> cordova build
```

Finally, you can run and test the generated Android project in the emulator by executing the following command:

```
> cordova emulate android
```

You might see the **ERROR: No emulator images (avds) found** message flash if no Android AVDs are available in your operating system. So, make sure you create one!

Refer to the *Creating an Android virtual device* section in *Chapter 3, Apache Cordova Development Tools*, to know how to create an Android AVD.

The following screenshot shows our Sound Recorder application's initial screen:

It is recommended that you make your code changes in the root www directory, and not in the `platforms/android/assets/www` directory (especially if you are targeting multiple platforms) as the `platforms` directory will be overridden every time you execute the `cordova build` command, unless you are willing to use Apache Cordova CLI to initialize the project for a single platform only.

Developing Sound Recorder application

After generating the initial application code, it's time to understand what to do next.

Sound Recorder functionality

The following screenshot shows our **Sound Recorder** page:

When the user clicks on the **Record Sound** button, they will be able to record their voices; they can stop recording their voices by clicking on the **Stop Recording** button. You can see this in the following screenshot:

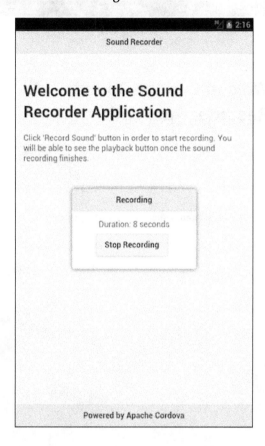

As shown in the following screenshot, when the user clicks on the **Playback** button, the recorded voice will be played back:

Sound Recorder preparation

In order to implement this functionality using Apache Cordova, we need to add the following plugins using the indicated commands, which should be executed from the application directory:

- `media`: This plugin is used to record and play back sound files:

    ```
    > cordova plugin add https://git-wip-us.apache.org/repos/asf/
    cordova-plugin-media.git
    ```

- `device`: This plugin is required to access the device information:

    ```
    > cordova plugin add https://git-wip-us.apache.org/repos/asf/
    cordova-plugin-device.git
    ```

- `file`: This plugin is used to access the device's filesystem:

    ```
    > cordova plugin add https://git-wip-us.apache.org/repos/asf/
    cordova-plugin-file.git
    ```

In order to apply these plugins to our Apache Cordova project, we need to run the `cordova build` command again from the `project` directory, as follows:

```
> cordova build
```

Sound Recorder details

Now we are done with the preparation of our Sound Recorder application. Before moving to the code details, let's see the hierarchy of our Sound Recorder application, as shown in the following screenshot:

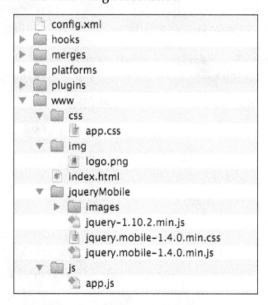

The application's www directory contains the following directories:

- css: This directory contains the custom application CSS file(s)
- img: This directory contains the custom application image file(s)
- js: This directory contains the custom application JavaScript code
- jqueryMobile: This directory (which is a newly added one) contains jQuery Mobile framework files

Finally, the index.html file contains the application's single page whose functionality was illustrated earlier in this section.

 It is important to note that Apache Cordova does not require you to use a JavaScript mobile **User Interface (UI)** framework. However, it is recommended that you use a JavaScript mobile UI framework in addition to Apache Cordova. This is in order to facilitate building the application UI and speed up the application development process. The jQuery Mobile framework is one of the best mobile UI frameworks, and as such will be used in all the Apache Cordova applications developed in this book.

Let's see the details of the index.html page of our Sound Recorder application. The following code snippet shows the included files in the page:

```
<link rel="stylesheet" type="text/css" href="css/app.css" />
<link rel="stylesheet" href="jqueryMobile/jquery.mobile-1.4.0.min.
css">
<script src="jqueryMobile/jquery-1.10.2.min.js"></script>
<script src="jqueryMobile/jquery.mobile-1.4.0.min.js"></script>
...
<script type="text/javascript" src="cordova.js"></script>
<script type="text/javascript" src="js/app.js"></script>
```

In the preceding code, the following files are included:

- app.css: This is the custom style file of our Sound Recorder application
- The files required by the jQuery Mobile framework, which are:
    - jquery.mobile-1.4.0.min.css
    - jquery-1.10.2.min.js
    - jquery.mobile-1.4.0.min.js
- cordova.js: This is the Apache Cordova JavaScript API's file
- app.js: This is the custom JavaScript file of our Sound Recorder application

It is important to know that you can download the jQuery Mobile framework files from `http://jquerymobile.com/download/`.

The following code snippet shows the HTML content of our application's single page, whose id is `"main"`:

```
<div data-role="page" id="main">
    <div data-role="header">
        <h1>Sound Recorder</h1>
    </div>
    <div data-role="content">
    <div data-role="fieldcontain">
        <h1>Welcome to the Sound Recorder Application</h1>
        <p>Click 'Record Sound' button in order to start
recording. You will be able to see
            the playback button once the sound recording
finishes.<br/><br/></p>
        <input type="hidden" id="location"/>
        <div class="center-wrapper">
            <input type="button" id="recordSound" data-
icon="audio" value="Record Sound" class="center-button" data-
inline="true"/>
            <input type="button" id="playSound" data-
icon="refresh" value="Playback" class="center-button" data-
inline="true"/><br/>
        </div>

        <div data-role="popup" id="recordSoundDialog" data-
dismissible="false" style="width:250px">
            <div data-role="header">
                <h1>Recording</h1>
            </div>

            <div data-role="content">
                <div class="center-wrapper">
                    <div id="soundDuration"></div>
                    <input type="button" id="stopRecordingSound"
value="Stop Recording"
                                class="center-button" data-
inline="true"/>
                </div>
            </div>
            </div>
        </div>
    </div>
```

```
        <div data-role="footer" data-position="fixed">
            <h1>Powered by Apache Cordova</h1>
        </div>
    </div>
```

Looking at the preceding code, our Sound Recording page ("main") is defined by setting a div's data-role attribute to "page". It has a header defined by setting a div's data-role to "header". It has content defined by setting a div's data-role to "content", which contains the recording and playback buttons.

The content also contains a "recordSoundDialog" pop up, which is defined by setting a div's data-role to "popup". The "recordSoundDialog" pop up has a header and content. The pop-up content displays the recorded audio duration in the "soundDuration" div, and it has a "stopRecordingSound" button that stops recording the sound.

Finally, the page has a footer defined by setting a div's data-role to "footer", which contains a statement about the application.

Now, it's time to learn how we can define event handlers on page HTML elements and use the Apache Cordova API inside our defined event handlers to implement the application's functionality.

The following code snippet shows the page initialization code:

```
(function() {

    $(document).on("pageinit", "#main", function(e) {
            e.preventDefault();

            function onDeviceReady() {
                    $("#recordSound").on("tap", function(e) {
                        // Action is defined here ...
                    });

                    $("#recordSoundDialog").on("popupafterclose",
    function(event, ui) {
                            // Action is defined here ...
                    });

                    $("#stopRecordingSound").on("tap", function(e) {
                        // Action is defined here ...
                    });

                    $("#playSound").on("tap", function(e) {
                        // Action is defined here ...
```

```
                    });
                }

            $(document).on('deviceready', onDeviceReady);

            initPage();
        });

        // Code is omitted here for simplicity

        function initPage() {
            $("#playSound").closest('.ui-btn').hide();
        }
    })();
```

In jQuery Mobile, the `"pageinit"` event is called once during page initialization. In this event, the event handlers are defined and the page is initialized. Note that all of the event handlers are defined after the `'deviceready'` event fires. The event handlers are defined for the following:

- Tapping the `"recordSound"` button
- Closing the `"recordSoundDailog"` dialog
- Tapping the `"stopRecordingSound"` button
- Tapping the `"playSound"` button

In `initPage()`, the `"playSound"` button is hidden as no voice has been recorded yet. As you noticed, in order to hide an element in jQuery Mobile, you just need to call its `hide()` method. We can now see the details of each event handler; the next code snippet shows the `"recordSound"` tap event handler:

```
var recInterval;
$("#recordSound").on("tap", function(e) {
    e.preventDefault();

    var recordingCallback = {};

    recordingCallback.recordSuccess = handleRecordSuccess;
    recordingCallback.recordError = handleRecordError;

    startRecordingSound(recordingCallback);

    var recTime = 0;
```

```
            $("#soundDuration").html("Duration: " + recTime + " seconds");

            $("#recordSoundDialog").popup("open");

            recInterval = setInterval(function() {
                                recTime = recTime + 1;
                                $("#soundDuration").html("Duration: "
    + recTime + " seconds");
                            }, 1000);
    });
```

The following actions are performed in the `"recordSound"` tap event handler:

1. A call to the `startRecordingSound(recordingCallback)` function is performed. The `startRecordingSound(recordingCallback)` function is a helper function that starts the sound recording process using the Apache Cordova Media API. Its `recordingCallback` parameter represents a JSON object, which has the `recordSuccess` and `recordError` callback attributes. The `recordSuccess` callback will be called if the recording operation is a success, and the `recordError` callback will be called if the recording operation is a failure.

2. Then, the `"recordSoundDialog"` dialog is opened and its `"soundDuration"` div is updated every second with the duration of the recorded sound.

The following code snippet shows the `startRecordingSound(recordingCallba ck)`, `stopRecordingSound()`, and `requestApplicationDirectory(callback)` functions:

```
var BASE_DIRECTORY = "CS_Recorder";
var recordingMedia;

function startRecordingSound(recordingCallback) {
    var recordVoice = function(dirPath) {
        var basePath = "";

        if (dirPath) {
            basePath = dirPath + "/";
        }

        var mediaFilePath = basePath + (new Date()).getTime() +
    ".wav";

        var recordingSuccess = function() {
```

```
            recordingCallback.recordSuccess(mediaFilePath);
        };
        recordingMedia = new Media(mediaFilePath,
recordingSuccess, recordingCallback.recordError);

        // Record audio
        recordingMedia.startRecord();
    };

    if (device.platform === "Android") {
        var callback = {};

        callback.requestSuccess = recordVoice;
        callback.requestError = recordingCallback.recordError;

        requestApplicationDirectory(callback);
    } else {

        recordVoice();
    }
}

function stopRecordingSound() {
    recordingMedia.stopRecord();
    recordingMedia.release();
}

function requestApplicationDirectory(callback) {
    var directoryReady = function (dirEntry) {
        callback.requestSuccess(dirEntry.toURL());
    };

    var fileSystemReady = function(fileSystem) {
        fileSystem.root.getDirectory(BASE_DIRECTORY, {create:
true}, directoryReady);
    };

    window.requestFileSystem(LocalFileSystem.PERSISTENT, 0,
fileSystemReady, callback.requestError);
}
```

The next section illustrates the preceding code snippet.

Recording and playing the audio files back

In order to record the audio files using Apache Cordova, we need to create a `Media` object, as follows:

```
recordingMedia = new Media(src, mediaSuccess, mediaError);
```

The `Media` object constructor has the following parameters:

- `src`: This refers to the URI of the media file
- `mediaSuccess`: This refers to the callback that will be invoked if the media operation (play/record or stop function) succeeds
- `mediaError`: This refers to the callback that will be invoked if the media operation (again a play/record or stop function) fails

In order to start recording an audio file, a call to the `startRecord()` method of the `Media` object must be performed. When the recording is over, a call to `stopRecord()` of the `Media` object method must be performed.

In `startRecordingSound(recordingCallback)`, the function gets the current device platform by using `device.platform`, as follows:

- If the current platform is Android, then a call to `requestApplicationDirectory(callback)` is performed in order to create an application directory (if it is not already created) called `"CS_Recorder"` under the device's SD card root directory using the Apache Cordova File API. If the directory creation operation succeeds, `recordVoice()` will be called by passing the application directory path as a parameter. The `recordVoice()` function starts recording the sound and saves the resulting audio file under the `application` directory. Note that if there is no SD card in your Android device, then the `application` directory will be created under the app's private data directory (`/data/data/[app_directory]`), and the audio file will be saved under it.

- In the `else` block which refers to the other supported platforms (Windows Phone 8 and iOS, which we will add using Cordova CLI in the next chapter), `recordVoice()` is called without creating an application-specific directory. At the time of writing this book, in iOS and Windows Phone 8, every application has a private directory, and applications cannot store their files in any place other than this directory, using the Apache Cordova APIs. In the case of iOS, the audio files will be stored under the `tmp` directory of the application's `sandbox` directory (the application's private directory). In the case of Windows Phone 8, the audio files will be stored under the application's local directory.

Note that using the native Windows Phone 8 API (Window. Storage), you can read and write files in an SD card with some restrictions. However, until the moment you cannot do this using Apache Cordova; hopefully this capability will soon be supported by Cordova (http://msdn.microsoft.com/en-us/library/ windows/apps/xaml/dn611857.aspx).

- In recordVoice(), it starts creating a media file using the Media object's startRecord() function. After calling the media file's stopRecord() function and after the success of the recording operation, recordingCallback. recordSuccess will be called by recordingSuccess. The recordingCallback.recordSuccess function calls handleRecordSuccess, passing the audio file's full path mediaFilePath as a parameter.

- The following code snippet shows the handleRecordSuccess function:

```
function handleRecordSuccess(currentFilePath) {

    $("#location").val(currentFilePath);
    $("#playSound").closest('.ui-btn').show();
}
```

- The handleRecordSuccess function stores the recorded audio filepath in the "location" hidden field, which is used later by the playback button, and shows the "playSound" button.

- In requestApplicationDirectory(callback), which is called in case of Android, it does the following:
    ○ Calls window.requestFileSystem in order to request the device filesystem before performing any file operation(s)
    ○ Calls fileSystem.root.getDirectory when the filesystem is ready in order to create our custom application directory
    ○ When our custom application directory is created successfully, the path of the created directory, or the existing directory, is passed to recordVoice() that was illustrated earlier

- In the other application actions, the following code snippet shows the "stopRecordingSound" tapping and "recordSoundDialog" closing event handlers:

```
$("#recordSoundDialog").on("popupafterclose", function(event, ui)
{
    clearInterval(recInterval);
    stopRecordingSound();
});
```

```
$("#stopRecordingSound").on("tap", function(e) {
    $("#recordSoundDialog").popup("close");
});

function stopRecordingSound(recordingCallback) {
    recordingMedia.stopRecord();
    recordingMedia.release();
}
```

In the "stopRecordingSound" tapping event handler, it closes the open
"recordSoundDialog" pop up. Generally, if "recordSoundDialog" is closed
by the "stopRecordingSound" button's tapping action or by pressing special
device keys, such as the back button in Android devices, then the recording timer
stops as a result of calling clearInterval(recInterval), and then it calls the
stopRecordingSound() function to stop recording the sound.

The stopRecordingSound() function calls the Media object's stopRecord() method,
and then releases it by calling the Media object's release() method. The following
code snippet shows the "playSound" tap event handler:

```
var audioMedia;
var recordingMedia;

$("#playSound").on("tap", function(e) {
    e.preventDefault();

    var playCallback = {};

    playCallback.playSuccess = handlePlaySuccess;
    playCallback.playError = handlePlayError;

    playSound($("#location").val(), playCallback);
});

function playSound(filePath, playCallback) {
    if (filePath) {
        cleanUpResources();

        audioMedia = new Media(filePath, playCallback.playSuccess,
playCallback.playError);

        // Play audio
        audioMedia.play();
    }
}
```

```
function cleanUpResources() {
    if (audioMedia) {
        audioMedia.stop();
        audioMedia.release();
        audioMedia = null;
    }

    if (recordingMedia) {
        recordingMedia.stop();
        recordingMedia.release();
        recordingMedia = null;
    }
}
```

In the "playSound" tap event handler, it calls the playSound(filePath, playCallback) function by passing the audio file location, which is stored in the "location" hidden field and playCallback.

The playSound(filePath, playCallback) function uses the Media object's play() method to play back the saved audio file after releasing used Media objects. Note that this is a requirement to avoid running out of system audio resources.

This is all you need to know about our Sound Recorder application. In order to see the complete application's source code, you can download it from the book page or get it from GitHub at https://github.com/hazems/soundRecorder.

Building and running Sound Recorder application

Now, after developing our application code, we can start building our application using the following cordova build command:

> **cordova build**

In order to run the application in your Android mobile or tablet, just make sure you enable USB debugging in your Android device. Then, plug your Android device into your development machine and execute the following command from the application directory:

> **cordova run android**

Downloading the example code

You can download the example code files for all Packt books you have purchased from your account at http://www.packtpub.com. If you purchased this book elsewhere, you can visit http://www.packtpub.com/support and register to have the files e-mailed directly to you.

Congratulations! After running this command, you will see the Sound Recorder application deployed in your Android device; you can now start testing it on your real device.

In order to learn how to enable USB debugging in your Android device, refer to the *Configuring the Android development environment* section in *Chapter 3, Apache Cordova Development Tools*.

Summary

In this chapter, you developed your first Apache Cordova application. You now know how to use the Apache Cordova Device API at a basic level. You also know how to use the Media and File APIs along with jQuery Mobile to develop the Sound Recorder application. You now understand how to use Apache Cordova CLI in order to manage your Cordova mobile application. In addition, you know how to create a Cordova project, add a new platform (in our case, Android), build your own Cordova mobile application, and deploy your Cordova mobile application to the emulator, and most importantly, to a real device!

In the next chapter, we will show you how to prepare your Android, iOS, and Windows Phone development environments. Along with this, you will see how to make our Sound Recorder application works on Windows Phone 8 and iOS.

3
Apache Cordova Development Tools

In the previous chapter, you developed, built, and deployed your first Apache Cordova application from scratch. In this chapter, you will learn:

- How to configure the Apache Cordova development tools for the most popular mobile platforms (Android, iOS, and Windows Phone 8) on your development machine(s)

- How to build the Sound Recorder application (which we developed in *Chapter 2, Developing Your First Cordova Application*) on these platforms

- How to deploy the Sound Recorder application on real Android, iOS, and Windows Phone 8 devices

- How to handle the common issues that you will face when supporting our Sound Recorder application (which we supported on Android in *Chapter 2, Developing Your First Cordova Application*) on the other mobile platforms (iOS and Windows Phone 8)

Configuring Android development environment

In order to install Android development environment, we first need to install **Java Development Kit (JDK)**. JDK 6 or 7 can work perfectly with Android development tools. In order to get JDK, use the following URLs:

- JDK 7 (`http://www.oracle.com/technetwork/java/javase/downloads/jdk7-downloads-1880260.html`)

- JDK 6 (`http://www.oracle.com/technetwork/java/javaee/downloads/java-ee-sdk-6u3-jdk-6u29-downloads-523388.html`)

Once the download page appears, accept the license and then download the JDK installer that matches your operating system, as shown in the following screenshot. After downloading the JDK installer, follow the steps of the JDK installer in order to properly install JDK.

Java SE Development Kit 7u55

You must accept the Oracle Binary Code License Agreement for Java SE to download this software.

Thank you for accepting the Oracle Binary Code License Agreement for Java SE; you may now download this software.

Product / File Description	File Size	Download
Linux x86	115.67 MB	jdk-7u55-linux-i586.rpm
Linux x86	133 MB	jdk-7u55-linux-i586.tar.gz
Linux x64	116.97 MB	jdk-7u55-linux-x64.rpm
Linux x64	131.82 MB	jdk-7u55-linux-x64.tar.gz
Mac OS X x64	179.56 MB	jdk-7u55-macosx-x64.dmg
Solaris x86 (SVR4 package)	138.86 MB	jdk-7u55-solaris-i586.tar.Z
Solaris x86	95.14 MB	jdk-7u55-solaris-i586.tar.gz
Solaris x64 (SVR4 package)	24.55 MB	jdk-7u55-solaris-x64.tar.Z
Solaris x64	16.25 MB	jdk-7u55-solaris-x64.tar.gz
Solaris SPARC (SVR4 package)	138.23 MB	jdk-7u55-solaris-sparc.tar.Z
Solaris SPARC	98.18 MB	jdk-7u55-solaris-sparc.tar.gz
Solaris SPARC 64-bit (SVR4 package)	24 MB	jdk-7u55-solaris-sparcv9.tar.Z
Solaris SPARC 64-bit	18.34 MB	jdk-7u55-solaris-sparcv9.tar.gz
Windows x86	123.67 MB	jdk-7u55-windows-i586.exe
Windows x64	125.49 MB	jdk-7u55-windows-x64.exe

Downloading JDK 1.7

If you want to have an Android development environment installed quickly on your machine, you can download **Android Developer Tools (ADT)** Bundle. The ADT Bundle includes the essential Android SDK components and a version of the Eclipse IDE with a built-in ADT to start developing your Android applications. You can download it from `http://developer.android.com/sdk/index.html`.

You can start downloading the ADT Bundle by clicking on the **Download the SDK** button, as shown in the following screenshot:

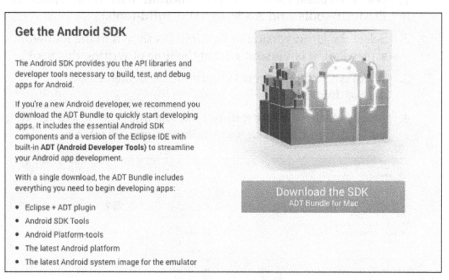

Downloading the ADT Bundle

Extending your existing Eclipse IDE

If you have an existing Eclipse IDE and you would prefer to use it as your Android development IDE, then you will need to configure things by yourself, start the configuration process by downloading the Android SDK tools from `http://developer.android.com/sdk/index.html#download`.

After downloading the Android SDK tools, and in order to start developing Android applications, you need to download at least one Android platform and the latest SDK platform tools using SDK Manager, as follows:

1. Open SDK Manager. If you use Linux or Mac, you can open a terminal and navigate to the `tools` directory under the Android SDK root directory and execute the following command:

   ```
   > android sdk
   ```

   If you use Windows, then open the `SDK Manager.exe` file under the Android SDK root directory.

2. After opening SDK Manager, follow these steps:

    1. Select the latest tools packages (**Android SDK Tools**, **Android SDK Platform-tools**, and **Android SDK Build-tools**).

    2. Select the latest version of Android (as shown in the following screenshot, it is Version 4.4.2 at the time of writing this book).

    3. Select **Android Support Library** that is located under the `Extras` folder.

    4. Finally, click on the **Install** button, and after the process is complete, you will find the packages installed on your machine.

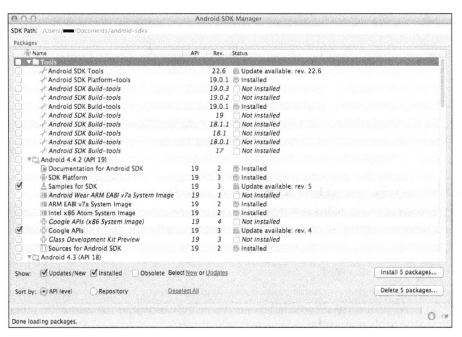

Android SDK Manager

Now, your Android environment is ready to develop your Android applications. However, in order to develop Android applications from your existing Eclipse IDE, Android provides an Eclipse plugin called ADT. This plugin provides a neat and integrated environment that you can use to develop your Android applications. ADT allows you to create new Android projects easily, build your Android application user interface, test and debug your Android applications, and export your application for distribution.

In order to install ADT in your Eclipse IDE, follow these steps:

1. Open Eclipse.

2. Choose **Install New Software** from the **Help** menu.

3. Click on the **Add** button.

4. In the **Add Repository** dialog, enter ADT for the name and the URL `https://dl-ssl.google.com/android/eclipse/` for the location.

5. Click on **OK**.

6. In the **Available Software** dialog, select **Developer Tools** and click on **Next**, as shown in the following screenshot:

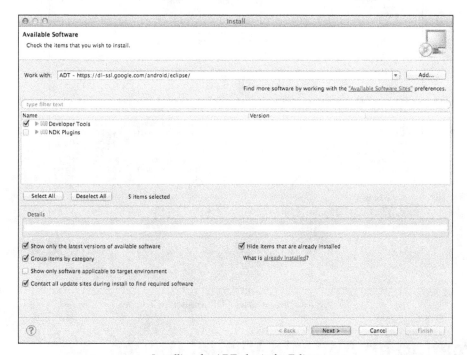

Installing the ADT plugin for Eclipse

7. The tools list to be downloaded will be shown to you. Then, click on **Next**.

8. Accept the license agreements, and finally, click on **Finish**.

 Sometimes, you will see a security warning telling you that you are installing software that contains unsigned content. Just ignore this message and click on **OK**, and then restart your Eclipse when the installation completes.

After restarting Eclipse, you need to specify the Android SDK path for Eclipse. You can do this by:

- Selecting the **Preferences** option from **Window** menu (in Windows or Linux), or by selecting **Preferences** from **Eclipse** menu in Mac

- Selecting the **Android** preference and specifying the SDK location, as shown in the following screenshot:

Configuring the Android SDK location in Eclipse

Creating an Android Virtual Device

In order to test your Android application in an emulator, you need to create an **Android Virtual Device (AVD)**. An AVD represents the Android emulator device configuration that allows you to model the different configurations of Android-powered devices. In order to create an AVD easily, you can use the graphical AVD Manager. To start AVD Manager from the command line, you can run the following command from the `tools` directory under the root of the Android SDK directory:

```
> android avd
```

After executing this command, the **Android Virtual Device Manager** window will appear, as shown in the following screenshot:

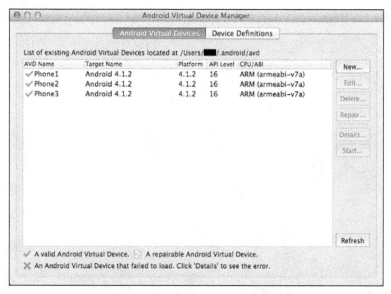

Android Virtual Device Manager

Note that while using Eclipse, you can also start AVD Manager by selecting **Android Virtual Device Manager** from the **Window** menu.

As shown in the preceding screenshot, using the AVD Manager, you can:

- Create a new AVD
- Delete an AVD
- Repair an AVD
- Check the details of an AVD
- Start running an AVD

In order to create a new AVD to test your Android applications, follow these steps:

1. Click on **New**.

2. Enter the details of your AVD, as shown in the following screenshot:

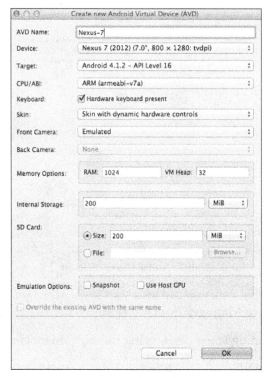

Creating a new Android Virtual Device (AVD)

As shown in the preceding screenshot, the following information is provided:

- **AVD Name**
- **Device**
- **Target**
- **CPU/ABI** (where ABI stands for Application Binary Interface)
- **Skin**

- ◦ **Front Camera**
- ◦ **Back Camera**
- ◦ **Memory Options**
- ◦ **Internal Storage**
- ◦ **SD Card**

3. Then, click on **OK**.

After this, you can start launching your AVD by clicking on the **Start** button; wait until your Android emulator is up and running, as shown in the following screenshot:

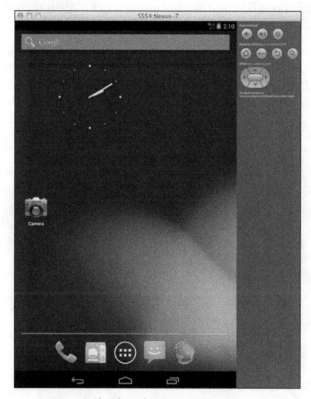

Android emulator start up screen

A best practice is to download the system images for all versions of Android that your application needs to support and test your application on them using the Android emulator. Another thing you need to consider is to select an AVD platform target that is greater than or equal to the API level used to compile your Android application.

Importing the Sound Recorder application in to Eclipse

Now, we have everything in place. We can now import our Sound Recorder Android application in our Eclipse IDE and start running it from the IDE. In order to import our project into Eclipse, follow these steps:

1. Before starting to import the project into your Eclipse IDE, and in order to avoid getting errors after importing the project into your IDE, make sure that our Sound Recorder project directories and subdirectories have **Read and Write** access for your user (that is, not read-only access).

2. Select the **Import** option from the **File** menu.

3. Select **Existing Android Code into workspace** from the **Android** menu.

4. In **Import Projects**, browse to the ${path_to_soundRecorder}/platforms/android directory in **Root Directory**, as shown in the following screenshot:

Importing the Sound Recorder project into Eclipse

5. Click on **Finish**.

By default, your HTML, CSS, and JavaScript Android resources under ${project_root}/assets are not shown in Eclipse; this shows your Android web resources.

1. Right-click on the project and then select **Properties**.

2. Select **Resource Filters** from the **Resources** dropdown.

3. Delete all the **Exclude all** rules, as shown in the following screenshot:

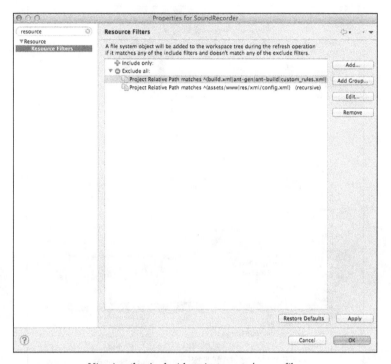

Viewing the Android project assets/www files

Now, you can view all the project assets/www files from the Eclipse workspace.

Do not forget that it is not recommended to edit the files under the platforms directory of your project as the cordova build command can overwrite your changes with the original resources in the root www directory. You can edit files under the platforms directory only if you want to use Apache Cordova to generate the initial artifacts of your project.

Before running our Sound Recorder Android project, make sure that the project is built by selecting **Build All** from **Project** menu (or select your project and choose **Build project** from the **Project** menu, or just select the **Build Automatically** option from the **Project** menu).

Now, you can run our Sound Recorder Android project from Eclipse by selecting the project and then selecting **Android Application** from the **Run as** menu, as shown in the following screenshot:

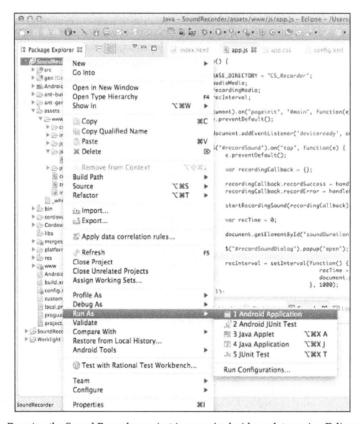

Running the Sound Recorder project in your Android emulator using Eclipse

You will have the option to select the emulator you want to run your project on, as shown in the following screenshot:

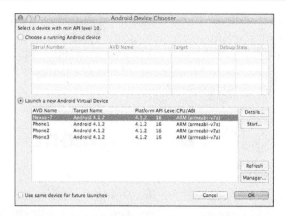

Selecting the Android emulator to run the project on

After selecting the Android emulator and clicking on the **OK** button, your selected Android emulator will be launched and your application will be installed on it for you to start testing.

Running the Sound Recorder application on a real Android device

In order to test your Android application on your Android mobile or tablet using the Eclipse IDE, just make sure that you enable USB debugging on your Android device. You can enable the **USB debugging** option on your device by clicking on **Developer Options** from the device **Settings** and then checking the **USB debugging** option, as shown in the following screenshot:

Enabling USB debugging on your Android device

Plug in your Android device to your development machine and then select **Android Application** again from the **Run as** menu. At this time, you will find your device available under the running Android device option in the **Android Device Chooser** dialog; select it, and you will find our Sound Recorder application deployed and launched in your device to start testing.

Configuring iOS development environment

Creating iOS development environment is a straightforward process if you meet the requirements. In order to have an iOS development environment, you need to:

- Have a Mac machine that runs OS X Mountain Lion (10.8) or higher versions
- Install Xcode on your Mac machine
- Install the iOS SDK on your Mac machine

Xcode is the official Apple IDE that allows you to develop applications for Mac, iPhone, and iPad. Xcode has a lot of great features, some of which are:

- Source code editor
- Assistant editor
- User-interface builder
- iOS simulator
- Static code analyzer
- A powerful built-in open source **low-level virtual machine (LLVM)** compiler for C, C++, and Objective-C
- The Live Issues feature, which highlights the common coding mistakes while coding your application, without the need to build your project
- Complete support for SCM systems (subversion and Git source control)

You can download the latest version of Xcode from the Apple App Store on your Mac machine. You will find the iOS SDK included with Xcode, so there is no need to download anything other than Xcode.

In order to download the latest version of Xcode, follow these steps:

1. Open the App Store application on your Mac machine.

2. In the search field of App Store, type in Xcode and press enter.

3. Download Xcode, and after completing the download, you will find it under your applications directory. The following screenshot shows the Xcode icon:

The Xcode icon

If you have an earlier version of OS X (less than 10.8), you need to upgrade it. In order to download Xcode, you need OS X Version 10.8 (or higher).

Importing the Sound Recorder application into Xcode

Now, it is time to make our Sound Recorder application support iPad and iPhone devices. The following command adds iOS platform support for our Sound Recorder application:

```
> cordova platform add ios
```

Then, build our application in the iOS platform using the following Cordova build command:

```
> cordova build ios
```

Open your Xcode environment, click on **Open other**, and then select the SoundRecorder.xcodeproj file under the platforms/ios directory to open our Sound Recorder iOS project.

You will find our Sound Recorder application open in Xcode. In order to run our project on an iPhone (or iPad) emulator, click on the **Build and run** button after selecting the iPhone emulator, as shown in the following screenshot:

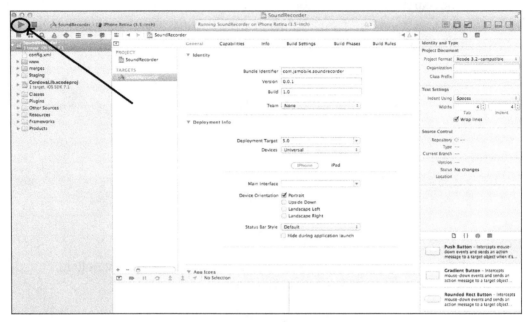

Running the Sound Recorder application in Xcode

After clicking on the **Build and run** button, the iPhone emulator will be launched with our Sound Recorder application and you can start using it.

An important point that you have to be aware of is that if you are deploying your application on iOS 7, and because of a bug in Apache Cordova 3.4, you will find an overlay between your application and the device status bar, as shown in the following screenshot:

Apache Cordova 3.4 bug with iOS 7

In order to fix this issue (which I hope to be fixed soon in the next releases of Apache Cordova 3.x), one of the possible workarounds is to hide the status bar by adding and setting two properties in our `SoundRecorder-info.plist` file, which is located under the `Resources` directory of our application, as shown in the following screenshot:

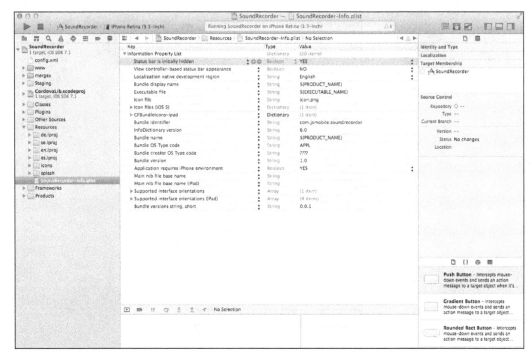

Adding properties to the SoundRecorder-info.plist file

The two properties and values are:

- The **Status bar is initially hidden** property set to the **YES** value
- The **View controller-based status bar appearance** property set to the **NO** value

 In order to add a property to the `*-info.plist` file, you can select the information list property in Xcode and then click on **Add Row**.

After setting these two properties, click on the **Build and run** button again to see the fixed screen in iOS 7, as shown in the following screenshot:

The Sound Recorder application fixed in iOS 7

Running the Sound Recorder application on a real iOS device

In order to deploy our Sound Recorder application on a real iOS device (iPhone or iPad), you will need to follow these 20 steps carefully:

1. Sign up for the iOS developer program at `https://developer.apple.com/programs/ios/`. There are two available enrollment types:

    ○ **Individual**: Select this enrollment type if you are an individual

    ○ **Company/Organization**: Select this enrollment type if you represent a company

 Sign up to the **Individual** program if you just want to develop applications in App Store. Note that at the time of writing this book, this will cost you 99 USD per year.

2. Generate a **Certificate Signing Request (CSR)** using the **Keychain Access** application, which you can get from the /Applications/Utilities directory. In order to generate the certificate signing request, follow these steps:

   1. Navigate to **Keychain Access | Certificate Assistant | Request a Certificate From a Certificate Authority**, as shown in the following screenshot:

   Creating a CSR using Keychain Access

   2. In the **Certificate Assistant** window, enter your e-mail address, click on the **Saved to disk** radio button, and check the **Let me specify key pair information** checkbox. Then, click on **Continue**.

   3. In the **Key Pair Information** window, choose **2048 bits** as the key size and **RSA** as the algorithm. Then, click on **Continue**.

   4. Use the default filename to save the certificate request to your disk, and click on **Save**.

By default, the generated certificate request file has the filename with the following extension CertificateSigningRequest. certSigningRequest.

3. Now, we need to use the iOS member center (`https://developer.apple.com/membercenter/`) in order to create the application ID, register your iOS device, generate a development certificate, and create a provision profile.

4. Click on the **Certificates, Identifiers & Profiles** link, as shown in the following screenshot. You will be introduced to the overview page, where you can click on the **Identifiers** link.

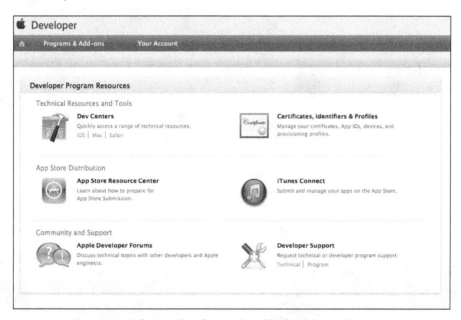

Managing certificates, identifiers, and profiles from the member center

5. Select **App IDs** from **Identifiers**. Register your application ID by entering an application name and the application bundle identifier (you can get the bundle identifier from the `SoundRecorder-info.plist` file), as shown in the following screenshot. Then, click on **Continue**.

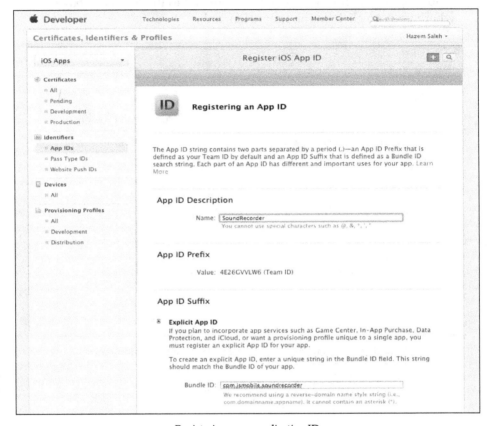

Registering your application ID

6. You will be introduced to the confirmation page. Click on **Submit** to confirm your application ID.

7. Select **All** from **Devices**. Register your iOS device by entering the device name and the device's **Unique Identifier** (**UDID**), as shown in the following screenshot. Then, click on **Continue**.

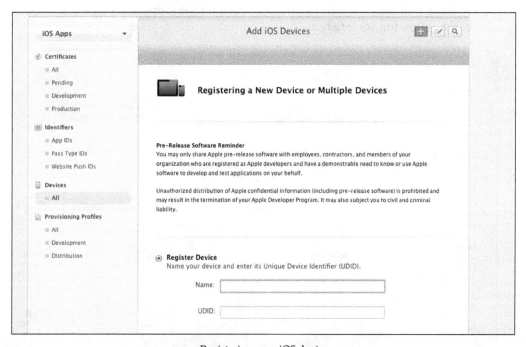

Registering your iOS device

 In order to get your iOS device's UDID, you can get it after connecting your iOS device to iTunes. Select your device from the left-hand side menu of iTunes and then click on **Serial Number**; you will find it changed to **Identifier (UDID)** with the device UDID.

8. You will be introduced to the review page. Click on **Register** to register your device.

9. Select **Development** in **Certificates** to create your development certificate file. Read the introduction page and click on **Continue**.

10. In the second step of the development certificate creation process, choose the CSR file that we created in step 2 and click on the **Generate** button, as shown in the following screenshot:

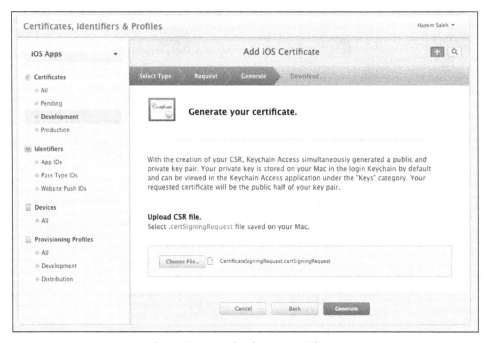

Generating your development certificate

11. In the last step of the development certificate creation process, click on the **Download** button to download the development certificate to your machine.

12. Select **All** from the **Provision Profiles** to create a provision profile, which will be installed on your iOS device. Choose the **iOS App Development** option from **Development**, as shown in the following screenshot, and then click on **Continue**:

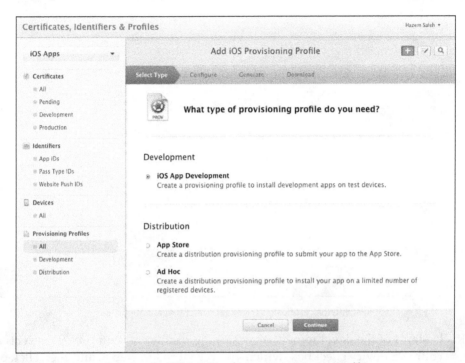

Selecting the iOS App Development provisioning profile

13. In the second step of the development provisioning profile creation process, select **App ID**, which we created in step 5, and then click on the **Continue** button.

14. In step 3 of the development provisioning profile creation process, select the **Development certificate** checkbox that we created in step 10, as shown in the following screenshot, and then click on the **Continue** button:

Selecting the certificate to include in the provisioning profile

15. In step 4 of the development provisioning profile creation process, select your iOS device checkbox, which you registered in step 8, and then click on the **Continue** button.

16. In step 5 of the development provisioning profile creation process, enter your preferred profile name (for example, **SoundRecorderProfile**) and then click on the **Generate** button.

17. In the last step of the development provisioning profile creation process, click on the **Download** button to download the provisioning profile to your machine.

18. Now that we have created and downloaded both the development certificate and the provisioning profile, we need to install them. Double-click on the `.cer` file that you downloaded in step 11 to install it onto a keychain on your Mac machine. If you are prompted with the **Add Certificates** dialog, click on **OK**.

19. In order to install the downloaded provisioning profile to your iOS device, connect your iOS device to your Mac, open the organizer application from your Xcode by selecting **Organizer** from **Window** menu, and then click on the **Add** button and select the `.mobileprovision` file. You should find that this profile is a valid one, as shown in the following screenshot:

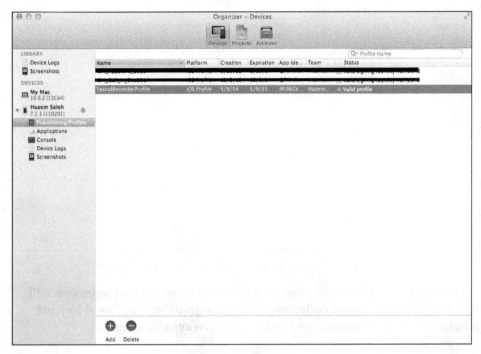

Adding a mobile provisioning profile to an iOS device

20. Finally, you can deploy your application on your iOS device by selecting your iOS device from the active scheme dropdown and clicking on the **Build and run** button, as shown in the following screenshot. After clicking on the button, you will find our Sound Recorder application finally launched on your iOS device.

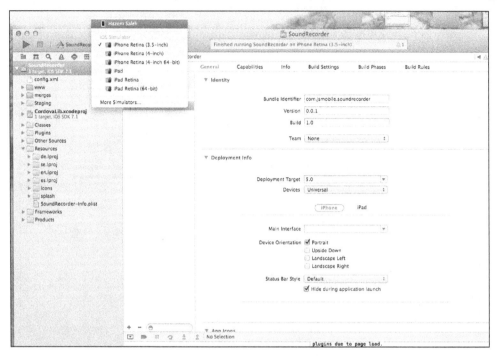

Deploying our Sound Recorder application to a real iOS device

When running your iOS application on a real device for the first time, you will receive the prompt message **codesign wants to sign using key "-----" in your keychain**. If you see this message, click on the **Always allow** button.

Configuring the Windows Phone development environment

In order to configure your Windows Phone 8 development environment, you will need the following:

- Windows 8 operating system or any higher compatible Windows versions.
- Windows Phone SDK 8.0, which includes a standalone Visual Studio Express 2012 for Windows Phone, Windows Phone emulators, and other useful tools to profile Windows Phone applications. The Windows Phone SDK can also work as an add-in to the Visual Studio 2012 Professional, Premium, or Ultimate editions.

In order to download Windows Phone SDK 8.0, go to `http://www.microsoft.com/en-us/download/details.aspx?id=35471`.

Visual Studio for Windows Phone is the official Microsoft IDE for Windows Phone development. It is a complete development environment to create Windows Phone applications and has many features, some of which are as follows:

- Source code editor
- User-interface builder
- Templates for Windows Phone projects
- Testing and debugging features on Windows Phone emulators or real Windows Phone devices
- Simulation, monitoring, and profiling capabilities for Windows Phone applications

After getting the Windows Phone 8.0 SDK, installing it onto your Windows machine is a very straightforward process. Launch the SDK installer and follow these steps:

1. Provide the path in which the SDK will be installed.

2. Check the **I agree to license terms and conditions** option.

3. Click on the **Install** button, and you will see the status of the SDK installation on your Windows machine, as shown in the following screenshot. After installation completes, you might be asked to reboot your operating system.

Installing Windows Phone SDK 8.0

Importing the Sound Recorder application into Visual Studio

Now, it is time to make our Sound Recorder application compatible on Windows Phone 8. The following command adds Windows Phone 8 platform support to our Sound Recorder application:

```
> cordova platform add wp8
```

Open your Visual Studio IDE and then follow these steps:

1. Select **Open File** from the **File** menu and then select the SoundRecorder. sln file under the platforms/wp8 directory to open our Sound Recorder Windows Phone 8 project.

2. Select **Build Solution** from the **Build** menu.

3. In order to run your project in the Windows Phone 8 emulator, click on the **Run** button by selecting a target emulator, as shown in the following screenshot:

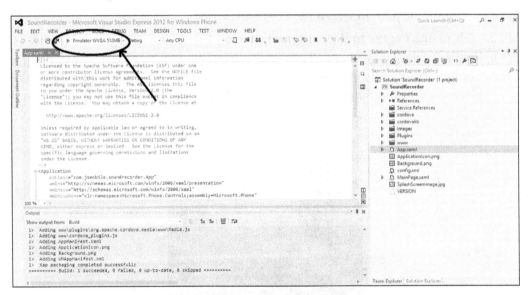

Running a Windows Phone 8 project in the Visual Studio IDE

After clicking on the **Run** button, the Windows Phone 8 emulator will be launched with our Sound Recorder application and you can start working with it, as shown in the following screenshot:

First run of our Sound Recorder application in WP8

If you notice in the preceding screenshot, there are two problems that occur when we run the application in a WP8 emulator:

- The header title is truncated
- The jQuery Mobile application footer is not aligned with the bottom of the page

The first problem appears because jQuery Mobile set the CSS overflow property of its header and title to `hidden`. In order to fix this issue, we need to change this behavior by setting the `overflow` property to visible in the `css/app.css` file, as shown in the following code:

```
.ui-header .ui-title {
    overflow: visible !important;
}
```

In order to fully align the application footer in both portrait and landscape modes of Windows Phone 8, you need to hide the system tray by setting `shell:SystemTray.IsVisible="False"` instead of `shell:SystemTray.IsVisible="True"` in `MainPage.xaml` (which is located under the `platforms/wp8` directory), as shown in the following code snippet:

```
<phone:PhoneApplicationPage
    x:Class="com.jsmobile.soundrecorder.MainPage"
    xmlns="http://schemas.microsoft.com/winfx/2006/xaml/presentation"
    ...
    xmlns:shell="clr-namespace:Microsoft.Phone.
Shell;assembly=Microsoft.Phone"
    shell:SystemTray.IsVisible="False" ...>
    ...
</phone:PhoneApplicationPage>
```

After performing these two fixes, we can rerun our Sound Recorder application; we will find that the screen is now fine, as shown in the following screenshot:

Fixed Sound Recorder application in WP8

Running the Sound Recorder application on a real Windows Phone

Now, it is time to deploy our Sound Recorder application on a real Windows Phone 8 device. In order to do this, you have to unlock your Windows Phone for development using the **Windows Phone Developer Registration** tool. In order to use and run this tool, note the following prerequisites:

- A registered Windows Phone developer account. You can create your registered Windows Phone developer account from `https://dev.windowsphone.com/en-us/join`. Note that creating a Windows Phone developer account is not free and the exact cost that you will pay depends on your country and region.
- A Microsoft account associated with your Windows Phone developer account.
- Connect your Windows Phone to your Windows machine and make sure that:
    - The mobile screen is unlocked
    - The date and time of your mobile are correct

Now, you can launch the **Windows Phone Developer Registration** tool by switching to Windows' **All Apps view** and select **Windows Phone Developer Registration** under **Windows Phone SDK 8.0**. When the tool starts, follow these steps in order to unlock your Windows Phone for development:

1. Make sure that the tool status displays the **Identified Windows Phone 8 device** message.

2. Click on the **Register** button to unlock your phone for development. If your phone is already registered, you will see an **Unregister** button, as shown in the following screenshot:

The Windows Phone Developer Registration tool

3. After clicking on the **Register** button, you will be introduced to the **Sign In** dialog box to enter your Microsoft account information (e-mail and password); you can then click on **Sign In**.

4. After clicking on **Sign In**, and assuming that you met all the prerequisites, your Windows Phone will be successfully unlocked for development, and you will be able to deploy your Windows Phone 8 application to it.

Now, in order to deploy our Sound Recorder application to your Windows Phone 8 device, select your Windows Phone8 device from the target device list and click on the **Run** button, as shown in the following screenshot:

Running the Sound Recorder application in WP8

After clicking on the **Run** button, you can enjoy testing our Sound Recorder application on your Windows Phone 8 device.

Summary

After reading and applying the steps mentioned in this chapter, you will have the three most popular mobile platform development environments (Android, iOS, and Windows Phone 8) installed on your machine(s). You can now build your Apache Cordova applications using these development tools and deploy your applications on their emulators. In this chapter, you learned how to deploy your Apache Cordova application on real devices of all these popular mobile platforms in detail. Finally, you learned the common problems and solutions that occur when you decide to support your Apache Cordova application on iOS and Windows Phone 8. In the next chapter, you will start learning how to use the different APIs provided by Apache Cordova in detail.

4

Cordova API in Action

In this chapter, we will start taking a deep dive in Apache Cordova API and see Apache Cordova API in action. You will learn how to work with the Cordova accelerometer, camera, compass, connection, contacts, device, geolocation, globalization, and the InAppBrowser APIs. This chapter as well as the next one illustrates a Cordova mobile app, Cordova Exhibition (which is developed using Apache Cordova and jQuery Mobile), that explores the main features of the Apache Cordova API in order to give you real-life usage examples of the Apache Cordova API in Android, iOS, and Windows Phone 8.

Exploring the Cordova Exhibition app

The Cordova Exhibition app aims at showing the main features of the Apache Cordova API. The demo shows practical examples of the following Apache Cordova API plugins:

- Accelerometer
- Camera
- Compass
- Connection
- Contacts
- Device
- Geolocation
- Globalization
- InAppBrowser
- Media, file, and capture
- Notification
- Storage

As well as Apache Cordova, the Cordova Exhibition app uses jQuery Mobile in order to create the app's user interface. The Cordova Exhibition app is supported on the following platforms:

- Android
- iOS
- Windows Phone 8

The following screenshot shows the home page of the Cordova Exhibition app. The home page displays a list from which users can choose the feature they want to try.

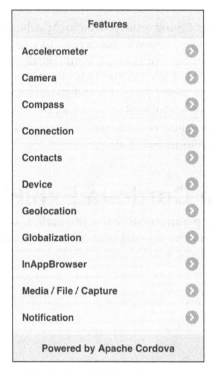

The Cordova Exhibition home page

In this chapter and the next one, we will explore each feature individually in its own section.

The Cordova Exhibition app structure

In order to create the Cordova Exhibition app from the **Command-line Interface** (**CLI**), we run the following `cordova create` command:

```
> cordova create cordova-exhibition com.jsmobile.cordovaexhibition
CordovaExhibition
```

In order to add Android, iOS, and Windows Phone 8 support from the CLI, we run the usual `cordova platform add` commands from the app directory as follows:

```
> cd cordova-exhibition
```

```
> cordova platform add android
```

```
> cordova platform add ios
```

```
> cordova platform add wp8
```

In order to add the different plugins to our Cordova Exhibition app, we use the usual `cordova plugin add` command (we will show the details of every plugin URL in its corresponding section).

To build and run the Cordova Exhibition app in your emulators and devices, you can follow the same steps that we used in *Chapter 3, Apache Cordova Development Tools*, to build and run the Sound Recorder application.

> The complete source code of our Cordova Exhibition app with all of the three supported platforms can be downloaded from the book's web page, or you can access the code directly from GitHub at `https://github.com/hazems/cordova-exhibition`.

Now, let's understand the structure of our Cordova Exhibition code. The following screenshot shows our Cordova Exhibition app's hierarchy:

The Cordova Exhibition application's structure

The www directory contains the following files and subdirectories:

- css: This directory contains the custom app's **Cascading Style Sheet (CSS)**.

- img: This directory contains the custom app's images.

- jqueryMobile: This directory contains the files of the jQuery Mobile framework and used plugins (the jQuery Mobile page params plugin and jQuery validation plugin).

- js: This directory contains all the custom app's JavaScript code. It has the following two subdirectories:

  - api: This directory contains the app managers that interact with the Apache Cordova API in order to decouple the Cordova API from the app event handlers. This gives us the ability to change the implementation of our app API without changing our app event handlers and, at the same time, the ability to keep our app event handlers small.

  - vc: This directory contains the app view controllers that register and implement the event handlers of every page and their user interface components. Event handlers usually call the app managers (the app API) in order to access the device's native features and, finally, they display the results in the app page.

The js directory also includes common.js file, which has common utilities. Finally, under the www directory, the index.html file contains all the app pages. The index. html file will be illustrated in *Finalizing the Cordova Exhibition app* section in *Chapter 5, Diving Deeper into the Cordova API*.

 It is important to note that not all Cordova features are supported across all platforms. In order to know the unsupported features, check out the last part in the *Overview of Cordova API* section in *Chapter 1, Introduction to Apache Cordova*.

Accelerometer

The accelerometer plugin provides access to the device's accelerometer in order to get the delta in movement relative to the current device's orientation in the x, y, and z axes.

In order to use the accelerometer in our Apache Cordova project, we need to use the following `cordova plugin add` command:

```
> cordova plugin add https://git-wip-us.apache.org/repos/asf/cordova-plugin-device-motion.git
```

Demo

In order to access the accelerometer demo, you need to click on the accelerometer list item. You will be introduced to the **Accelerometer** page. You can then click on the **Start Watch Acceleration** button in order to start watching the accelerometer. You will then be able to get the acceleration information in the x, y, and z axes, as shown in the following screenshot:

The Accelerometer page in action

You can click on the **Stop Watch Acceleration** button to stop watching the accelerometer at any time.

The HTML page

The following code snippet shows the `"accelerometer"` page:

```
<div data-role="page" id="accelerometer">
    <div data-role="header">
        <h1>Accelerometer</h1>
        <a href="#" data-role="button" data-rel="back" data-
icon="back">Back</a>
    </div>
    <div data-role="content">
        <h1>Welcome to the Accelerometer Gallery</h1>
        <p>Click 'Start Watch Acceleration' button below to start
watch acceleration.</p>
        <input type="button" id="startWatchAcceleration"
value="Start Watch Acceleration"/>
        <input type="button" id="stopWatchAcceleration"
value="Stop Watch Acceleration"/>
        <div id="acceleration">
        </div>
    </div>
</div>
```

As shown in the preceding `"accelerometer"` page code snippet, it contains the following:

- A page header that includes a back button
- Page content that includes the following main elements:
    - `"startWatchAcceleration"`: This button is used to start watching acceleration
    - `"stopWatchAcceleration"`: This button is used to stop watching acceleration
    - `"acceleration"`: This div is used to display the acceleration result

View controller

The following code snippet shows the page view controller JavaScript object, which includes the event handlers of the page (`accelerometer.js`):

```
(function() {
    var accelerometerManager = AccelerometerManager.getInstance();
    var watchID;

    $(document).on("pageinit", "#accelerometer", function(e) {
        e.preventDefault();

        $("#startWatchAcceleration").on("tap", function(e) {
            e.preventDefault();

            enableStartWatchAccelerationButton(false);

            var callback = {};

            callback.onSuccess = onSuccess;
            callback.onError = onError;

            watchID = accelerometerManager.
startWatchAcceleration(callback);
        });

        $("#stopWatchAcceleration").on("tap", function(e) {
            e.preventDefault();

            enableStartWatchAccelerationButton(true);

            accelerometerManager.stopWatchAcceleration(watchID);
        });

        initPage();
    });

    $(document).on("pagebeforehide", "#accelerometer", function(e) {
        accelerometerManager.stopWatchAcceleration(watchID);
        enableStartWatchAccelerationButton(true);
    });

    function initPage() {
        $("#stopWatchAcceleration").closest('.ui-btn').hide();
    }
```

```
    function onSuccess(acceleration) {
        $("#acceleration").html("Acceleration X: " + acceleration.x +
"<br/>" +
            "Acceleration Y: " + acceleration.y + "<br/>" +
            "Acceleration Z: " + acceleration.z + "<br/>" +
            "Timestamp: "      + acceleration.timestamp + "<br/>");
    }


    function onError() {
        $("#acceleration").html("An error occurs during watching
acceleration.");
    }


    function enableStartWatchAccelerationButton(enable) {
        if (enable) {
            $("#startWatchAcceleration").button("enable");
            $("#stopWatchAcceleration").closest('.ui-btn').hide();
        } else {
            $("#startWatchAcceleration").button("disable");
            $("#stopWatchAcceleration").closest('.ui-btn').show();
        }

        $("#startWatchAcceleration").button("refresh");
    }

})();
```

The "pageinit" event handler, which is called once in the page initialization, registers the "startWatchAcceleration" tap event handler. The "startWatchAcceleration" tap event handler does the following:

- It disables the "startWatchAcceleration" button and shows the "stopWatchAcceleration" button by calling enableStartWatchAccelerat ionButton(false)
- It starts watching the acceleration by calling accelerometerManager.star tWatchAcceleration(callback), specifying a callback object that contains the following:

    ◦ The onSuccess callback that will be called if the operation succeeds
    ◦ The onError callback that will be called if the operation fails

The `accelerometerManager.startWatchAcceleration(callback)` function returns `watchID`, which will be used in order to stop watching the acceleration.

The `"pageinit"` event handler, which is called once in the page initialization, registers the `"stopWatchAcceleration"` tap event handler. The `"stopWatchAcceleration"` tap event handler does the following:

- It hides the `"stopWatchAcceleration"` button and enables the `"startWatchAcceleration"` button by calling `enableStartWatchAccelerationButton(true)`

- It stops watching the acceleration by calling `accelerometerManager.stopWatchAcceleration(watchID)` and specifying `watchID`, which we get from the `accelerometerManager.startWatchAcceleration(callback)` call

The `"pageinit"` event handler also calls `initPage()` in order to hide the `"stopWatchAcceleration"` button at the beginning. In `onSuccess(acceleration)`, which will be called if `accelerometerManager.startWatchAcceleration(callback)` succeeds, the x, y, and z acceleration is shown with the current timestamp. In `onError()`, which will be called if `accelerometerManager.startWatchAcceleration(callback)` fails, an error message is displayed.

Finally, in order to stop watching acceleration before leaving the page, `accelerometerManager.stopWatchAcceleration()` is called in the `"pagebeforehide"` event, which will be called every time we transition away from the page.

API

The following code snippet shows the accelerometer manager JavaScript object that interacts with the Apache Cordova Accelerometer API (`AccelerometerManager.js`). Note that the manager files are always included in the `index.html` file before the view controller files so that the manager objects can be used by view controller objects:

```
var AccelerometerManager = (function () {
    var instance;

    function createObject() {
        return {
            startWatchAcceleration: function (callback) {
                return navigator.accelerometer.
watchAcceleration(callback.onSuccess,
callback.onError,
```

```
{frequency: 2000});
        },
        stopWatchAcceleration: function (watchID) {
            if (watchID) {
                navigator.accelerometer.clearWatch(watchID);
            }
        }
    };
};

return {
  getInstance: function () {
    if (!instance) {
        instance = createObject();
    }

    return instance;
  }
};
})();
```

As you can see, `AccelerometerManager` is a singleton object that has the following two methods, as highlighted in the preceding code:

- `startWatchAcceleration(callback)`: This uses the Cordova `navigator.accelerometer.watchAcceleration()` method to watch acceleration. The `navigator.accelerometer.watchAcceleration(accelerometerSuccess, accelerometerError, [accelerometerOptions])` method has the following parameters:

  - `accelerometerSuccess`: This will be called if the operation succeeds with an object that contains the current acceleration along the x, y, and z axes and the timestamp. In `AccelerometerManager`, `accelerometerSuccess` is set to `callback.onSuccess`.

  - `accelerometerError`: This will be called if the operation fails. In `AccelerometerManager`, `accelerometerError` is set to `callback.onError`.

  - `accelerometerOptions`: This is an optional parameter that holds the accelerometer's configuration. It has a `frequency` attribute to specify how often to retrieve acceleration in milliseconds. In `AccelerometerManager`, the `frequency` parameter is set to `2000` milliseconds (note that this parameter is `10000` milliseconds by default).

- stopWatchAcceleration(watchID): This uses the Cordova `navigator.accelerometer.clearWatch()` method to remove watching acceleration. `navigator.accelerometer.clearWatch(watchID)` has the following parameter:

  ○ watchID: This represents the ID returned by `navigator.accelerometer.watchAcceleration()`.

We are now done with the `Accelerometer` functionality in our Cordova Exhibition app. However, before exploring the `Camera` functionality, note that the `navigator.accelerometer` object has also the method shown in the following table:

Method name	Description
navigator.accelerometer.getCurrentAcceleration (accelerometerSuccess, accelerometerError)	This method retrieves the current acceleration along the *x*, *y*, and *z* axes. Acceleration values are returned to the accelerometerSuccess callback function.

Camera

The camera plugin provides access to the device's camera in order to take pictures. This plugin also allows you to pick images from the device's image library.

In order to use the camera in our Apache Cordova project, we need to use the following `cordova plugin add` command:

```
> cordova plugin add https://git-wip-us.apache.org/repos/asf/cordova-plugin-camera.git
```

Demo

In order to access the camera demo, you need to click on the camera list item. You will be introduced to the **Camera** page. You can click on the **Get Picture** button in order to select whether to get a picture from the device's gallery or the device's camera. If you choose the **Camera** menu item, the default camera application of the device will be launched for you to capture a picture. If you choose the **Gallery** menu item, the device's gallery will be opened for you to pick an image. After getting the image from the camera or the gallery, you will be able to view the image on the **Camera** page, as shown in the following screenshot:

A selected image is shown on the camera page

The HTML page

The following code snippet shows the `"camera"` page:

```
<div data-role="page" id="camera">
    <div data-role="header">
        <h1>Camera</h1>
        <a href="#" data-role="button" data-rel="back" data-
icon="back">Back</a>
    </div>
    <div data-role="content">
        <h1>Welcome to the Camera Gallery</h1>
        <p>Click 'Get Picture' button below</p>
        <div class="center-wrapper">
            <input type="button" id="getPicture" data-
icon="camera" value="Get Picture"
```

```
                    class="center-button" data-inline="true"/>
            </div>
            <br/>

            <div style="width: 100%;">
                <img id="imageView" style="width: 100%;"></img>
            </div>

            <div data-role="popup" id="pictureTypeSelection">
                <ul data-role="listview" data-inset="true" style="min-
width:210px;">
                    <li data-role="divider" data-theme="a">Get Picture
From</li>
                    <li><a id="pictureFromGallery"
href="#">Gallery</a></li>
                    <li><a id="pictureFromCamera"
href="#">Camera</a></li>
                </ul>
            </div>
        </div>
</div>
```

As shown in the preceding `"camera"` page code snippet, it contains the following:

- A page header that includes a back button
- Page content that includes the following main elements:
    - `"getPicture"`: This button is used to get a picture
    - `"imageView"`: This is used in order to display the selected or captured image
    - `"pictureTypeSelection"`: This div element is a pop up that will be displayed to allow the user to select whether to get a picture from the camera or from the gallery

View controller

The following code snippet shows the page view controller JavaScript object that includes the action handlers of the page (`camera.js`):

```
(function() {
    var cameraManager = CameraManager.getInstance();

    $(document).on("pageinit", "#camera", function(e) {
        e.preventDefault();
```

```
        $("#imageView").hide();

        $("#getPicture").on("tap", function(e) {
            e.preventDefault();

            $("#pictureTypeSelection").popup("open");
        });

        $("#pictureFromGallery").on("tap", function(e) {
            e.preventDefault();
            $("#pictureTypeSelection").popup("close");

            getPhoto(true);
        });

        $("#pictureFromCamera").on("tap", function(e) {
            e.preventDefault();
            $("#pictureTypeSelection").popup("close");

            getPhoto(false);
        });
    });

    function getPhoto(fromGallery) {
        var callback = {};

        callback.onSuccess = onSuccess;
        callback.onError = onError;

        cameraManager.getPicture(callback, fromGallery);
    }

    function onSuccess(fileURI) {
        $("#imageView").show();
        $("#imageView").attr("src", fileURI);
    }

    function onError(message) {
        console.log("Camera capture error");
    }
})();
```

The `"pageinit"` event handler registers the following event handlers:

- `"getPicture"` tap event handler: This opens the `"pictureTypeSelection"` pop up to allow the user to select the way to get a picture

- `"pictureFromGallery"` tap event handler: This closes the currently opened `"pictureTypeSelection"` pop up and calls `getPhoto(true)` to pick a photo from the device's gallery

- `"pictureFromCamera"` tap event handler: This closes the currently opened `"pictureTypeSelection"` pop up and calls `getPhoto(false)` to capture a photo using the device's camera

The `getPhoto(fromGallery)` method can get a photo (from the gallery or using the camera) by calling `cameraManager.getPicture(callback, fromGallery)` and specifying the following parameters:

- The `callback` object that contains the following attributes:
    - `onSuccess`: This callback will be called if the operation succeeds. It receives the `fileURI` of the picked image as a parameter, this allows the callback to display the picked image in `"imageView"`.
    - `onError`: This callback will be called if the operation fails.

- The `fromGallery` parameter informs `cameraManager.getPicture()` to get the photo from the device's gallery if it is set to `true`, and if `fromGallery` is set to `false`, then it informs `cameraManager.getPicture()` to get the photo using the device's camera

API

The following code snippet shows the camera manager JavaScript object that interacts with the Apache Cordova Camera API (`CameraManager.js`):

```
var CameraManager = (function () {
  var instance;

  function createObject() {
      var fileManager = FileManager.getInstance();

      return {
          getPicture: function (callback, fromGallery) {
              var source = Camera.PictureSourceType.CAMERA;
```

```
            if (fromGallery) {
                source = Camera.PictureSourceType.PHOTOLIBRARY;
            }

            navigator.camera.getPicture(callback.onSuccess,
                                        callback.onError,
                                        {
                                            quality: 80,
                                            destinationType:
Camera.DestinationType.FILE_URI,

                                            sourceType: source,
                                            correctOrientation: true
                                        });
        }
    };
  };

  return {
    getInstance: function () {
      if (!instance) {
          instance = createObject();
      }

      return instance;
    }
  };
})();
```

As you can see, `CameraManager` is a singleton object that has a single method as highlighted in the preceding code. The `getPicture(callback, fromGallery)` function uses the Cordova `navigator.camera.getPicture()` method to get a picture.

The `navigator.camera.getPicture(cameraSuccess, cameraError, [cameraOptions])` function has the following parameters:

- `cameraSuccess`: This callback will be called if the operation succeeds. It receives a parameter that represents a file URI, or a native URI, or a Base-64 encoded string based on the specified `cameraOptions` parameter. In `CameraManager`, `cameraSuccess` is set to `callback.onSuccess`.

- `cameraError`: This parameter will be called if the operation fails. In `CameraManager`, `cameraError` is set to `callback.onError`. Note that `CameraError` receives a string that represents the error description.

- `cameraOptions`: This is an optional parameter that holds the camera's configuration.

The `cameraOptions` parameter has many attributes. The attributes in the following table are used by our `CameraManager` object:

Attribute name	Description
`quality`	This represents the quality of the saved image. It is expressed in a range of 0-100, where 100 is typically the full resolution with no loss due to file compression. In our `CameraManager` object, the quality is set to `80`.
	As per the Cordova documentation, setting the quality below 50 is recommended to avoid memory errors on some iOS devices. Setting the quality to `80` has always given me a good picture quality and has worked fine with me in my Cordova projects; however, if you find any memory errors because of the `navigator.camera.getPicture()` method, then please set the quality below 50 and rebuild/rerun the project again in your iOS device.
`destinationType`	This represents the type of the operation's returned value. It can have one of the following values:
	• `Camera.DestinationType.DATA_URL`: This means that the returned value will be a Base64-encoded string that represents the image
	• `Camera.DestinationType.FILE_URI`: This means that the returned value will be a file URI of the image
	• `Camera.DestinationType.NATIVE_URI`: This means that the returned value will be a native URI of the image
	In our `CameraManager` object, `destinationType` is set to `Camera.DestinationType.FILE_URI`, which means that the success callback of the `navigator.camera.getPicture()` method will receive the image file URI.
`sourceType`	This represents the source of the picture. It can have one of the following values:
	• `Camera.PictureSourceType.PHOTOLIBRARY`
	• `Camera.PictureSourceType.CAMERA`
	• `Camera.PictureSourceType.SAVEDPHOTOALBUM`
	In our `CameraManager` object, `sourceType` is set to `Camera.PictureSourceType.PHOTOLIBRARY` if `fromGallery` is set to `true`. If `fromGallery` is set to `false`, then `sourceType` is set to `Camera.PictureSourceType.CAMERA`.
`correctOrientation`	If this is set to `true`, then it will rotate the image to correct it for the orientation of the device during capture.

We are now done with the Camera functionality in our Cordova Exhibition app. However, before exploring the compass functionality, note that the navigator. camera.getPicture() function's CameraOptions parameter has also the attributes shown in the following table:

Attribute name	Description
allowEdit	If set to true, this will allow the user to edit an image before selection.
cameraDirection	This represents the type of camera to use (front facing or back facing). It can have one of the following values: • Camera.Direction.BACK • Camera.Direction.FRONT
encodingType	This represents the returned image file's encoding; it can have one of the following values: • Camera.EncodingType.JPEG • Camera.EncodingType.PNG
mediaType	This represents the type of media to select from. It only works when PictureSourceType is set to PHOTOLIBRARY or SAVEDPHOTOALBUM. It can have one of the following values: • Camera.MediaType.PICTURE: This allows the selection of only pictures • Camera.MediaType.VIDEO: This allows the selection of only videos • Camera.MediaType.ALLMEDIA: This allows the selection of all media types
popoverOptions	This represents the popover location in iPad. It works only for iOS.
saveToPhotoAlbum	If set to true, then this will save the image to the photo album on the device after capture.
targetWidth	This represents the width in pixels to scale image. It must be used with targetHeight.
targetHeight	This represents the height in pixels to scale image. It must be used with targetWidth.

The `navigator.camera` object has also the method shown in the following table:

Method name	Description

`navigator.camera.`
`cleanup(cameraSuccess,`
`cameraError)`
	This forces the removal of the intermediate image files that are kept in temporary storage after calling the `camera.getPicture()` method. This API applies only when the value of `Camera.sourceType` is `Camera.PictureSourceType.CAMERA` and the value of `Camera.destinationType` is `Camera.DestinationType.FILE_URI`. This works only on iOS.

	In iOS, the temporary images in `/tmp` might be deleted when exiting the application. Using this API will force an instant cleanup of the temporary images.

Compass

The compass plugin provides access to the device's compass in order to detect the direction (heading) that the device is pointed to (the compass measures the heading in degrees from 0 to 359.99, where 0 represents north). In order to use the compass in our Apache Cordova project, we need to use the following `cordova plugin add` command:

```
>cordova plugin add https://git-wip-us.apache.org/repos/asf/cordova-plugin-device-orientation.git
```

Demo

In order to access the compass demo, you need to click on the **Compass** list item. You will be introduced to the **Compass** page. Then, you can click on the **Start Watch Heading** button in order to start watching the compass heading. You will be able to get the heading value, as shown in the following screenshot:

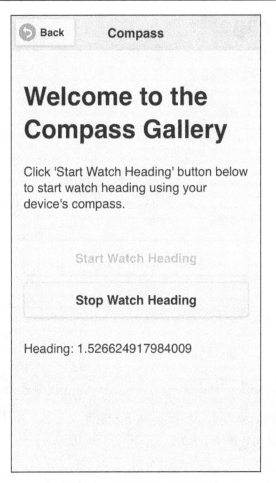

The Compass page in action

You can click on the **Stop Watch Heading** button to stop watching the compass heading at any time.

The HTML page

The following code snippet shows the "compass" page:

```
<div data-role="page" id="compass">
    <div data-role="header">
        <h1>Compass</h1>
        <a href="#" data-role="button" data-rel="back" data-
icon="back">Back</a>
    </div>
    <div data-role="content">
        <h1>Welcome to the Compass Gallery</h1>
        <p>Click 'Start Watch Heading' button below to start watch
heading using your device's compass.</p>
        <input type="button" id="startWatchHeading" value="Start
Watch Heading"/>
        <input type="button" id="stopWatchHeading" value="Stop
Watch Heading"/><br/>

        <div id="compassHeading">
        </div>
    </div>
</div>
```

As shown in the preceding "compass" page code snippet, it contains the following:

- A page header that includes a back button
- Page content that includes the following main elements:
    - "startWatchHeading": This button is used to start watching the compass heading
    - "stopWatchHeading": This button is used to stop watching the compass heading
    - "compassHeading": This div is used to display the compass heading result

View controller

The following code snippet shows the page view controller JavaScript object that includes the event handlers of the page (compass.js):

```javascript
(function() {
    var compassManager = CompassManager.getInstance();
    var watchID;

    $(document).on("pageinit", "#compass", function(e) {
        e.preventDefault();

        $("#startWatchHeading").on("tap", function(e) {
            e.preventDefault();

            enableStartWatchHeadingButton(false);

            var callback = {};

            callback.onSuccess = onSuccess;
            callback.onError = onError;

            watchID = compassManager.startWatchHeading(callback);
        });

        $("#stopWatchHeading").on("tap", function(e) {
            e.preventDefault();

            enableStartWatchHeadingButton(true);

            compassManager.stopWatchHeading(watchID);
        });

        initPage();
    });
```

```
$(document).on("pagebeforehide", "#compass", function(e) {
    compassManager.stopWatchHeading(watchID);
    enableStartWatchHeadingButton(true);
});

function initPage() {
    $("#stopWatchHeading").closest('.ui-btn').hide();
}

function onSuccess(heading) {
    $("#compassHeading").html("Heading: " +
heading.magneticHeading);
}

function onError(error) {
    $("#compassHeading").html("An error occurs during watch
heading: " + error.code);
}

function enableStartWatchHeadingButton(enable) {

    if (enable) {
        $("#startWatchHeading").button("enable");
        $("#stopWatchHeading").closest('.ui-btn').hide();
    } else {
        $("#startWatchHeading").button("disable");
        $("#stopWatchHeading").closest('.ui-btn').show();
    }

    $("#startWatchHeading").button("refresh");
}

})();
```

The "pageinit" event handler registers the "startWatchHeading" tap event handler. The "startWatchHeading" tap event handler does the following:

- It disables the "startWatchHeading" button and shows the "stopWatchHeading" button by calling enableStartWatchHeadingButton(false)

- It starts to watch the heading by calling `compassManager.startWatchHeading(callback)` and specifying the `callback` object parameter, which contains the following attributes:

  - `onSuccess`: This callback will be called if the operation succeeds
  - `onError`: This callback will be called if the operation fails

The `compassManager.startWatchHeading(callback)` function returns `watchID` that we will be using in order to stop watching the compass heading.

The `"pageinit"` event handler also registers the `"stopWatchHeading"` tap event handler. The `"stopWatchHeading"` tap event handler does the following:

- It hides the `"stopWatchHeading"` button and enables the `"startWatchHeading"` button by calling `enableStartWatchHeadingButton(true)`

- It stops watching the heading by calling `compassManager.stopWatchHeading(watchID)` and specifying `watchID` parameter, which we get from the `compassManager.startWatchHeading(callback)` call

The `"pageinit"` event handler also calls `initPage()` in order to hide the `"stopWatchHeading"` button at the beginning.

In `onSuccess(heading)`, which will be called if `compassManager.startWatchHeading(callback)` succeeds, `heading.magneticHeading` (which represents the heading in degrees) is displayed in the `"compassHeading"` div. In `onError()`, which will be called if `compassManager.startWatchHeading(callback)` fails, an error message is displayed in the `"compassHeading"` div. Finally, in order to make sure to stop watching the heading before leaving the page, `compassManager.stopWatchHeading()` is called in the `"pagebeforehide"` event.

API

The following code snippet shows the compass manager JavaScript object that interacts with the Apache Cordova Compass API (`CompassManager.js`):

```
var CompassManager = (function () {
  var instance;

  function createObject() {
      return {
```

```
        startWatchHeading: function (callback) {
            return navigator.compass.watchHeading(callback.
onSuccess,
                                            callback.onError,
                                            {frequency:
2000});
        },
        stopWatchHeading: function (watchID) {
            if (watchID) {
                navigator.compass.clearWatch(watchID);
            }
        }
    };
};

return {
  getInstance: function () {
    if (!instance) {
        instance = createObject();
    }

    return instance;
  }
};
})();
```

As you can see in the preceding code, CompassManager is a singleton object that has the following two methods, as highlighted in the code:

- startWatchHeading(callback): This uses the Cordova navigator. compass.watchHeading() method to watch the compass heading. The navigator.compass.watchHeading(compassSuccess, compassError, [compassOptions]) method has the following parameters:

  - compassSuccess(heading): This callback will be called if the operation succeeds. It receives an object (heading) that contains the current heading's information as a parameter. In CompassManager, compassSuccess is set to callback.onSuccess.

  - compassError: This callback will be called if the operation fails. In CompassManager, compassError is set to callback.onError.

- ° compassOptions: This is an optional parameter that holds the compass' configuration. It has a frequency attribute to specify how often to retrieve the compass heading in milliseconds. In CompassManager, the frequency parameter is set to 2000 milliseconds (note that this parameter is 100 milliseconds by default).

- stopWatchHeading(watchID): This uses the Cordova navigator.compass. clearWatch() method to remove the compass heading. The navigator. compass.clearWatch(watchID) method has the following parameter:

  - ° watchID: This represents the ID returned by navigator.compass. watchHeading().

This compassOptions object (which is passed as the last parameter to navigator. compass.watchHeading method) has the attributes shown in the following table:

Attribute name	Description
frequency	This represents the frequency of compass heading retrieval in milliseconds. By default, it is 100 milliseconds.
filter	This represents the change in degrees that is required in order to initiate a watchHeading success callback. It is not supported in Android, Windows Phone 7 and 8, Tizen, Firefox OS, and Amazon Fire OS.

The heading object (which is passed as a parameter to the compassSuccess callback) has the attributes shown in the following table:

Attribute name	Description
magneticHeading	This represents the heading in degrees from 0 to 359.99 at a single point of time.
trueHeading	This represents the heading relative to the geographic North Pole in degrees from 0 to 359.99 at a single point of time. A negative value indicates that the true heading cannot be determined.
headingAccuracy	This is the deviation in degrees between the reported heading and the true heading.
timestamp	This is the time in which the compass heading was retrieved.

We are now done with the Compass functionality in our Cordova Exhibition app. However, before exploring the Connection functionality, note that the navigator.compass object has also the method shown in the following table:

Method name	Description
navigator.compass.getCurrentHeading (compassSuccess, compassError, compassOptions)	This retrieves the information of the current compass heading. When the operation succeeds, the heading information is passed to the compassSuccess callback as a parameter.

Connection

The connection plugin provides information about the connection type of the device. In order to use the connection plugin in our Apache Cordova project, we need to use the following cordova plugin add command:

```
> cordova plugin add https://git-wip-us.apache.org/repos/asf/cordova-
plugin-network-information.git
```

Demo

In order to access the connection demo, you can click on the **Connection** list item. You will be introduced to the **Connection** page. You can click on the **Get Connection Type** button in order to know the current connection type of your device, as shown in the following screenshot:

Getting the device's connection type

The HTML page

The following code snippet shows the "connection" page:

```html
<div data-role="page" id="connection">
    <div data-role="header">
        <h1>Connection</h1>
        <a href="#" data-role="button" data-rel="back" data-
icon="back">Back</a>
    </div>
    <div data-role="content">
        <h1>Welcome to the Connection Gallery</h1>
        <p>Click 'Get Connection Type' button below to know the
connection type.</p>
        <input type="button" id="getConnectionType" value="Get
Connection Type"/><br/>
        <div id="connectionType">
        </div>
    </div>
</div>
```

As shown in the preceding "connection" page code snippet, it contains
the following:

- A page header that includes a back button
- Page content that includes only one button, "getConnectionType",
  and one div, "connectionType", to display the connection type

View controller

The following code snippet shows the page view controller JavaScript object that
includes the action handlers of the page (connection.js):

```javascript
(function() {
    var connectionManager = ConnectionManager.getInstance();
    $(document).on("pageinit", "#connection", function(e) {
        e.preventDefault();

        $("#getConnectionType").on("tap", function(e) {
            e.preventDefault();

            $("#connectionType").html("Current Connection: " +
connectionManager.getCurrentConnection());
        });
    });
})();
```

The `"pageinit"` event handler registers the `"getConnectionType"` tap event handler. In the `"getConnectionType"` tap event handler, it displays the current connection of the device, which is retrieved by calling the `connectionManager.getCurrentConnection()` method.

API

The following code snippet shows the connection manager JavaScript object that interacts with the Apache Cordova Connection API (`ConnectionManager.js`):

```
var ConnectionManager = (function () {
    var instance;

    function createObject() {
        return {
            getCurrentConnection: function () {
                var connectionType = navigator.connection.type;

                switch(connectionType) {
                    case Connection.UNKNOWN:
                        return "Unknown connection";
                    case Connection.ETHERNET:
                        return "Ethernet connection";
                    case Connection.WIFI:
                        return "WiFi connection";
                    case Connection.CELL_2G:
                        return "Cell 2G connection";
                    case Connection.CELL_3G:
                        return "Cell 3G connection";
                    case Connection.CELL_4G:
                        return "Cell 4G connection";
                    case Connection.CELL:
                        return "Cell generic connection";
                    case Connection.NONE:
```

```
                        return "No network connection";
                    default:
                        return "Un-recognized connection";
                }
            }
        };
    };
    return {
      getInstance: function () {
        if (!instance) {
            instance = createObject();
        }

        return instance;
      }
    };
})();
```

As you can see, `ConnectionManager` is a singleton object that has a single method as highlighted in the code. The `getCurrentConnection()` method uses the Cordova `navigator.connection.type` property in order to get the currently active network connection (Ethernet, Wi-Fi, cell 2G, cell 3G, and so on).

Contacts

The contacts plugin provides access to the device's contacts database in order to find and create contacts. In order to use the contacts plugin in our Apache Cordova project, we need to use the following `cordova plugin add` command:

```
> cordova plugin add https://git-wip-us.apache.org/repos/asf/cordova-
plugin-contacts.git
```

Demo

In order to access the contacts demo, you can click on the **Contacts** list item. You will be introduced to the **Contacts** page. You can search for contacts by typing in the search field (you have to type at least three characters), as shown in the following screenshot:

Searching for contacts

You can click on any of the filtered contacts, and you will be introduced to the **Contact Details** page in order to check the contact details, as shown in the following screenshot:

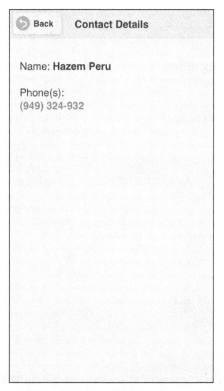

Viewing contact details

The HTML page

The following code snippet shows the `"contacts"` page:

```
<div data-role="page" id="contacts">
    <div data-role="header">
        <h1>Contacts</h1>
        <a href="#" data-role="button" data-rel="back" data-
icon="back">Back</a>
    </div>
    <div data-role="content">
        <ul data-role="listview" id="contactList" data-
filter="true" data-filter-placeholder="Enter 3+ chars to search
...">
        </ul>
    </div>
</div>
```

As shown in the preceding `"contacts"` page code snippet, it contains the following:

- A page header that includes a back button.
- Page content that includes a jQuery Mobile list view element (`"contactList"`) that is defined by setting the `data-role` attribute to `"listview"`. Setting the `data-filter` attribute to `true` tells jQuery Mobile to provide a search field for our list view. Finally, the `placeholder` attribute informs the user to enter at least three characters in order to search for contacts.

When the user clicks on any of the filtered contacts, the user will be introduced to the `"contactDetails"` page. The following code snippet shows the `"contactDetails"` page:

```
<div data-role="page" id="contactDetails">
    <div data-role="header">
        <h1>Contact Details</h1>
        <a href="#" data-role="button" data-rel="back" data-
icon="back">Back</a>
    </div>
    <div data-role="content">
        <div id="contactInfo"></div>
    </div>
</div>
```

As shown in the preceding `"contact details"` page code snippet, it contains the following:

- A page header that includes a back button
- Page content that includes a `"contactInfo"` div to display information on contact details

View controller

The following code snippet shows the contacts page view controller JavaScript object that includes the event handlers of the page (`contacts.js`):

```
(function() {
    var contactsManager = ContactsManager.getInstance();

    $(document).on("pageinit", "#contacts", function(e) {
        e.preventDefault();

        $("#contactList").on("filterablebeforefilter", function
(e, data) {
            e.preventDefault();
```

```
                var filterText = data.input.val();

            if (filterText && filterText.length > 2) {
                var callback = {};

                callback.onSuccess = function (contacts) {
                    updateContactsList(contacts);
                };

                callback.onError = function (error) {
                    $("#contactList").empty();
                    $("<li>Error displaying contacts</li>").
appendTo("#contactList");
                };

                contactsManager.getAllContacts(callback,
filterText);
            }
        });
    });

    function updateContactsList(contacts) {
        $("#contactList").empty();

        if (jQuery.isEmptyObject(contacts)) {
            $("<li>No Contacts Available</li>").
appendTo("#contactList");
        } else {
            var i;

            //Display the top 50 elements
            for (i = 0; i < contacts.length || i < 50; ++i) {
                if (contacts[i]) {
                    $("<li><a href='#contactDetails?contact=" +
encodeURIComponent(JSON.stringify(contacts[i])) + "'>" +
                        contacts[i].name.formatted +
"</a></li>").appendTo("#contactList");
                }
            }
        }

        $("#contactList").listview('refresh');
    }
})();
```

As highlighted in the preceding code snippet, the `"pageinit"` event handler registers the `"filterablebeforefilter"` event handler on the `"contactList"` list view in order to create our custom contacts filter. In the `"filterablebeforefilter"` event handler, the current filter text entered by the user is retrieved by calling `data.input.val()`. In order to minimize the search space, the filter text has to be at least three characters. If the filter text's length exceeds two characters, then a call to the `contactsManager.getAllContacts(callback, filterText)` method is performed in order to get all the contacts that match the entered filter text.

In order to call the `contactsManager.getAllContacts(callback, filterText)` method, we specified a callback object that contains two attributes: the `onSuccess` attribute (which represents a success callback) and the `onError` attribute (which represents a failure callback). The `onSuccess` callback receives the filtered contacts list and then calls the `updateContactsList()` method in order to update the current contacts list view with the new filtered contacts list. The `onError` callback just displays an error message to the user. The second parameter `filterText` represents the input filter text.

The `updateContactsList(contacts)` method clears the `"contactList"` list view, and if the contacts list (`contacts`) is not empty, contacts are appended to the `"contactList"` list view, and finally, the `"contactList"` list view is refreshed with new updates.

You might notice that every contact item in the list view is linked to the `"contactDetails"` page and passes the item's contact object as a parameter (after converting the contact object to an encoded JSON string).

Thanks to the jQuery Mobile page parameters plugin (which can be downloaded from `https://github.com/jblas/jquery-mobile-plugins/tree/master/page-params`) and its inclusion in the `index.html` file, we can pass parameters between pages easily using `"#pageID?param1=value1&param2=value2 ...etc.`

However, in our application, in the `js/common.js` file (which contains common utilities across all of the app pages and is included after the plugin, that is, the `jqm.page.params.js` file), we added a small utility over the plugin in order to retrieve page parameters at any event of the `"to"` page. In order to implement this, we create an event handler for the `"pagebeforechange"` event in order to get the passed parameter(s), as shown in the following code snippet:

```
$(document).bind("pagebeforechange", function(event, data) {
    $.mobile.pageData = (data && data.options &&
data.options.pageData)
                    ? data.options.pageData : null;
});
```

By checking `data.options.pageData`, we can determine whether there are any passed parameters from the `"from"` page to the `"to"` page, thanks to the page parameters plugin. After getting the passed parameters, we set them in `$.mobile.pageData`, which can be accessible from any event in the `"to"` page. If there are no passed parameters, then `$.mobile.pageData` will be set to `null`.

The following code snippet shows `contactDetails.js`, which is the view controller of the `"contactDetails"` page:

```
(function() {
    $(document).on("pageshow", "#contactDetails", function(e) {
        e.preventDefault();

        var contactDetailsParam = $.mobile.pageData.contact ||
null;
        var contactDetails = JSON.parse(decodeURIComponent(contactDet
ailsParam));
        var i;
        var numbers = "";

        if (contactDetails.phoneNumbers) {
            for (i = 0; i < contactDetails.phoneNumbers.length; ++i)
{
                numbers = "<a href='tel:" + contactDetails.
phoneNumbers[i].value + "'>" +
                        contactDetails.phoneNumbers[i].value +
"</a><br/>";
            }
        } else {
            numbers = "NA<br/>";
        }

        $("#contactInfo").html("<p>" +
                "Name: <strong>" + contactDetails.name.formatted +
"</strong><br/><br/>" +
                "Phone(s): " + "<br/>" +
                numbers +
                "</p>");
    });
})();
```

In the "pageshow" event handler of the "contactDetails" page, contactDetails is retrieved using $.mobile.pageData.contact and then decoded and parsed to be converted to a JavaScript object. Finally, the contact names and numbers are acquired from contactDetails using contactDetails.name.formatted and contactDetails.phoneNumbers and are displayed in the "contactInfo" div.

The jQuery Mobile "pageshow" event is triggered on the "to" page after the transition completes.

API

The following code snippet shows the contacts manager JavaScript object that wraps the Apache Cordova Contacts API (ContactsManager.js):

```
var ContactsManager = (function () {
    var instance;

    function createObject() {
        return {
            getAllContacts: function (callback, filterText) {
                var options = new ContactFindOptions();

                options.filter = filterText || "";
                options.multiple = true;

                var fields = ["id", "name", "phoneNumbers"];

                navigator.contacts.find(callback.onSuccess, callback.onError, fields, options);
            }
        };
    };

    return {
        getInstance: function () {
            if (!instance) {
                instance = createObject();
            }

            return instance;
        }
    };
})();
```

As you can see, `ContactsManager` is a singleton object that has a single method as highlighted in the preceding code. The `getAllContacts(callback, filterText)` method uses the Cordova `navigator.contacts.find()` method to retrieve contacts.

The `navigator.contacts.find(contactSuccess, contactError, contactFields, contactFindOptions)` method has the following parameters:

- `contactSuccess`: This callback will be called if the operation succeeds. It receives the retrieved contacts array as a parameter. In `ContactsManager`, `contactSuccess` is set to `callback.onSuccess`.

- `contactError`: This callback will be called if the operation fails. In `ContactsManager`, `contactError` is set to `callback.onError`.

- `contactFields`: This object specifies the fields of every contact object in the returned result of `navigator.contacts.find()`. In `ContactsManager`, we specified the `["id", "name", "phoneNumbers"]` contact fields.

- `contactFindOptions`: This is an optional parameter that is used to filter contacts.

The `contactFindOptions` parameter has the attributes shown in the following table:

Attribute name	Description
filter	This represents the search string used to filter contacts. In `ContactsManager`, the value is set to `filterText`.
multiple	This specifies whether the `find` operation returns multiple contacts. By default, it is `false`. In our `ContactsManager`, it is set to `true`.

We are now done with the `Contacts` functionality in the Cordova Exhibition app. However, before exploring the device's API functionality, note that the `navigator.contacts.find()` method's `contactFields` parameter can have one or more attribute(s) from the `Contact` object, whose attributes are specified in the following table:

Attribute name	Description
id	This represents a globally unique identifier for the contact. It is used in our contacts example.
displayName	This represents the name of this contact.
name	This represents a `ContactName` object that contains all the components of a name, which will be illustrated later. It is used in our contacts example.
nickname	This represents the contact's nickname.

Attribute name	Description
phoneNumbers	This represents a ContactField array of all the contacts' phone numbers. It is used in our contacts example. The ContactField object will be illustrated later.
Emails	This represents a ContactField array of all the contacts' e-mail addresses.
addresses	This represents a ContactAddress array of all the contacts' addresses. It will be illustrated later.
ims	This represents a ContactField array of all the contacts' IM addresses.
organizations	This represents a ContactOrganization array of all the contacts' organizations. It will be illustrated later.
birthday	This represents the contact's birthday.
note	This represents a note about the contact.
photos	This represents a ContactField array of the contacts' photos.
categories	This represents a ContactField array of all the user-defined categories associated with the contact.
urls	This represents a ContactField array of web pages associated with the contact.

The ContactName object has the attributes shown in the following table:

Attribute name	Description
formatted	This represents the complete name of the contact.
familyName	This represents the contact's family name.
givenName	This represents the contact's given name.
middleName	This represents the contact's middle name.
honorificPrefix	This represents the contact's prefix (such as Mr or Mrs).
honorificSuffix	This represents the contact's suffix.

The ContactField object has the attributes shown in the following table:

Attribute name	Description
type	This represents a string that indicates what type of field it is.
value	This represents the value of the field, for example, a phone number.
pref	If this is set to true, it means that this ContactField object contains the user's preferred value.

The ContactAddress object has the attributes shown in the following table:

Attribute name	Description
type	This represents a string that indicates what type of field it is.
pref	If this is set to true, it means that this ContactAddress object contains the user's preferred value.
formatted	This represents the formatted full address for display.
streetAddress	This represents the full street address.
locality	This represents the city or locality.
region	This represents the state or region.
postalCode	This represents the zip code or postal code.
country	This represents the country name.

The ContactOrganization object has the attributes shown in the following table:

Attribute name	Description
type	This represents a string that indicates what type of field it is, for example, "home".
pref	If this is set to true, it means that this ContactOrganization contains the user's preferred value.
name	This represents the contact's organization name.
department	This represents the contact's department name inside the organization.
title	This represent the contact's title in the organization.

The navigator.contacts object has also the method shown in the following table:

Method name	Description
navigator.contacts.create(properties)	This is used to return a Contact object that you can use, for example, to save a contact in the device contacts database by calling the save() method of the Contact object.

Device

The device plugin defines a global device object that describes the device's hardware and software. It is very important to note that the device object is available after the "deviceready" event occurs. In order to use the device plugin in our Apache Cordova project, we need to use the following cordova plugin add command:

```
> cordova plugin add https://git-wip-us.apache.org/repos/asf/cordova-plugin-device.git
```

Demo

In order to access the device demo, you can click on the **Device** list item. You will be introduced to the **Device** page. You can click on the **Get Device Info** button in order to get your device information, as shown in the following screenshot:

Getting device information

The HTML page

The following code snippet shows the `"device"` page:

```html
<div data-role="page" id="device">
    <div data-role="header">
        <h1>Device</h1>
        <a href="#" data-role="button" data-rel="back" data-
icon="back">Back</a>
    </div>
    <div data-role="content">
        <h1>Welcome to the Device Gallery</h1>
        <p>Click 'Get Device Info' button below to get the device
information.</p>
        <input type="button" id="getDeviceInfo" value="Get Device
Info"/><br/>

        <div id="deviceInfo">
        </div>
    </div>
</div>
```

As shown in the preceding `"device"` page code snippet, it contains the following:

- A page header that includes a back button
- Page content that includes a `"getDeviceInfo"` button to get the device information and a `"deviceInfo"` div in order to display device information

View controller

The following code snippet shows the `"device"` page view controller JavaScript object that includes the event handlers of the page (`device.js`):

```javascript
(function() {
    var deviceManager = DeviceManager.getInstance();

    $(document).on("pageinit", "#device", function(e) {
        e.preventDefault();

        $("#getDeviceInfo").on("tap", function(e) {
            e.preventDefault();

            $("#deviceInfo").html(deviceManager.getDeviceInfo());
        });
    });
})();
```

As shown in the preceding code snippet, the `"pageinit"` event handler registers the `"tap"` event handler on the `"getDeviceInfo"` button. In the `"tap"` event handler of the `"getDeviceInfo"` button, the device information is displayed in the `"deviceInfo"` div and retrieved by calling the `deviceManager.getDeviceInfo()` method.

API

The following code snippet shows the device manager JavaScript object that uses the Apache Cordova device object (`DeviceManager.js`):

```
var DeviceManager = (function () {
    var instance;

    function createObject() {
        return {
            getDeviceInfo: function () {
                return "Device Model: "    + device.model    + "<br
/>" +
                       "Device Cordova: "  + device.cordova  + "<br
/>" +
                       "Device Platform: " + device.platform + "<br
/>" +
                       "Device UUID: "     + device.uuid     + "<br
/>" +
                       "Device Version: "  + device.version  + "<br
/>";
            }
        };
    };

    return {
        getInstance: function () {
            if (!instance) {
                instance = createObject();
            }
```

```
            return instance;
        }
    };
})();
```

The `DeviceManager` object is a singleton object that has a single method as highlighted in the preceding code. The `getDeviceInfo()` function uses the Cordova device object to retrieve the device information.

The `DeviceManager` object uses the attributes of the device object, as shown in the following table:

Attribute name	Description
`model`	This represents the device's model name.
`cordova`	This represents the version of Apache Cordova that runs on this device.
`platform`	This represents the device's operating system name.
`uuid`	This represents the device's **Universally Unique Identifier (UUID)**.
`version`	This represents the device's operating system version.

Geolocation

The geolocation plugin provides information about the device's current location that can be retrieved via **Global Positioning System (GPS)**, network signals, and GSM/CDMA cell IDs. Note that there is no guarantee that the API returns the device's actual location.

In order to use the geolocation plugin in our Apache Cordova project, we need to use the following `cordova plugin add` command:

```
> cordova plugin add https://git-wip-us.apache.org/repos/asf/cordova-plugin-geolocation.git
```

Demo

In order to access the geolocation demo, you can click on the **Geolocation** list item. You will be introduced to the **Geolocation** page. You can click on the **Get Current Position** button in order to get your device's current position, as shown in the following screenshot:

Getting the device's position

The HTML page

The following code snippet shows the "geolocation" page:

```html
<div data-role="page" id="geolocation">
    <div data-role="header">
        <h1>Geolocation</h1>
        <a href="#" data-role="button" data-rel="back" data-icon="back">Back</a>
    </div>
    <div data-role="content">
        <h1>Welcome to the Geolocation Gallery</h1>
        <p>Click 'Get Current Position' button below to know where you are.</p>
        <input type="button" id="getCurrentPosition" value="Get Current Position"/><br/>

        <div id="position">
        </div>
    </div>
</div>
```

As shown in the preceding "geolocation" page code snippet, it contains the following:

- A page header that includes a back button
- Page content that includes a "getCurrentPosition" button to get the device's current position and a "position" div in order to display it

View controller

The following code snippet shows the "geolocation" page view controller JavaScript object that includes the event handlers of the page (geolocation.js):

```javascript
(function() {
    var geolocationManager = GeolocationManager.getInstance();

    $(document).on("pageinit", "#geolocation", function(e) {
        e.preventDefault();

        $("#getCurrentPosition").on("tap", function(e) {
            e.preventDefault();

            var callback = {};
```

```
        callback.onSuccess = onSuccess;
        callback.onError = onError;

        geolocationManager.getCurrentPosition(callback);
    });
});

function onSuccess(position) {
    console.log("position is retrieved successfully");

    $("#position").html("Latitude: "  +
position.coords.latitude + "<br />" +
                        "Longitude: " +
position.coords.longitude);
    }

function onError(error) {
    $("#position").html("Error code: " + error.code + ",
message: " + error.message);
    }
})();
```

As shown in the preceding code snippet, the `"pageinit"` event handler registers the `"tap"` event handler on the `"getCurrentPosition"` button. In the `"tap"` event handler of the `"getCurrentPosition"` button, the device's current position is retrieved by calling the `geolocationManager.getCurrentPosition()` method.

The `geolocationManager.getCurrentPosition(callback)` method takes a `callback` object as a parameter that contains two attributes (`onSuccess` and `onError`) that refer to the following callbacks:

- `onSuccess(position)`: This callback will be called if the operation succeeds. It receives a position object (which represents the device's current position) as a parameter. Inside the success callback, the position's longitude and latitude information are displayed in the `"position"` div.

- `onError(error)`: This callback will be called if the operation fails. It receives an `error` object that contains the error information (error code and error message) as a parameter.

API

The following code snippet shows the geolocation manager JavaScript object that interacts with the Apache Cordova geolocation API (GeolocationManager.js):

```
var GeolocationManager = (function () {
    var instance;

    function createObject() {
        return {
            getCurrentPosition: function (callback) {
                navigator.geolocation.getCurrentPosition(callback.
onSuccess,
callback.onError,
                                                                       {
timeout: 15000,
enableHighAccuracy: true
                                                                       });
            }
        };
    };

    return {
        getInstance: function () {
            if (!instance) {
                instance = createObject();
            }

            return instance;
        }
    };
})();
```

As shown, GeolocationManager is a singleton object that has a single method, getCurrentPosition(callback), as highlighted in the preceding code. This method uses the Cordova navigator.geolocation.getCurrentPosition() method in order to retrieve the device's current position.

The `navigator.geolocation.getCurrentPosition(geolocationSuccess,` `[geolocationError],` `[geolocationOptions])` method has the following parameters:

- `geolocationSuccess`: This represents the successful callback that will be called when the operation succeeds. It receives a `Position` object that holds the current position information as a parameter. In `GeolocationManager`, `geolocationSuccess` is set to `callback.onSuccess`.

- `geolocationError`: This is an optional parameter that represents the error callback that will be called when the operation fails. It receives a `PositionError` object that holds the error information (the code that represents the error code and the message that represents the error message) as a parameter. In `GeolocationManager`, `geolocationError` is set to `callback.onError`.

- `geolocationOptions`: This is an optional parameter that represents the geolocation options.

The `geolocationOptions` object has the attributes shown in the following table:

Attribute name	Description
`enableHighAccuracy`	If this attribute is set to `true`, it informs the plugin to use more accurate methods in order to get the current position, such as satellite positioning. In `GeolocationManager.getCurrentPosition()`, `enableHighAccuracy` is set to `true`.
`timeout`	This represents the time in milliseconds after which the operation times out. In `GeolocationManager.getCurrentPosition()`, `timeout` is set to `15000`.
`maximumAge`	This is the maximum time in milliseconds for cached position.

The `Position` object has the attributes shown in the following table:

Attribute name	Description
`coords`	This represents a `Coordinates` object that represents coordinates of the position.
`timestamp`	This represents the creation timestamp of `coords`.

The `Coordinates` object has the attributes shown in the following table:

Attribute name	Description
latitude	This represents the position's latitude. It is used in our geolocation example.
longitude	This represents the position's longitude. It is used in our geolocation example.
altitude	This represents the height of the position in meters above the ellipsoid.
accuracy	This represents the accuracy level of the latitude and longitude coordinates in meters.
altitudeAccuracy	This represents the accuracy level of the altitude coordinate in meters.
heading	This represents the direction of travel, specified in degrees, counting clockwise relative to true north.
speed	This represents the current ground speed of the device, specified in meters per second.

Note that `navigator.geolocation` has the following two more methods:

- `watchPosition(geolocationSuccess, [geolocationError], [geolocationOptions])`: This can watch for changes in the device's current position. It returns a watch ID that should be used with `clearWatch()` to stop watching for changes in position.
- `clearWatch(watchID)`: This can stop watching the changes to the device's position referenced by the `watchID` parameter.

We are now done with the geolocation functionality in the Cordova Exhibition app.

Globalization

The globalization plugin can be used in order to get the user locale and language and to perform operations specific to the user's locale and time zone.

In order to use the globalization plugin in our Apache Cordova project, we need to use the following `cordova plugin add` command:

```
> cordova plugin add https://git-wip-us.apache.org/repos/asf/cordova-
plugin-globalization.git
```

Demo

In order to access the globalization demo, you can click on the **Globalization** list item. You will be introduced to the **Globalization** page. You can click on the **Get Locale Name** button in order to get the user's locale name or the **Get Preferred Language** button in order to get the user's preferred language, as shown in the following screenshot:

Getting the user's locale and preferred language

The HTML page

The following code snippet shows the `"globalization"` page:

```html
<div data-role="page" id="globalization">
    <div data-role="header">
        <h1>Globalization</h1>
        <a href="#" data-role="button" data-rel="back" data-
icon="back">Back</a>
    </div>
    <div data-role="content">
        <h1>Welcome to the Globalization Gallery</h1>
        <p>Click the buttons below to explore globalization.</p>
        <input type="button" id="getLocaleName" value="Get Locale
Name"/>
        <input type="button" id="getPreferredLanguage" value="Get
Preferred Language"/><br/>

        <div id="globInfo">
        </div>
    </div>
</div>
```

As shown in the preceding `"globalization"` page code snippet, it contains the following:

- A page header that includes a back button
- Page content that includes a `"getLocaleName"` button to get the user locale, a `"getPreferredLanguage"` button to get the user preferred language, and a `"globInfo"` div in order to display the results

View controller

The following code snippet shows the `"globalization"` page view controller JavaScript object that includes the event handlers of the page (`globalization.js`):

```javascript
(function() {
    var globalizationManager = GlobalizationManager.getInstance();

    $(document).on("pageinit", "#globalization", function(e) {
        e.preventDefault();
```

```
        $("#getLocaleName").on("tap", function(e) {
            e.preventDefault();

            var callback = {};

            callback.onSuccess = handleLocaleSuccess;
            callback.onError = handleLocaleError;

            globalizationManager.getLocaleName(callback);
        });

        $("#getPreferredLanguage").on("tap", function(e) {
            e.preventDefault();

            var callback = {};

            callback.onSuccess = handleLangSuccess;
            callback.onError = handleLangError;

            globalizationManager.getPreferredLanguage(callback);
        });
    });

    function handleLocaleSuccess(locale) {
        $("#globInfo").html("Locale Name: " + locale.value +
"<br/>");
    }

    function handleLocaleError() {
        $("#globInfo").html("Unable to get Locale name<br/>");
    }

    function handleLangSuccess(language) {
        $("#globInfo").html("Preferred language name: " +
language.value + "<br/");
    }

    function handleLangError() {
        $("#globInfo").html("Unable to get preferred language
name<br/>");
    }
})();
```

As shown in the preceding code snippet, the `"pageinit"` event handler registers the `"tap"` event handler on the `"getLocaleName"` button. In the `"tap"` event handler of the `"getLocaleName"` button, the user locale is retrieved by calling the `globalizationManager.getLocaleName()` method.

The `globalizationManager.getLocaleName(callback)` method takes a callback object as a parameter that contains two attributes (`onSuccess` and `onError`) that refer to the following callbacks in order:

- `handleLocaleSuccess(locale)`: This callback will be called if the operation succeeds; it receives a locale object that represents the user's current locale as a parameter. In the success callback, the locale value is displayed in the `"globInfo"` div.

- `handleLocaleError()`: This callback will be called if the operation fails.

The `"pageinit"` event handler also registers the `"tap"` event handler on the `"getPreferredLanguage"` button. In the `"tap"` event handler of the `"getPreferredLanguage"` button, the user's preferred language is retrieved by calling the `globalizationManager.getPreferredLanguage()` method.

The `globalizationManager.getPreferredLanguage(callback)` method takes a callback object as a parameter that contains two attributes (`onSuccess` and `onError`) that refer to the following callbacks in order:

- `handleLangSuccess(language)`: This callback will be called if the operation succeeds; it receives a language object that represents the user's preferred language as a parameter. In the success callback, the preferred language value is displayed in the `"globInfo"` div.

- `handleLangError()`: This callback will be called if the operation fails.

API

The following code snippet shows the globalization manager JavaScript object that interacts with the Apache Cordova Globalization API (`GlobalizationManager.js`):

```
var GlobalizationManager = (function () {
    var instance;

    function createObject() {
        return {
            getLocaleName: function (callback) {
                navigator.globalization.getLocaleName(callback.
onSuccess, callback.onError);
            },
```

```
          getPreferredLanguage: function (callback) {
               navigator.globalization.getPreferredLanguage(callback.
onSuccess,
callback.onError);
               }
          };
     };

     return {
          getInstance: function () {
               if (!instance) {
                    instance = createObject();
               }

               return instance;
          }
     };
})();
```

As shown, `GlobalizationManager` is a singleton object that has two methods as highlighted in the preceding code. The first one is `getLocaleName(callback)`, which uses the Cordova `navigator.globalization.getLocaleName()` method in order to retrieve the user's current locale.

The `navigator.globalization.getLocaleName(successCallback, errorCallback)` method has the following parameters:

- `successCallback`: This represents the successful callback that will be called when the operation succeeds. It receives a locale object that holds the current locale information as a parameter. In `GlobalizationManager`, `sucessCallback` is set to `callback.onSuccess`.

- `errorCallback`: This represents the error callback that will be called when the operation fails. It receives a `GlobalizationError` object that holds the error information (the code that represents the error code and the message that represents the error message) as a parameter. In `GlobalizationManager`, `errorCallback` is set to `callback.onError`.

The second method is `getPreferredLanguage(callback)` that uses the Cordova `navigator.globalization.getPreferredLanguage()` method in order to retrieve the user's preferred language.

The `navigator.globalization.getPreferredLanguage(successCallback, errorCallback)` method has the following parameters:

- `successCallback`: This represents the successful callback that will be called when the operation succeeds. It receives a `language` object that holds the user's preferred language information as a parameter. In `GlobalizationManager`, `sucessCallback` is set to `callback.onSuccess`.

- `errorCallback`: This represents the error callback that will be called when the operation fails. It receives a `GlobalizationError` object that holds the error information (the code that represents the error code and the message that represents the error message). In `GlobalizationManager`, `errorCallback` is set to `callback.onError`.

> The `navigator.globalization` object has more methods that you can check out in the Apache Cordova documentation at `https://github.com/apache/cordova-plugin-globalization/blob/master/doc/index.md`.

We are now done with the globalization functionality in the Cordova Exhibition app.

InAppBrowser

The InAppBrowser plugin can provide a web browser view that is displayed when calling the `window.open()` function or when opening a link formed as `<a target="_blank">`.

In order to use the `InAppBrowser` plugin in our Apache Cordova project, we need to use the following `cordova plugin add` command:

```
> cordova plugin add https://git-wip-us.apache.org/repos/asf/cordova-plugin-inappbrowser.git
```

Demo

In order to access the `InAppBrowser` demo, you can click on the InAppBrowser list item. You will be introduced to the **InAppBrowser** page. As shown in the following screenshot, you can click on the **Open and Close web page** button in order to open the `http://www.google.com/` web page using InAppBrowser. Note that the opened web page will be closed after 10 seconds.

Opening an external page using InAppBrowser

The HTML page

The following code snippet shows the `"inAppBrowser"` page:

```
<div data-role="page" id="inAppBrowser">
    <div data-role="header">
        <h1>InAppBrowser</h1>
        <a href="#" data-role="button" data-rel="back" data-
icon="back">Back</a>
    </div>
    <div data-role="content">
        <h1>Welcome to the InAppBrowser Gallery</h1>
        <p>Click the button below to open the inAppBrowser which
will close after 10 seconds.</p>

        <input type="button" id="openGoogleSearchPage" value="Open
and Close web page"/>
    </div>
</div>
```

As shown in the preceding `"inAppBrowser"` page code snippet, it contains the following:

- A page header that includes a back button
- Page content that includes a `"openGoogleSearchPage"` button to open a web page (`http://www.google.com/`) and close it after 10 seconds

View controller

The following code snippet shows the InAppBrowser page view controller JavaScript object that includes the event handlers of the page (inAppBrowser.js):

```
(function() {
    var inAppBrowserManager = InAppBrowserManager.getInstance();

    $(document).on("pageinit", "#inAppBrowser", function(e) {
        e.preventDefault();

        $("#openGoogleSearchPage").on("tap", function(e) {
            e.preventDefault();

            var windowRef = inAppBrowserManager.openWindow("http://
www.google.com");
```

```
              //Close the window after 10 seconds...
              window.setTimeout(function() {
                    console.log("It is over. Time to close the
    window...");
                       inAppBrowserManager.closeWindow(windowRef);
                 }, 10000);
           });
      });
 })();
```

As shown in the preceding code snippet, the `"pageinit"` event handler registers the `"tap"` event handler on the `"openGoogleSearchPage"` button. In the `"tap"` event handler of the `"openGoogleSearchPage"` button, a new window is opened by calling the `inAppBrowserManager.openWindow()` method that specifies the URL to open `"http://www.google.com/"`.

When the `window.setTimeout()` function is executed after 10 seconds using `windowRef`, which is returned from the `inAppBrowserManager.openWindow()` method, the opened window is closed by calling `inAppBrowserManager.closeWindow(windowRef)`.

API

The following code snippet shows `InAppBrowserManager.js`:

```
 var InAppBrowserManager = (function () {
     var instance;

     function createObject() {
         return {
             openWindow: function (url) {
                 var windowRef = window.open(url, '_blank',
 'location=no');

                 return windowRef;
             },
             closeWindow: function (windowRef) {
                 if (windowRef) {
                     windowRef.close();
                 }
             }
         };
     };
```

```
    return {
        getInstance: function () {
            if (!instance) {
                instance = createObject();
            }

            return instance;
        }
    };
})();
```

As shown in the preceding code, `InAppBrowserManager` is a singleton object that has two simple methods, as highlighted in the preceding code:

- `openWindow(url)`: This is used to open a new window by calling the `window.open()` method. The `window.open(url, target, options)` method has the following parameters:
    - `url`: This represents the URL to be loaded.
    - `target`: This represents the target in which to load the URL. It can be `_self` (default value), which means that the URL opens in the Cordova WebView if it is in the white list; otherwise, it opens in `InAppBrowser` or `_blank` (a specified value by `InAppBrowserManager`). This `_blank` means that the URL opens in `InAppBrowser` or `_system`, which means that the URL opens in the web browser of the system.
    - `options`: This represents the options for the `InAppBrowser`. It is a string that must not have any empty spaces, and it consists of key/value pairs, where key represents a feature's name and value represents a feature's value. The separator between any two features in the `options` string must be a comma. A `location` string is one of the available features that can be used in the `options` string. It specifies whether the location bar will be shown or not. In `InAppBrowserManager`, the `location` feature is set to no to hide the location bar, as it is by default set to `yes`.

`window.open()` returns a reference to the **InAppBrowser** window. This can be used to close the opened window later.

- `closeWindow(windowRef)`: This is used to close an opened window by calling the `close()` method of the reference to the **InAppBrowser** window (the `windowRef` object).

 InAppBrowser has more methods that you can check out in the Apache Cordova documentation at `https://github.com/apache/cordova-plugin-inappbrowser/blob/master/doc/index.md`.

We are now done with the InAppBrowser functionality in the Cordova Exhibition app.

Summary

In this chapter, we covered a lot of information regarding the Apache Cordova API. You saw the Apache Cordova API in action by exploring some features of the Cordova Exhibition app. You learned how to work with the Cordova accelerometer, camera, compass, connection, contacts, device, geolocation, globalization, and InAppBrowser APIs. In the next chapter, we will continue our look at the Apache Cordova API by exploring the remaining features of the Cordova Exhibition app.

5
Diving Deeper into the Cordova API

In this chapter, we will continue our journey in the Apache Cordova API by exploring the remaining main features of the Cordova Exhibition app. You will learn how to work with Cordova's media, file, capture, notification, and storage APIs. You will also learn how to utilize the Apache Cordova events in your Cordova mobile app.

Media, file, and capture

The media plugin provides the ability to record and play back audio files on a device.

In order to use the media plugin in our Apache Cordova project, we need to use the following `cordova plugin add` command:

```
> cordova plugin add https://git-wip-us.apache.org/repos/asf/cordova-plugin-media.git
```

The capture plugin provides access to the device's audio, image, and video capture capabilities. In order to use the capture plugin in our Apache Cordova project, we need to use the following `cordova plugin add` command:

```
> cordova plugin add https://git-wip-us.apache.org/repos/asf/cordova-plugin-media-capture.git
```

The file plugin provides access to the device's filesystem. In order to use the file plugin in our Apache Cordova project, we need to use the following `cordova plugin add` command:

```
> cordova plugin add https://git-wip-us.apache.org/repos/asf/cordova-plugin-file.git
```

Demo

In order to access the media, file, and capture demo, you can click on the **Media**, **File**, and **Capture** list item, respectively. You will then be introduced to the **Media / File / Capture** page. You can click on the **Record Sound** button in order to start recording. Once you complete recording, you can click on the **Stop Recording** button, as shown in the following screenshot, and you will be able to play back your recorded sound by clicking on the **Playback** button:

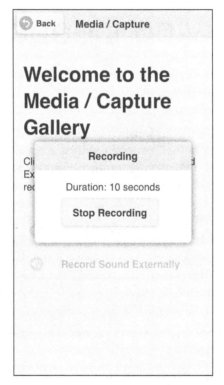

Record your voice

You also have the option to click on **Record Sound Externally**, which will open your device's default recording application in order to perform recording. Once you are done, you will return to the page, and then, you can use the **Playback** button to play back your recorded sound again.

The HTML page

The following code snippet shows the media page ("mediaFC"):

```
<div data-role="page" id="mediaFC">
    <div data-role="header">
        <h1>Media / Capture</h1>
        <a href="#" data-role="button" data-rel="back" data-
icon="back">Back</a>
    </div>
    <div data-role="content">
        <h1>Welcome to the Media / Capture Gallery</h1>
        <p>Click 'Record Sound' or 'Record Sound Externally'
button below to start recording your voice.</p>
        <input type="hidden" id="location"/>
        <div class="center-wrapper">
            <input type="button" id="recordSound" data-
icon="audio" value="Record Sound"/>
            <input type="button" id="recordSoundExt" data-
icon="audio" value="Record Sound Externally"/>
            <input type="button" id="playSound" data-
icon="refresh" value="Playback"/><br/>
        </div>

        <div data-role="popup" id="recordSoundDialog" data-
dismissible="false" style="width:250px">
            <div data-role="header">
                <h1>Recording</h1>
            </div>

            <div data-role="content">
                <div class="center-wrapper">
                    <div id="soundDuration"></div>
                    <input type="button" id="stopRecordingSound"
value="Stop Recording"
                            class="center-button" data-
inline="true"/>
                </div>
            </div>
        </div>
    </div>
</div>
```

As shown in the preceding `"mediaFC"` page, it contains the following:

- A page header that includes a back button
- Page content that includes the following elements:
  - `"recordSound"`: This button is used to record sound using our app interface. Clicking on this button will show the `"recordSoundDialog"` pop up to allow the user to stop the recording when the operation is finished.
  - `"recordSoundExt"`: This button is used to record sound externally using the device's default recording app.
  - `"playSound"`: This button is used to play the recorded sound.
  - `"recordSoundDialog"`: This is a custom pop up that will be shown when the user clicks on the `"recordSound"` button. It contains the `"stopRecordingSound"` button, which is used to stop recording sound when the recording is finished.

View controller

The following code snippet shows the first main part of the `"mediaFC"` page view controller JavaScript object:

```
(function() {
    var mediaManager = MediaManager.getInstance(), recInterval;

    $(document).on("pageinit", "#mediaFC", function(e) {
        e.preventDefault();

        $("#recordSound").on("tap", function(e) {
            e.preventDefault();

            disableActionButtons();

            var callback = {};

            callback.onSuccess = handleRecordSuccess;
            callback.onError = handleRecordError;

            mediaManager.startRecording(callback);

            var recTime = 0;
```

```
        $("#soundDuration").html("Duration: " + recTime + "
seconds");

        $("#recordSoundDialog").popup("open");

        recInterval = setInterval(function() {
                        recTime = recTime + 1;
                        $("#soundDuration").html("Duration:
" + recTime + " seconds");
                    }, 1000);
    });

    $("#recordSoundExt").on("tap", function(e) {
        e.preventDefault();

        disableActionButtons();

        var callback = {};

        callback.onSuccess = handleRecordSuccess;
        callback.onError = handleRecordError;

        mediaManager.recordVoiceExternally(callback);
    });

    $("#recordSoundDialog").on("popupafterclose", function(e,
ui) {
        e.preventDefault();

        clearInterval(recInterval);
        mediaManager.stopRecording();
    });

    $("#stopRecordingSound").on("tap", function(e) {
        e.preventDefault();

        $("#recordSoundDialog").popup("close");
    });

    $("#playSound").on("tap", function(e) {
        e.preventDefault();

        disableActionButtons();
```

```
            var callback = {};

            callback.onSuccess = handlePlaySuccess;
            callback.onError = handlePlayError;

            mediaManager.playVoice($("#location").val(),
   callback);
         });

         initPage();
      });

      $(document).on("pagebeforehide", "#mediaFC", function(e) {
         mediaManager.cleanUpResources();
         enableActionButtons();
      });

      // code is omitted for simplicity ...
   })();
```

The `"pageinit"` event handler registers the `"tap"` event handler on the `"recordSound"`, `"recordSoundExt"`, `"playSound"`, and `"stopRecordingSound"` buttons.

In the `"tap"` event handler of the `"recordSound"` button:

- Sound recording and playing buttons are disabled by calling the `disableActionButtons()` method
- In order to start recording sound:
  - A call to `mediaManager.startRecording(callback)` is performed specifying a callback parameter with the success and error callbacks
  - The `"recordSoundDialog"` pop up is shown, and its `"soundDuration"` div is updated every second with the current recording duration using the `window's` `setInterval()` method

In the `"tap"` event handler of the `"recordSoundExt"` button:

- Sound recording and playing buttons are disabled by calling the `disableActionButtons()` method
- In order to start recording sound externally, a call to `mediaManager.recordVoiceExternally(callback)` is performed specifying a callback parameter with the success and error callbacks

In the `"tap"` event handler of the `"stopRecordingSound"` button, it closes the `"recordSoundDialog"` pop up in order to trigger the `"popupafterclose"` event of the `"recordSoundDialog"` pop up in the `"popupafterclose"` event handler of the `"recordSoundDialog"` pop up:

- The recording timer is stopped using the `window's clearInterval()` method
- In order to stop recording sound, a call to `mediaManager.stopRecording()` is performed

In the `"tap"` event handler of the `"playSound"` button:

- Sound recording and playing buttons are disabled by calling the `disableActionButtons()` method
- In order to start playing the recorded sound, a call to `mediaManager.playVoice(filePath, callback)` is performed specifying a `filePath` parameter with the media file location to play (media file location is stored in the `"location"` hidden field when the recording operation succeeds) and a `callback` parameter with the success and error callbacks

The `"pageinit"` event handler also calls `initPage()`, whose code will be shown in the following code snippet. Finally, in the `"pagebeforehide"` event handler, which will be called every time, we are transitioning away from the page. A call to `mediaManager.cleanUpResources()` is performed in order to stop any playing sounds and clean up any used media resources when the media page is left.

The following code snippet shows the second main part of the `"mediaFC"` page view controller, which mainly includes the callback handlers and the `initPage()` method:

```
(function() {
    // code is omitted here for simplicity

    function initPage() {
        $("#playSound").closest('.ui-btn').hide();
    }

    function handleRecordSuccess(filePath) {
        $("#location").val(filePath);
        enableActionButtons();
        $("#playSound").closest('.ui-btn').show();
    }

    function handleRecordError(error) {
        console.log("An error occurs during recording: " +
error.code);
```

```
            enableActionButtons();
    }

    function handlePlaySuccess() {
        console.log("Sound file is played successfully ...");
        enableActionButtons();
    }

    function handlePlayError(error) {
        if (error.code) {
            console.log("An error happens when playing sound file
...");

            enableActionButtons();
        }
    }

    // Code is omitted here for simplicity ...
})();
```

As shown in the preceding code, we have the following methods:

- `initPage()`: This is called in the `"pageinit"` event. It initially hides the `"playSound"` button.

- `handleRecordSuccess(filePath)`: This represents the success callback of `mediaManager.startRecording(callback)` and `mediaManager.recordVoiceExternally(callback)`. It does the following:
    - It receives `filePath` of the recorded file as a parameter and saves it in the `"location"` hidden field in order to be used by the playback operation
    - It enables the sound recording (`"recordSound"` and `"recordSoundExt"`) and playback (`"playsound"`) buttons
    - It shows the `"playSound"` button

- `handleRecordError(error)`: This represents the error callback of `mediaManager.startRecording(callback)` and `mediaManager.recordVoiceExternally(callback)`. It does the following:
    - It receives an `error` object as a parameter and the error code is logged in the console
    - It enables the sound recording and playback buttons

- `handlePlaySuccess()`: This represents the success callback of `mediaManager.playVoice(filePath, callback)`. It does the following:
    - It logs a successful message in the console
    - It enables the sound recording and playing buttons
- `handlePlayError(error)`: This represents the error callback of `mediaManager.playVoice(filePath, callback)`. It does the following:
    - It logs an error message in the console
    - It enables the sound recording and playing buttons

API

The following code snippet shows the first part of `MediaManager.js` that interacts with the Cordova media and capture APIs:

```
var MediaManager = (function () {
    var instance;

    function createObject() {
        var fileManager = FileManager.getInstance();
        var recordingMedia;
        var audioMedia;

        return {
            startRecording : function (callback) {
                var recordVoice = function(dirEntry) {
                    var basePath = "";

                    if (dirEntry) {
                        basePath = dirEntry.toURL() + "/";
                    }

                    var mediaFilePath = basePath + (new Date()).
getTime() + ".wav";

                    var recordingSuccess = function() {
                        callback.onSuccess(mediaFilePath);
                    };

                    recordingMedia = new Media(mediaFilePath,
recordingSuccess, callback.onError);
```

```
                    // Record audio
                    recordingMedia.startRecord();
                };

                if (device.platform === "Android") {
                    var cb = {};

                    cb.requestSuccess = recordVoice;
                    cb.requestError = callback.onError;

                    fileManager.requestApplicationDirectory(cb);
                } else {
                    recordVoice();
                }
            },
            stopRecording : function () {
                if (recordingMedia) {
                    recordingMedia.stopRecord();
                    recordingMedia.release();

                    recordingMedia = null;
                }
            },
            playVoice : function (filePath, callback) {
                if (filePath) {
                    this.cleanUpResources();

                    audioMedia = new Media(filePath,
callback.onSuccess, callback.onError);

                    // Play audio
                    audioMedia.play();
                }
            },
            recordVoiceExternally: function (callback) {
                // code is omitted for simplicity ...
            },
            cleanUpResources : function () {
                // code is omitted for simplicity ...
            }
        };
    };
```

```
        return {
            getInstance: function () {
                if (!instance) {
                    instance = createObject();
                }

                return instance;
            }
        };
    })();
```

As you can see in the preceding highlighted code, `MediaManager` is a singleton object that has five methods. In order to record audio files using Apache Cordova, we can create a `Media` object as follows:

```
recordingMedia = new Media(src, [mediaSuccess], [mediaError],
[mediaStatus]);
```

The `Media` object constructor has the following parameters in order:

- `src`: This refers to the URI of the media file
- `mediaSuccess`: This is an optional parameter that refers to the callback, which will be called if the media operation (play/record or stop function) succeeds
- `mediaError`: This is an optional parameter that refers to the callback, which will be called if the media operation (play/record or stop function) fails
- `mediaStatus`: This is an optional parameter that executes to indicate status changes

In order to start recording an audio file, a call to the `startRecord()` method of the `Media` object must be performed. When the recording is finished, a call to the `stopRecord()` method of the `Media` object must be performed. Now, let's check out the details of the `MediaManager` methods:

- `startRecording(callback)`: This starts the audio recording by doing the following:
    - Getting the current device platform by calling `device.platform`.

- ○ If the current platform is Android, then a call to `fileManager.requestApplicationDirectory(cb)` is performed in order to create an application directory (if it hasn't already been created) under the device SD card's root directory using the `fileManager` object. If the directory creation operation succeeds, then `cb.requestSuccess` will be called, in this case, and the application directory path will be passed as a parameter. The `recordVoice()` method starts recording the sound and saves the result audio file under the application directory. Note that if there is no SD card in your Android device, then the application directory will be created under the app's private data directory (`/data/data/[app_directory]`), and the audio file will be saved under it.

- ○ In the `else` block, which refers to the other supported platforms (Windows Phone 8 and iOS), `recordVoice()` is called without creating an application-specific directory. As you know from *Chapter 2*, *Developing Your First Cordova Application*, in iOS and Windows Phone 8, every application has a private directory, and applications cannot store their files in any place other than this directory using Apache Cordova APIs. In the case of iOS, the application audio files will be stored under the `tmp` directory of the application `sandbox` directory (the application private directory). In the case of Windows Phone 8, the audio files will be stored under the application's local directory. As you know from *Chapter 2*, *Developing Your First Cordova Application*, using the Windows Phone 8 native API (`Window.Storage`), you can read and write files in an SD card with some restrictions; however, until this moment, you cannot do this using the Apache Cordova API.

- ○ In `recordVoice()`, `startRecording(callback)` starts creating a media file using the `Media` object's (`recordingMedia`) `startRecord()` method. After calling the `recordingMedia` object's `stopRecord()` method and if the recording operation succeeds, then `callback.onSuccess` will be called and the audio file's full path, `mediaFilePath` will be passed as a parameter. If the recording operation fails, then `callback.onError` will be called.

- `stopRecording()`: This stops the audio recording by doing the following:
  - ○ Calling `stopRecord()` of `recordingMedia` in order to stop recording
  - ○ Calling `release()` of `recordingMedia` in order to release the underlying operating system's audio resources

- `playVoice(filePath, callback)`: This plays an audio file by doing the following:

    ° Cleaning up resources before playing the audio file by calling the `cleanUpResources()` method, which will be shown in the following code snippet

    ° Creating a `Media` object (`audioMedia`) specifying `filePath` as the media source, `callback.onSuccess` as the media success callback, and `callback.onError` as the media error callback

    ° Calling the `play()` method of the `audioMedia` object

The following code snippet shows the second part of `MediaManager.js`:

```
var MediaManager = (function () {
    var instance;

    function createObject() {
        // ...
        return {
            // ...
            recordVoiceExternally: function (callback) {
                var onSuccess = function (mediaFiles) {
                    if (mediaFiles && mediaFiles[0]) {
                        var currentFilePath =
mediaFiles[0].fullPath;

                        if (device.platform === "Android") {
                            var fileCopyCallback = {};

                            fileCopyCallback.copySuccess =
function(filePath) {
                                callback.onSuccess(filePath);
                            };

                            fileCopyCallback.copyError =
callback.onError;

                            fileManager.copyFileToAppDirectory(current
FilePath, fileCopyCallback);
                        } else {
                            callback.onSuccess(currentFilePath);
                        }
                    }
                };
```

```
                       navigator.device.capture.captureAudio(onSuccess,
        callback.onError, {limit: 1});
                },
                cleanUpResources : function () {
                    if (audioMedia) {
                        audioMedia.stop();
                        audioMedia.release();
                        audioMedia = null;
                    }

                    if (recordingMedia) {
                        recordingMedia.stop();
                        recordingMedia.release();
                        recordingMedia = null;
                    }
                }
            };
        };
        // ...
    })();
```

In order to record the audio files using the device's default audio recording app, we can use the `captureAudio` method of Cordova's `capture` object as follows:

```
navigator.device.capture.captureAudio(captureSuccess,
captureError,  [options])
```

The `captureAudio()` method has the following parameters:

- `captureSuccess`: This will be called when the audio capture operation is performed successfully. It receives an array of `MediaFile` as a parameter. As shown in the following table, these are the attributes of `MediaFile`:

Attribute name	Description
name	This is the name of the file
fullPath	This is the full path of the file, including the name
type	This is the file's mime type
lastModifiedDate	This is the date and time when the file was last modified
size	This is the file size in bytes

- captureError: This will be called when the audio capture operation fails. It receives a CaptureError object as a parameter. The CaptureError object has a code attribute, which represents the error code.

- options: This represents the options of capture configuration. The following table shows the options attributes:

Attribute name	Description
limit	This is the maximum number of audio clips that the device user can record in a single capture operation. The value must be greater than or equal to 1 (defaults to 1).
duration	This is the maximum duration in seconds of an audio sound clip.

The preceding code snippet shows the other methods of the MediaManager object as follows:

- recordVoiceExternally(callback): This starts audio recording using the device's default recording app by doing the following:

    ○ In order to start audio recording using the device's default recording app, navigator.device.capture.captureAudio(onSuccess, callback.onError, {limit: 1}) is called. This means that onSuccess is set as the success callback, callback.onError is set as the error callback, and finally, options is set to {limit: 1} in order to limit the maximum number of audio clips that the device user can record in a single capture to 1.

    ○ In the onSuccess callback, if the current platform is Android, then a call to fileManager.copyFileToAppDirectory(currentFilePath, fileCopyCallback) is performed in order to copy the recorded file to the app directory using the fileManager object. If the copy operation succeeds, then the original recordVoiceExternally() method's callback.onSuccess(filePath) will be called in this case and the new copied file path under the app directory (filePath) will be passed as a parameter.

    ○ If the current platform is not Android (in our case, Windows Phone 8 and iOS), callback.onSuccess(currentFilePath) will be called and the current filepath (currentFilePath) will be passed as a parameter.

- cleanUpResources(): This makes sure that all resources are cleaned up by calling stop() and release() methods of all the Media objects.

As the current implementation of the media plugin does not adhere to the W3C specification for media capture, a future implementation is considered for compliance with the W3C specification, and the current APIs might be deprecated.

Before going into the details of the `FileManager.js` file, note that the `Media` object has more methods that you can check out in the Apache Cordova Documentation at `https://github.com/apache/cordova-plugin-media/blob/master/doc/index.md`.

Cordova Capture also has more objects and methods that you can look at in the Apache Cordova Documentation at `https://github.com/apache/cordova-plugin-media-capture/blob/master/doc/index.md`.

The following code snippet shows the first part of `FileManager.js`, which is used by `MediaManager.js`:

```
var FileManager = (function () {
    var instance;

    function createObject() {
        var BASE_DIRECTORY = "CExhibition";
        var FILE_BASE = "file:///";

        return {
            copyFileToAppDirectory: function (filePath, cb) {
                var callback = {};

                callback.requestSuccess = function (dirEntry) {
                    if (filePath.indexOf(FILE_BASE) != 0) {
                        filePath = filePath.replace("file:/",
FILE_BASE);
                    }

                    window.resolveLocalFileSystemURL(filePath,
function(file) {
                        var filename = filePath.replace(/^.*[\\\/]/,
'');

                        var copyToSuccess = function (fileEntry) {
                            console.log("file is copied to: " +
fileEntry.toURL());

                            cb.copySuccess(fileEntry.toURL());
                        };
```

```
                        file.copyTo(dirEntry, filename,
copyToSuccess, cb.copyError);
                    }, cb.copyError);
                };

                callback.requestError = function (error) {
                    console.log(error);
                };

                this.requestApplicationDirectory(callback);
            },
            requestApplicationDirectory: function (callback) {
                var fileSystemReady = function(fileSystem) {
                    fileSystem.root.getDirectory(BASE_DIRECTORY,
{create: true}, callback.requestSuccess);
                };

                window.requestFileSystem(LocalFileSystem.PERSISTENT,
0,
fileSystemReady, callback.requestError);
            }
        };
    };

    return {
        getInstance: function () {
            if (!instance) {
                instance = createObject();
            }

            return instance;
        }
    };
})();
```

As you can see in the preceding highlighted code, `FileManager` is a singleton object that has two methods. In order to work with directories or files using Apache Cordova, we first need to request a filesystem using the `requestFileSystem()` method as `window.requestFileSystem(type, size, successCallback, errorCallback)`.

The `window.requestFileSystem` method has the following parameters in order:

- `type`: This refers to the local filesystem type
- `Size`: This indicates how much storage space, in bytes, the application expects to need
- `successCallback`: This will be called if the operation succeeds, and it will receive a `FileSystem` object as a parameter
- `errorCallback`: This will be called if an operation error occurs

In order to create a directory after getting the `FileSystem` object, we can use the `getDirectory()` method of the `DirectoryEntry` object as `fileSystem.root.getDirectory(path, options, successCallback, errorCallback)`.

The `directoryEntry.getDirectory` method takes the following parameters:

- `path`: This is either a relative or absolute path of the directory in which we can look up or create a directory
- `options`: This refers to an `options` JSON object that specifies the `create` directory using `{create: true}` or exclusively creates the directory using `{create: true, exclusive: true}`
- `successCallback`: This will be called if the operation succeeds, and it receives the new or existing `DirectoryEntry` as a parameter
- `errorCallback`: This will be called if an operation error occurs

If you look at the first method `requestApplicationDirectory(callback)` of the `FileManager` object, you will find that it creates a directory called `"CExhibition"` if it has not already been created (in the case of an Android device with an SD card, `"CExhibition"` will be created under the SD card root).

In order to get an `Entry` object of a specific URI to perform a file or directory operation, we need to use `resolveLocalFileSystemURL()` as `window.resolveLocalFileSystemURL(uri, successCallback, errorCallback)`.

The `window.resolveLocalFileSystemURL` method takes the following parameters:

- `uri`: This is a URI that refers to a local file or directory
- `successCallback`: This will be called if the operation succeeds, and it will receive an `Entry` object that corresponds to the specified URI (it can be `DirectoryEntry` or `FileEntry`) as a parameter
- `errorCallback`: This will be called if an operation error occurs

In order to copy a file, we need to use the `copyTo()` method of the `Entry` object as `fileEntry.copyTo(parent, newName, successCallback, errorCallback)` the `Entry` object.

The `fileEntry.copyTo` method takes the following parameters:

- `parent`: This represents the directory to which the entry will be copied
- `newName`: This represents the new name of the copied file, and it defaults to the current name
- `successCallback`: This will be called if the operation succeeds, and it will receive the new entry object as a parameter
- `errorCallback`: This will be called if an operation error occurs

If you look at the second method `copyFileToAppDirectory (filePath, cb)` of the `FileManager` object, you will find that it creates an `app` directory called `"CExhibition"` if it has not already been created. Then, it copies the file specified in `filePath` under the `app` directory using the `copyTo()` method of the `fileEntry` object. Finally, if the copy operation succeeds, then the `cb.copySuccess()` callback will be called and the new copied file path will be passed as a parameter.

> The Cordova file has more objects and methods that you can have a look at in the Apache Cordova Documentation at https://github.com/apache/cordova-plugin-file/blob/master/doc/index.md.

Now, we are done with the media, file, and capture functionalities in the Cordova Exhibition app.

Notification

The notification plugin provides the ability to create visual, audible, and tactile device notifications. In order to use the notification plugin in our Apache Cordova project, we need to use the following `cordova plugin add` command:

```
> cordova plugin add https://git-wip-us.apache.org/repos/asf/cordova-plugin-vibration.git
```

```
> cordova plugin add https://git-wip-us.apache.org/repos/asf/cordova-plugin-dialogs.git
```

Demo

In order to access the notification demo, you can click on the **Notification** list item. You will be introduced to the **Notification** page. You can click on one of the available buttons to see, hear, and feel the different available notifications. The following screenshot shows the result of clicking on the **Show Prompt** button, which shows a prompt dialog to have the user input:

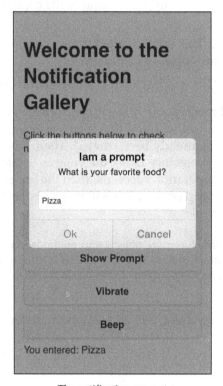

The notification prompt

You also have the option to show an alert message and confirmation dialog. You can vibrate the device by clicking on the **Vibrate** button, and finally, you can make the device beep by clicking on the **Beep** button.

The HTML page

The following code snippet shows the "notification" page:

```html
<div data-role="page" id="notification">
    <div data-role="header">
        <h1>Notification</h1>
        <a href="#" data-role="button" data-rel="back" data-
icon="back">Back</a>
    </div>
    <div data-role="content">
        <h1>Welcome to the Notification Gallery</h1>
        <p>Click the buttons below to check notifications.</p>
        <input type="button" id="showAlert" value="Show Alert"/>
        <input type="button" id="showConfirm" value="Show
Confirm"/>
        <input type="button" id="showPrompt" value="Show Prompt"/>
        <input type="button" id="vibrate" value="Vibrate"/>
        <input type="button" id="beep" value="Beep"/>

        <div id="notificationResult">
        </div>
    </div>
</div>
```

The preceding "notification" page contains the following:

- A page header that includes a back button.
- Page content that includes five buttons: "showAlert" to show an alert, "showConfirm" to show a confirmation dialog, "showPrompt" to show a prompt dialog, "vibrate" to vibrate the device, and finally, "beep" to make the device beep. It also has a "notificationResult" div to display the notification result.

View controller

The following code snippet shows the "notification" page view controller JavaScript object, which includes the event handlers of the page (notification.js):

```javascript
(function() {
    var notificationManager = NotificationManager.getInstance();

    $(document).on("pageinit", "#notification", function(e) {
        e.preventDefault();
```

```
    $("#showAlert").on("tap", function(e) {
        e.preventDefault();

        notificationManager.showAlert("This is an Alert",
onOk, "Iam an Alert", "Ok");
    });

    $("#showConfirm").on("tap", function(e) {
        e.preventDefault();

        notificationManager.showConfirm("This is a
confirmation", onConfirm, "Iam a confirmation", "Ok,Cancel");
    });

    $("#showPrompt").on("tap", function(e) {
        e.preventDefault();

        notificationManager.showPrompt("What is your favorite
food?", onPrompt, "Iam a prompt", ["Ok", "Cancel"], "Pizza");
    });

    $("#vibrate").on("tap", function(e) {
        e.preventDefault();

        notificationManager.vibrate(2000);
    });

    $("#beep").on("tap", function(e) {
        e.preventDefault();

        notificationManager.beep(3);
    });

});

function onOk() {
    $("#notificationResult").html("You clicked Ok<br/>");
}

function onConfirm(index) {
    $("#notificationResult").html("You clicked " + ((index ==
1) ? "Ok":"Cancel") + "<br/>");
}
```

```
        function onPrompt(result) {
            if (result.buttonIndex == 1) {
                $("#notificationResult").html("You entered: " +
    result.input1);
            }
        }
    })();
```

As shown in the preceding code snippet, the `"pageinit"` event handler registers the `"tap"` event handlers on the `"showAlert"`, `"showConfirm"`, `"showPrompt"`, `"vibrate"`, and `"beep"` buttons.

In the `"tap"` event handler of the `"showAlert"` button, an alert is shown by calling the `notificationManager.showAlert(message, callback, title, buttonName)` method specifying the message to display (`"This is an Alert"`), the callback to be called when the dialog is dismissed (`onOk`), the dialog title (`"I am an Alert"`), and finally, the button name (`Ok`). In `onOk`, the `"You clicked Ok"` message is displayed in the `"notificationResult"` div.

In the `"tap"` event handler of the `"showConfirm"` button, a confirmation dialog is shown by calling the `notificationManager.showConfirm(message, callback, title, buttonLabels)` method specifying the message to display (`"This is a confirmation"`), the callback to be called when the dialog is dismissed or if any of the confirmation dialog buttons is clicked (`onConfirm`), the dialog title (`"I am a confirmation"`), and finally, the button labels, which are represented using a comma-separated string that specify button labels (`"Ok,Cancel"`). In `onConfirm(index)`, the clicked button is displayed in the `notificationResult` div using the received `index` callback parameter, which represents the index of the pressed button. Note that `index` uses one-based indexing, which means that the `"Ok"` button has the index 1 and the `"Cancel"` button has the index 2.

In the `"tap"` event handler of the `"showPrompt"` button, a confirmation dialog is shown by calling the `notificationManager.showPrompt(message, callback, title, buttonLabels, defaultText)` method specifying the message to display (`"What is your favorite food?"`), the callback to be called when any of the prompt dialog buttons is clicked (`onPrompt`), the dialog title (`"I am a prompt"`), the button labels, which are represented as an array of strings that specify button labels (`["Ok", "Cancel"]`), and finally, the default input text (`"Pizza"`). In `onPrompt(result)`, `result.buttonIndex` represents the button index (which is one-based indexing) that is clicked. If the `"Ok"` button (which has the index 1) is clicked, then the user input is obtained using `result.input1`.

In the "tap" event handler of the "vibrate" button, the device is vibrated by calling the notificationManager.vibrate(milliseconds) method specifying milliseconds to vibrate the device (2,000 milliseconds).

In the "tap" event handler of the "beep" button, the device is made to beep by calling the notificationManager.beep(times) method specifying the times to repeat the beep (three times).

API

The following code snippet shows NotificationManager.js:

```
var NotificationManager = (function () {
    var instance;

    function createObject() {
        return {
            showAlert: function (message, callback, title,
buttonName) {
                navigator.notification.alert(message, callback,
title, buttonName);
            },
            showConfirm: function (message, callback, title,
buttonLabels) {
                navigator.notification.confirm(message, callback,
title, buttonLabels);
            },
            showPrompt: function (message, callback, title,
buttonLabels, defaultText) {
                navigator.notification.prompt(message, callback,
title, buttonLabels, defaultText);
            },
            beep: function (times) {
                navigator.notification.beep(times);
            },
            vibrate: function (milliseconds) {
                navigator.notification.vibrate(milliseconds);
            }
        };
    };

    return {
        getInstance: function () {
            if (!instance) {
```

```
            instance = createObject();
        }

        return instance;
    }
    };
})();
```

As shown, `NotificationManager` is a singleton object that does a simple wrapping for the Cordova Notification API. It has the following methods:

- `showAlert(message, callback, title, buttonName)`: This shows an alert by calling the `navigator.notification.alert()` method. The `navigator.notification.alert(message, callback, [title], [buttonName])` method has the following parameters:
    - `message`: This represents the alert message
    - `Callback`: This represents the callback to be called when the alert is dismissed
    - `Title`: This is an optional parameter that represents the alert title (the default value is `"Alert"`)
    - `buttonName`: This represents the button name (the default value is `"Ok"`)

- `showConfirm(message, callback, title, buttonLabels)`: This shows a confirmation dialog by calling the `navigator.notification.confirm()` method. The `navigator.notification.confirm(message, callback, [title], [buttonLabels])` method has the following parameters:
    - `message`: This represents the dialog message.
    - `callback(index)`: This represents the callback to be called when the user presses one of the buttons in the confirmation dialog. It receives an `index` parameter that represents the pressed button's index, which starts from 1.
    - `title`: This is an optional parameter that represents the dialog title (the default value is `"Confirm"`).
    - `buttonLabels`: This is an optional parameter that represents a comma-separated string that specifies button labels (the default value is `"Ok", Cancel"`).

- showPrompt(message, callback, title, buttonLabels, defaultText): This shows a prompt dialog by calling the navigator. notification.prompt() method. The navigator.notification. prompt(message, promptCallback, [title], [buttonLabels], [defaultText]) method has the following parameters:

    ○ Message: This represents the dialog message.

    ○ promptCallback(results): This represents the callback to be called when the user presses one of the buttons in the prompt dialog. It receives a results parameter that has the following attributes: buttonIndex, which represents the pressed button's index, which starts from 1 and input1, which represents the text entered by the user in the prompt dialog box.

    ○ title: This is an optional parameter that represents the dialog title (the default value is "Prompt").

    ○ buttonLabels: This is an optional parameter that represents a string array, which specifies button labels (the default value is ["OK","Cancel"]).

    ○ defaultText: This is an optional parameter that represents the default text input value of the prompt dialog (the default value is an empty string).

- beep(times): This makes the device beeps by calling the navigator. notification.beep() method. The navigator.notification. beep(times) method has the following parameter:

    ○ times: This represents the number of times to repeat the beep.

- vibrate(milliseconds): This vibrates the device by calling the navigator. notification.vibrate() method. The navigator.notification. vibrate(milliseconds) method has the following parameter:

    ○ milliseconds: This represents the milliseconds to vibrate the device.

Now, we are done with the notification functionality in the Cordova Exhibition app.

Storage

The Cordova Storage API provides the ability to access the device storage options based on three popular W3C specifications:

- Web Storage API Specification, which allows you to access data using simple key/value pairs (which we will demonstrate in our `"Storage"` demo).

- Web SQL Database Specification, which offers full-featured database tables, which can be accessed using SQL. Note that this option is only available in Android, iOS, BlackBerry 10, and Tizen and not supported on other platforms.

- IndexedDB Specification is an API for the client-side storage and high performance. It searches on the stored data using indexes. Note that this option is available in Windows Phone 8 and BlackBerry 10.

Demo

In order to use the Storage API, there is no need for a CLI command to run, as it is built in Cordova. In order to access the **Storage** demo, you can do it by clicking on the **Storage** list item. You will be introduced to the **Storage** page. On the **Storage** page, the users can enter their names and valid e-mails and then click on the **Save** button in order to save the information, as shown in the following screenshot:

Saving user information

You can exit the app and then open the **Storage** page again; you will find that your saved information is reflected in the **Name** and **Email** fields. At any point, you can click on the **Reload** button in order to reload input fields with your saved data.

The HTML page

The following code snippet shows the `"storage"` page:

```
<div data-role="page" id="storage">
    <div data-role="header">
        <h1>Storage</h1>
        <a href="#" data-role="button" data-rel="back" data-
icon="back">Back</a>
    </div>
    <div data-role="content">
        <h1>Welcome to the Storage Gallery</h1>
        <p>Persist your information using Cordova Web Storage
API.</p>
        <form id="storageForm">
            <div class="ui-field-contain">
                <label for="userName">Name</label>
                <input type="text" id="userName" name="userName"></
input>
            </div>
            <div class="ui-field-contain">
                <label for="userEmail">Email</label>
                <input type="text" id="userEmail" name="userEmail"></
input>
            </div>

            <div class="center-wrapper">
                <input type="button" id="saveInfo" data-
icon="action" value="Save" data-inline="true"/>
                <input type="button" id="reloadInfo" data-
icon="refresh" value="Reload" data-inline="true"/>
            </div>

            <ul id="storageMessageBox"></ul>

            <div id="storageResult">
            </div>
        </form>
    </div>
</div>
```

The preceding `"storage"` page contains the following:

- A page header that includes a back button
- Page content that includes the `"storageForm"` form, which includes the following elements:
  - `"userName"`: This is the user's name text field
  - `"userEmail"`: This is the user's email text field
  - `"saveInfo"`: This button is used to persist user information
  - `"reloadInfo"`: This button is used to reload saved user information in the `"userName"` and `"userEmail"` fields
  - `"messageBox"`: This is an unordered list that displays form validation errors
  - `"storageResult"`: This is a div that displays the storage operation result

View controller

The following code snippet shows the `"storage"` page view controller JavaScript object that includes the event handlers of the page (`storage.js`):

```javascript
(function() {
    var storageManager = StorageManager.getInstance();
    var INFO_KEY = "cordovaExhibition.userInfo";

    $(document).on("pageinit", "#storage", function(e) {
        e.preventDefault();

        $("#saveInfo").on("tap", function(e) {
            e.preventDefault();


            if (! $("#storageForm").valid()) {
                return;
            }

            storageManager.set(INFO_KEY, JSON.stringify({
                                        userName:
$("#userName").val(),
                                        userEmail:
$("#userEmail").val()
                })
```

```
                                    );

                    $("#storageResult").html("User Information are saved");
            });

            $("#reloadInfo").on("tap", function(e) {
                e.preventDefault();

                reloadUserInfo();

                $("#storageResult").html("Reloading completes");
            });
    });

    $(document).on("pageshow", "#storage", function(e) {
        e.preventDefault();

        $("#storageForm").validate({
            errorLabelContainer: "#storageMessageBox",
            wrapper: "li",
            rules: {
                userName: "required",
                userEmail: {
                    required: true,
                    email: true
                }
            },
            messages: {
                userName: "Please specify user name",
                userEmail: {
                    required: "Please specify email",
                    email: "Please enter valid email"
                }
            }
        });

        reloadUserInfo();
    });

    function reloadUserInfo() {
        var userInfo = JSON.parse(storageManager.get(INFO_KEY));

        populateFormFields(userInfo);
    }
```

```
function populateFormFields(userInfo) {
    if (userInfo) {
        $("#userName").val(userInfo.userName);
        $("#userEmail").val(userInfo.userEmail);
    }
  }
})();
```

As shown in the preceding highlighted code snippet, the "pageinit" event handler registers the "tap" event handlers on the "saveInfo" and "reloadInfo" buttons.

> In order to validate our "storage" form, we use the jQuery validation plugin, which can be found at http://jqueryvalidation.org. In order to use the plugin, all we need to do is include the jquery. validate.min.js file below the jquery.js file that will be shown in the index.html file in *Finalizing the Cordova Exhibition App* section. After including the jQuery validation plugin JS file, we can simply use the plugin by defining the validation rules on the form fields using the form's validate() method and then validate the form using the form's valid() method, as shown in the "storage" page view controller code.

In the "tap" event handler of the "saveInfo" button:

- The "storageForm" is validated using the $("#storageForm").valid() method.
- If the form is valid, then both the "userName" and "userEmail" valid input text values are set as attributes in a JSON object, which is converted to a string using JSON.stringify(). Finally, the stringified JSON object is persisted in the device storage by calling the storageManager.set(key, value) specifying key to be INFO_KEY and the value to be the stringified JSON object.

In the "tap" event handler of the "reloadInfo" button:

- The user information is retrieved by calling reloadUserInfo(). The reloadUserInfo() method calls storageManager.get(INFO_KEY) in order to get the stored stringified JSON object and then use JSON.parse() in order to convert the stringified JSON object to a JSON object (userInfo).
- Using populateFormFields(userInfo), userInfo is populated to both "userName" and "userEmail" input text elements.

In the `"pageshow"` event of the `"storage"` page, our `"storageForm"` form validation is constructed by specifying the `options` parameter of the form's `validate()` method as follows:

- `errorLabelContainer`: This is set to `"storageMessageBox"` to display the validation errors
- `wrapper`: This is set to `"li"` to wrap the error messages in list items
- `rules` object is set as follows:
    - `userName`: This is set to required
    - `userEmail`: This is set to be an e-mail and required
- `messages` object specifies `userName` and `userEmail` validation error messages

Finally, in the `"pageshow"` event of the `"storage"` page, `reloadUserInfo()` is called to reload the user information in the `"userName"` and `"userEmail"` input text elements.

API

The following code snippet shows `StorageManager.js` that does a simple wrapping for two `localStorage` methods:

```
var StorageManager = (function () {
    var instance;

    function createObject() {
        return {
            set: function (key, value) {
                window.localStorage.setItem(key, value);
            },
            get: function (key) {
                return window.localStorage.getItem(key);
            }
        };
    };

    return {
        getInstance: function () {
            if (!instance) {
                instance = createObject();
            }
```

```
            return instance;
        }
    };
})();
```

As you can see in the preceding highlighted code, `StorageManager` is a singleton object that has the following methods:

- `set(key, value)`: This persists the key/value pair in the local storage by calling the `window.localStorage.setItem(key, value)` method
- `get(key)`: This gets the stored value using the passed key parameter by calling the `window.localStorage.getItem(key)` method

 The complete W3C Web Storage specification is available at `http://www.w3.org/TR/webstorage/`, and you can also look at the W3C Web SQL Database specification at `http://dev.w3.org/html5/webdatabase/`. Finally, you can look at the W3C IndexedDB specification at `http://www.w3.org/TR/IndexedDB/`.

Now, we are done with the storage functionality in the Cordova Exhibition app.

Finalizing the Cordova Exhibition app

The last part we need to check is `index.html`; the following code snippet shows this part, which is the most important, of the `index.html` page:

```html
<!DOCTYPE html>
<html>
    <head>
        <!-- omitted code ... -->
        <link rel="stylesheet" type="text/css" href="css/app.css"
/>
        <link rel="stylesheet" href="jqueryMobile/jquery.mobile-
1.4.0.min.css">

        <script src="jqueryMobile/jquery-1.10.2.min.js"></script>
        <script src="jqueryMobile/jquery.mobile-
1.4.0.min.js"></script>

        <script>
            var deviceReadyDeferred = $.Deferred();
            var jqmReadyDeferred = $.Deferred();
```

```
        $(document).ready(function() {
            document.addEventListener("deviceready", function() {
                deviceReadyDeferred.resolve();
            }, false);
        });

        $(document).on("mobileinit", function () {
            jqmReadyDeferred.resolve();
        });

        $.when(deviceReadyDeferred, jqmReadyDeferred).
then(function () {

            //Now everything loads fine, you can safely go to the
app home ...
            $.mobile.changePage("#features");
        });
    </script>

    <script src="jqueryMobile/jqm.page.params.js"></script>
    <script src="jqueryMobile/jquery.validate.min.js"></script>
    <script src="js/common.js"></script>

    <title>Cordova Exhibition</title>
</head>
<body>
    <div id="loading" data-role="page">
        <div class="center-screen">Please wait ...</div>
    </div>

    <!-- Other pages are placed here ... -->

    <script type="text/javascript" src="cordova.js"></script>

    <!-- API JS files -->
    <script type="text/javascript" src="js/api/
AccelerometerManager.js"></script>
        <script type="text/javascript" src="js/api/FileManager.js"></
script>
        <script type="text/javascript" src="js/api/CameraManager.
js"></script>
        <script type="text/javascript" src="js/api/CompassManager.
js"></script>
        <script type="text/javascript" src="js/api/ConnectionManager.
js"></script>
```

```
        <script type="text/javascript" src="js/api/ContactsManager.
js"></script>
        <script type="text/javascript" src="js/api/DeviceManager.
js"></script>
        <script type="text/javascript" src="js/api/GeolocationManager.
js"></script>
        <script type="text/javascript" src="js/api/
GlobalizationManager.js"></script>
        <script type="text/javascript" src="js/api/
InAppBrowserManager.js"></script>
        <script type="text/javascript" src="js/api/MediaManager.js"></
script>
        <script type="text/javascript" src="js/api/
NotificationManager.js"></script>
        <script type="text/javascript" src="js/api/StorageManager.
js"></script>

        <!-- View controller files -->
        <script type="text/javascript" src="js/vc/accelerometer.js"></
script>
        <script type="text/javascript" src="js/vc/camera.js"></script>
        <script type="text/javascript" src="js/vc/compass.js"></
script>
        <script type="text/javascript" src="js/vc/connection.js"></
script>
        <script type="text/javascript" src="js/vc/contacts.js"></
script>
        <script type="text/javascript" src="js/vc/contactDetails.
js"></script>
        <script type="text/javascript" src="js/vc/device.js"></script>
        <script type="text/javascript" src="js/vc/geolocation.js"></
script>
        <script type="text/javascript" src="js/vc/globalization.js"></
script>
        <script type="text/javascript" src="js/vc/inAppBrowser.js"></
script>
        <script type="text/javascript" src="js/vc/media.js"></script>
        <script type="text/javascript" src="js/vc/notification.js"></
script>
        <script type="text/javascript" src="js/vc/storage.js"></
script>
    </body>
</html>
```

As shown in the preceding code, `index.html` includes the following:

- App custom CSS file (`app.css`)
- jQuery Mobile library files
- A jQuery Page Params plugin file (`jqm.page.params.js`)
- A jQuery Validation plugin file (`jquery.validate.min.js`)
- A Common JS (`common.js`) file, app manager JS files, and finally, app view controller JS files

The preceding highlighted code shows you how to make sure that Apache Cordova and jQuery Mobile are loaded correctly (using the jQuery Deferred object) before proceeding to the app pages. Doing this step is important to make sure that our app's code will not access any API that is not ready yet to avoid any unexpected errors. If Apache Cordova and jQuery Mobile are loaded correctly, then the user will leave the `"loading"` page and will be forwarded to the app's home page (the `"features"` page) to start exploring the Cordova features.

 To learn the jQuery Deferred object by example, check out `http://learn.jquery.com/code-organization/deferreds/examples/`.

It's worth mentioning that in order to boost the performance of jQuery Mobile 1.4 with Apache Cordova, it is recommended that you disable transition effects. The `common.js` file applies this tip in the Cordova Exhibition app as follows:

```
$.mobile.defaultPageTransition   = 'none';
$.mobile.defaultDialogTransition = 'none';
$.mobile.buttonMarkup.hoverDelay = 0;
```

Finally, in order to exit the application when the user clicks on the back button (which exists in the Android and Windows Phone 8 devices) on the app's home page, `common.js` also implements this behavior, as shown in the following code snippet:

```
var homePage = "features";

//Handle back buttons decently for Android and Windows Phone 8 ...
function onDeviceReady() {
    document.addEventListener("backbutton", function(e){

        if ($.mobile.activePage.is('#' + homePage)){
            e.preventDefault();
            navigator.app.exitApp();
```

```
        } else {
            history.back();
        }
    }, false);
}

$(document).ready(function() {
    document.addEventListener("deviceready", onDeviceReady,
false);
});
```

We create an event listener on the device's `"backbutton"` after Cordova is loaded. If the user clicks on the back button, we check whether the user is on the home page using `$.mobile.activePage.is()`. If the user is on the home page, then the app exits using `navigator.app.exitApp()`; otherwise, we simply use `history.back()` to forward the user to the previous page.

>
> The complete source code of our Cordova Exhibition app with all the three supported platforms can be downloaded from the book's web page, or you can access the code directly from GitHub at `https://github.com/hazems/cordova-exhibition`.

Cordova events

Cordova allows listening and creating handlers for its life cycle events. The following table shows the description of these events:

Event name	Description
Deviceready	This fires once Apache Cordova is fully loaded. Once this event fires, you can safely make calls to the Cordova API.
Pause	This fires if the application is put into the background.
Resume	This fires if the application is resumed from the background.
Online	This fires if the application becomes connected to the Internet.
offline	This fires if the application becomes disconnected from the Internet.
backbutton	This fires if the user clicks on the device's back button (some devices such as Android and Windows Phone devices have a back button).

Event name	Description
batterycritical	This fires if the device's battery power reaches a critical state (that is, reached the critical-level threshold).
batterylow	This fires if the device's battery power reaches the low-level threshold.
batterystatus	This fires if there is a change in the battery status.
menubutton	This fires if the user presses the device's menu button (the menu button is popular in Android and BlackBerry devices).
searchbutton	This fires if the user presses the device's search button (the search button can be found in Android devices).
startcallbutton	This fires when the user presses the start call button of the device.
endcallbutton	This fires when the user presses the end call button of the device.
volumeupbutton	This fires when the user presses the volume up button of the device.
volumedownbutton	This fires when the user presses the volume down button of the device.

Access to all of the events, which are not related to the battery status, are enabled by default. In order to use the events related to the battery status, use the following CLI cordova plugin add command:

```
> cordova plugin add https://git-wip-us.apache.org/repos/
asf/cordova-plugin-battery-status.git
```

We can create our Cordova event listener using the document.addEventListener() method once DOM is loaded as follows:

```
document.addEventListener("eventName", eventHandler, false)
```

Let's see an example; let's assume that we have the following div element in our HTML page, which displays the log of our Cordova app pause and resume events:

```
<div id="results"></div>
```

In our JavaScript code, once the DOM is loaded, we can define our Cordova event listeners for the `"pause"` and `"resume"` events once the `"deviceready"` event is triggered, as follows:

```
function onPause() {
    document.getElementById("results").innerHTML += "App is paused
...<br/>";
};

function onResume() {
    document.getElementById("results").innerHTML += "App is
resumed ...<br/>";
};

function onDeviceReady() {
    document.addEventListener("pause", onPause, false);
    document.addEventListener("resume", onResume, false);
};

$(document).ready(function() {
    document.addEventListener("deviceready", onDeviceReady,
false);
});
```

Summary

In this chapter, you learned how to utilize the most important features in Apache Cordova API by understanding the Cordova Exhibition app. You learned how to work with Cordova media, file, capture, notification, and storage APIs. You also learned how to utilize the Apache Cordova events in your mobile app. In the next chapter, you will learn the advanced part of Apache Cordova, which is building your own custom Cordova plugin on the different mobile platforms (Android, iOS, and Windows Phone 8).

6
Developing Custom Cordova Plugins

In this chapter, we will continue to deep dive into Apache Cordova. You will learn how to create your own custom Cordova plugin on the three most popular mobile platforms: Android (using the Java programming language), iOS (using the Objective-C programming language), and Windows Phone 8 (using the C# programming language).

Developing a custom Cordova plugin

Before going into the details of the plugin, it is important to note that developing custom Cordova plugins is not a common scenario if you are developing Apache Cordova apps. This is because the Apache Cordova core and community custom plugins already cover many of the use cases that are needed to access device's native functions. So, make sure of two things:

- You are not developing a custom plugin that already exists in the Apache Cordova core plugins, which were illustrated in the previous two chapters.

- You are not developing a custom plugin whose functionality already exists in other good Apache Cordova custom plugin(s) that have been developed by the Apache Cordova development community. Building plugins from scratch can consume precious time from your project; otherwise, you can save time by reusing one of the available good custom plugins.

Another thing to note is that developing custom Cordova plugins is an advanced topic. It requires you to be aware of the native programming languages of the mobile platforms, so make sure you have an overview of Java, Objective-C, and C# (or at least one of them) before reading this chapter. This will be helpful in understanding all the plugin development steps (plugin structuring, JavaScript interface definition, and native plugin implementation).

Now, let's start developing our custom Cordova plugin. It can be used in order to send SMS messages from one of the three most popular mobile platforms (Android, iOS, and Windows Phone 8). Before we start creating our plugin, we need to define its API. The following code listing shows you how to call the `sms.sendMessage` method of our plugin, which will be used in order to send an SMS across platforms:

```
var messageInfo = {
    phoneNumber: "xxxxxxxxxx",
    textMessage: "This is a test message"
};

sms.sendMessage(messageInfo, function(message) {
    console.log("success: " + message);
}, function(error) {
    console.log("code: " + error.code + ", message: " +
error.message);
});
```

The `sms.sendMessage` method has the following parameters:

- `messageInfo`: This is a JSON object that contains two main attributes: `phoneNumber`, which represents the phone number that will receive the SMS message, and `textMessage`, which represents the text message to be sent.

- `successCallback`: This is a callback that will be called if the message is sent successfully.

- `errorCallback`: This is a callback that will be called if the message is not sent successfully. This callback receives an `error` object as a parameter. The error object has `code` (the error code) and `message` (the error message) attributes.

Using plugman

In addition to the Apache Cordova CLI utility, you can use the `plugman` utility in order to add or remove plugin(s) to/from your Apache Cordova projects. However, it's worth mentioning that `plugman` is a lower-level tool that you can use if your Apache Cordova application follows a **platform-centered workflow** and not a **cross-platform workflow**. If your application follows a **cross-platform workflow**, then Apache Cordova CLI should be your choice.

If you want your application to run on different mobile platforms (which is a common use case if you want to use Apache Cordova), it's recommend that you follow a **cross-platform workflow**. Use a **platform-centered workflow** if you want to develop your Apache Cordova application on a single platform and modify your application using the platform-specific SDK.

Besides adding and removing plugins to/from a **platform-centered workflow**, the Cordova projects `plugman` can also be used:

- To create basic scaffolding for your custom Cordova plugin
- To add and remove a platform to/from your custom Cordova plugin
- To add user(s) to the Cordova plugin registry (a repository that hosts the different Apache Cordova core and custom plugins)
- To publish your custom Cordova plugin(s) to the Cordova plugin registry
- To unpublish your custom plugin(s) from the Cordova plugin registry
- To search for plugin(s) in the Cordova plugin registry

In this section, we will use the `plugman` utility to create the basic scaffolding of our custom SMS plugin. In order to install `plugman`, you need to make sure that Node.js is installed on your operating system. Then, to install `plugman`, execute the following command:

```
> npm install -g plugman
```

After installing `plugman`, we can start generating our initial custom plugin artifacts using the `plugman create` command as follows:

```
> plugman create --name sms --plugin_id  com.jsmobile.plugins.sms --
plugin_version 0.0.1
```

It is important to note the following parameters:

- `--name`: This specifies the plugin name (in our case, `sms`)
- `--plugin_id`: This specifies an ID for the plugin (in our case, `com.jsmobile.plugins.sms`)
- `--plugin_version`: This specifies the plugin version (in our case, 0.0.1)

The following are two parameters that the `plugman create` command can accept as well:

- `--path`: This specifies the directory path of the plugin
- `--variable`: This can specify extra variables such as author or description

After executing the previous command, we will have initial artifacts for our custom plugin. As we will be supporting multiple platforms, we can use the `plugman` `platform add` command. The following two commands add the Android and iOS platforms to our custom plugin:

```
> plugman platform add --platform_name android
> plugman platform add --platform_name ios
```

In order to run the `plugman platform add` command, we need to run it from the `plugin` directory. Unfortunately, for Windows Phone 8 platform support, we need to add it manually later to our plugin.

Now, let's check the initial scaffolding of our custom plugin code. The following screenshot shows the hierarchy of our initial plugin code:

Hierarchy of our initial plugin code

As shown in the preceding screenshot, there is one file and two parent directories. They are as follows:

- `plugin.xml` file: This contains the plugin definition.

- `src` directory: This contains the plugin native implementation code for each platform. For now, it contains two subdirectories: `android` and `ios`. The `android` subdirectory contains `sms.java`. This represents the initial implementation of the plugin in `Android`. `ios` subdirectory contains `sms.m`, which represents the initial implementation of the plugin in iOS.

- `www` directory: This mainly contains the JavaScript interface of the plugin. It contains `sms.js`, which represents the initial implementation of the plugin's JavaScript API.

We will need to edit these generated files (and maybe, refactor and add new implementation files) in order to implement our custom SMS plugin. The details of our SMS plugin definition, JavaScript interface, and native implementations will be illustrated in detail in the upcoming sections.

Plugin definition

First of all, we need to define our plugin structure. In order to do so, we need to define our plugin in the `plugin.xml` file. The following code listing shows our `plugin.xml` code:

```xml
<?xml version='1.0' encoding='utf-8'?>
<plugin id="com.jsmobile.plugins.sms" version="0.0.1"
    xmlns="http://apache.org/cordova/ns/plugins/1.0"
    xmlns:android="http://schemas.android.com/apk/res/android">

    <name>sms</name>
    <description>A plugin for sending sms messages</description>
    <license>Apache 2.0</license>
    <keywords>cordova,plugins,sms</keywords>

    <js-module name="sms" src="www/sms.js">
        <clobbers target="window.sms" />
    </js-module>

    <platform name="android">
        <config-file parent="/*" target="res/xml/config.xml">
            <feature name="Sms">
                <param name="android-package" value="com.jsmobile.
plugins.sms.Sms" />
            </feature>
        </config-file>

        <config-file target="AndroidManifest.xml" parent="/manifest">
            <uses-permission android:name="android.permission.SEND_
SMS" />
        </config-file>

        <source-file src="src/android/Sms.java"
                     target-dir="src/com/jsmobile/plugins/sms" />
    </platform>

    <platform name="ios">
        <config-file parent="/*" target="config.xml">
```

```
            <feature name="Sms">
                <param name="ios-package" value="Sms" />
            </feature>
        </config-file>

        <source-file src="src/ios/Sms.h" />
        <source-file src="src/ios/Sms.m" />

        <framework src="MessageUI.framework" weak="true" />
    </platform>

    <platform name="wp8">
        <config-file target="config.xml" parent="/*">
            <feature name="Sms">
                <param name="wp-package" value="Sms" />
            </feature>
        </config-file>

        <source-file src="src/wp8/Sms.cs" />
    </platform>

</plugin>
```

The `plugin.xml` file defines the plugin structure and contains a top-level element `<plugin>`, which contains the following attributes:

- xmlns: This attribute represents the plugin namespace which is `http://apache.org/cordova/ns/plugins/1.0`

- id: This attribute represents the plugin ID; in our case, it is `com.jsmobile.plugins.sms`

- version: This attribute represents the plugin version number, 0.0.1

The `<plugin>` element contains the following subelements:

- `<name>`: This element represents the plugin name; in our case, it is sms.

- `<description>`: This element represents the plugin description; in our case, it is "A plugin for sending sms messages".

- `<licence>`: This element represents the plugin license; in our case, it is Apache 2.0.

- `<keywords>`: This element represents the keywords of the plugin; in our case, it is cordova, plugins, sms.

- `<js-module>`: This element represents the plugin JavaScript module, and it corresponds to a JavaScript file. It has a `name` attribute that represents the JavaScript module name (in our case, `"sms"`). It also has an `src` attribute that represents the JavaScript module file. The `src` attribute references a JavaScript file in the `plugin` directory that is relative to the `plugin.xml` file (in our case, `"www/sms.js"`). The `<clobbers>` element is a subelement of `<js-module>`. It has a `target` attribute, whose value, in our case, is `"window.sms"`. The `<clobbers target="window.sms" />` element mainly inserts the `smsExport` JavaScript object that is defined in the `www/sms.js` file and exported using `module.exports` (the `smsExport` object will be illustrated in the *Defining the plugin's JavaScript interface* section) into the `window` object as `window.sms`. This means that our plugin users will be able to access our plugin's API using the `window.sms` object (this will be shown in detail in the *Testing our Cordova plugin* section).

A `<plugin>` element can contain one or more `<platform>` element(s). A `<platform>` element specifies a platform-specific plugin's configuration. It has mainly one attribute name that specifies the platform name (`android`, `ios`, `wp8`, `bb10`, `wp7`, and so on). The `<platform>` element can have the following sub-elements:

- `<source-file>`: This element represents the native platform source code that will be installed and executed in the plugin-client project. The `<source-file>` element has the following two main attributes:
    - `src`: This attribute represents the location of the source file relative to `plugin.xml`.
    - `target-dir`: This attribute represents the `target` directory (that is relative to the project root) in which the source file will be placed when the plugin is installed in the client project. This attribute is mainly needed in Java platform (Android), because a file under the `x.y.z` package must be placed under `x/y/z` directories. For iOS and Windows platforms, this parameter should be ignored.

- `<config-file>`: This element represents the configuration file that will be modified. This is required for many cases; for example, in Android, in order to send an SMS from your Android application, you need to modify the Android configuration file for asking to have the permission to send an SMS from the device. The `<config-file>` element has two main attributes:
    - `target`: This attribute represents the file to be modified and the path relative to the project root.
    - `parent`: This attribute represents an XPath selector that references the parent of the elements to be added to the configuration file.

- `<framework>`: This element specifies a platform-specific framework that the plugin depends on. It mainly has the `src` attribute to specify the framework name and `weak` attributes to indicate whether the specified framework should be weakly linked.

Given this explanation for the `<platform>` element and getting back to our `plugin.xml` file, you will notice that we have the following three `<platform>` elements:

- Android (`<platform name="android">`) performs the following operations:
  - It creates a `<feature>` element for our SMS plugin under the root element of the `res/xml/config.xml` file to register our plugin in the Android project. In Android, the `<feature>` element's `name` attribute represents the service name, and its `"android-package"` parameter represents the fully qualified name of the Java plugin class:

    ```
    <feature name="Sms">
        <param name="android-package"
    value="com.jsmobile.plugins.sms.Sms" />
    </feature>
    ```

  - It modifies the `AndroidManifest.xml` file to add the `<uses-permission android:name="android.permission.SEND_SMS" />` element (to have permission to send an SMS in Android platform) under the `<manifest>` element.

  - Finally, it specifies the plugin's implementation source file, `"src/android/Sms.java"`, and its `target` directory, `"src/com/jsmobile/plugins/sms"` (we will explore the contents of this file in the *Developing Android code* section).

- iOS (`<platform name="ios">`) performs the following operations:
  - It creates a `<feature>` element for our SMS plugin under the root element of the `config.xml` file to register our plugin in the iOS project. In iOS, the `<feature>` element's `name` attribute represents the service name, and its `"ios-package"` parameter represents the Objective-C plugin class name:

    ```
    <feature name="Sms">
        <param name="ios-package" value="Sms" />
    </feature>
    ```

  - It specifies the plugin implementation source files: `Sms.h` (the header file) and `Sms.m` (the methods file). We will explore the contents of these files in the *Developing iOS code* section.

- It adds `"MessageUI.framework"` as a weakly linked dependency for our iOS plugin.

- Windows Phone 8 (`<platform name="wp8">`) performs the following operations:

  - It creates a `<feature>` element for our SMS plugin under the root element of the `config.xml` file to register our plugin in the Windows Phone 8 project. The `<feature>` element's name attribute represents the service name, and its `"wp-package"` parameter represents the C# service class name:

    ```
    <feature name="Sms">
            <param name="wp-package" value="Sms" />
    </feature>
    ```

  - It specifies the plugin implementation source file, `"src/wp8/Sms.cs"` (we will explore the contents of this file in the *Developing Windows Phone 8 code* section).

This is all we need to know in order to understand the structure of our custom plugin; however, there are many more attributes and elements that are not mentioned here, as we didn't use them in our example. In order to get the complete list of attributes and elements of plugin.xml, you can check out the plugin specification page in the Apache Cordova documentation at http://cordova.apache.org/docs/en/3.4.0/plugin_ref_spec.md.html#Plugin%20Specification.

Defining the plugin's JavaScript interface

As indicated in the plugin definition file (plugin.xml), our plugin's JavaScript interface is defined in sms.js, which is located under the www directory. The following code snippet shows the sms.js file content:

```javascript
var smsExport = {};

smsExport.sendMessage = function(messageInfo, successCallback,
errorCallback) {
    if (messageInfo == null || typeof messageInfo !== 'object') {
        if (errorCallback) {
            errorCallback({
                code: "INVALID_INPUT",
```

```
                message: "Invalid Input"
        });
    }

    return;
}

var phoneNumber = messageInfo.phoneNumber;
var textMessage = messageInfo.textMessage || "Default Text
from SMS plugin";

if (! phoneNumber) {
    console.log("Missing Phone Number");

    if (errorCallback) {
        errorCallback({
            code: "MISSING_PHONE_NUMBER",
            message: "Missing Phone number"
        });
    }

    return;
}

cordova.exec(successCallback, errorCallback, "Sms",
"sendMessage", [phoneNumber, textMessage]);
};

module.exports = smsExport;
```

The `smsExport` object contains a single method, `sendMessage(messageInfo, successCallback, errorCallback)`. In the `sendMessage` method, `phoneNumber` and `textMessage` are extracted from the `messageInfo` object. If a phone number is not specified by the user, then `errorCallback` will be called with a JSON error object, which has a `code` attribute set to `"MISSING_PHONE_NUMBER"` and a `message` attribute set to `"Missing Phone number"`. After passing this validation, a call is performed to the `cordova.exec()` API in order to call the native code (whether it is Android, iOS, Windows Phone 8, or any other supported platform) from Apache Cordova JavaScript.

It is important to note that the `cordova.exec(successCallback, errorCallback, "service", "action", [args])` API has the following parameters:

- `successCallback`: This represents the success callback function that will be called (with any specified parameter(s)) if the Cordova `exec` call completes successfully

- `errorCallback`: This represents the error callback function that will be called (with any specified error parameter(s)) if the Cordova `exec` call does not complete successfully

- `"service"`: This represents the native service name that is mapped to a native class using the `<feature>` element (in `sms.js`, the native service name is `"Sms"`)

- `"action"`: This represents the action name to be executed, and an action is mapped to a class method in some platforms (in `sms.js`, the action name is `"sendMessage"`)

- `[args]`: This is an array that represents the action arguments (in `sms.js`, the action arguments are `[phoneNumber, textMessage]`)

> It is very important to note that in `cordova.exec(successCallback, errorCallback, "service", "action", [args])`, the `"service"` parameter must match the name of the `<feature>` element, which we set in our `plugin.xml` file in order to call the mapped native plugin class correctly.

Finally, the `smsExport` object is exported using `module.exports`. Do not forget that our JavaScript module is mapped to `window.sms` using the `<clobbers target="window.sms" />` element inside `<js-module src="www/sms.js">` element, which we discussed in the `plugin.xml` file. This means that in order to call the `sendMessage` method of the `smsExport` object from our plugin-client application, we use the `sms.sendMessage()` method.

In the upcoming sections, we will explore the implementation of our custom Cordova plugin in Android, iOS, and Windows Phone 8 platforms.

Developing Android code

As specified in our `plugin.xml` file's platform section for Android, the implementation of our plugin in Android is located at `src/android/Sms.java`. The following code snippet shows the first part of the `Sms.java` file:

```java
package com.jsmobile.plugins.sms;

import org.apache.cordova.CordovaPlugin;
import org.apache.cordova.CallbackContext;
import org.apache.cordova.PluginResult;
import org.apache.cordova.PluginResult.Status;
import org.json.JSONArray;
import org.json.JSONException;
import org.json.JSONObject;

import android.app.Activity;
import android.app.PendingIntent;
import android.content.BroadcastReceiver;
import android.content.Context;
import android.content.Intent;
import android.content.IntentFilter;
import android.content.pm.PackageManager;
import android.telephony.SmsManager;

public class Sms extends CordovaPlugin {
    private static final String SMS_GENERAL_ERROR =
"SMS_GENERAL_ERROR";
    private static final String NO_SMS_SERVICE_AVAILABLE =
"NO_SMS_SERVICE_AVAILABLE";
    private static final String SMS_FEATURE_NOT_SUPPORTED =
"SMS_FEATURE_NOT_SUPPORTED";
    private static final String SENDING_SMS_ID = "SENDING_SMS";

    @Override
    public boolean execute(String action, JSONArray args,
CallbackContext callbackContext) throws JSONException {
        if (action.equals("sendMessage")) {
            String phoneNumber = args.getString(0);
            String message = args.getString(1);

            boolean isSupported = getActivity().getPackageManager().ha
sSystemFeature(PackageManager.
FEATURE_TELEPHONY);
```

```
        if (! isSupported) {
            JSONObject errorObject = new JSONObject();

            errorObject.put("code", SMS_FEATURE_NOT_SUPPORTED);
            errorObject.put("message", "SMS feature is not
supported on this device");

            callbackContext.sendPluginResult(new
PluginResult(Status.ERROR, errorObject));
            return false;
        }

        this.sendSMS(phoneNumber, message, callbackContext);

        return true;
    }

    return false;
}

// Code is omitted here for simplicity ...

private Activity getActivity() {
    return this.cordova.getActivity();
}
}
```

In order to create our Cordova Android plugin class, our Android plugin class must extend the `CordovaPlugin` class and must override one of the `execute()` methods of `CordovaPlugin`. In our `Sms` Java class, the `execute(String action, JSONArray args, CallbackContext callbackContext)` execute method, which has the following parameters, is overridden:

- `String action`: This represents the action to be performed, and it matches the specified action parameter in the `cordova.exec()` JavaScript API

- `JSONArray args`: This represents the action arguments, and it matches the `[args]` parameter in the `cordova.exec()` JavaScript API

- `CallbackContext callbackContext`: This represents the callback context used when calling back into JavaScript

In the `execute()` method of our `Sms` class, the `phoneNumber` and `message` parameters are retrieved from the `args` parameter. Using `getActivity().getPackageManager().hasSystemFeature(PackageManager.FEATURE_TELEPHONY)`, we can check whether the device has a telephony radio with data communication support. If the device does not have this feature, this API returns `false`, so we create `errorObject` of the `JSONObject` type that contains an error code attribute (`"code"`) and an error message attribute (`"message"`) that inform the plugin user that the SMS feature is not supported on this device. The plugin tells the JavaScript caller that the operation failed by calling `callbackContext.sendPluginResult()` and specifying a `PluginResult` object as a parameter (the `PluginResult` object's status is set to `Status.ERROR`, and message is set to `errorObject`).

 As indicated in our Android implementation, in order to send a plugin result to JavaScript from Android, we use the `callbackContext.sendPluginResult()` method specifying the `PluginResult` status and message. Other platforms (iOS and Windows Phone 8) have much a similar way, as we will see in the upcoming sections.

If an Android device supports sending SMS messages, then a call to the `sendSMS()` private method is performed. The following code snippet shows the `sendSMS()` method:

```
private void sendSMS(String phoneNumber, String message, final
CallbackContext callbackContext) throws JSONException {
    PendingIntent sentPI =
PendingIntent.getBroadcast(getActivity(), 0, new
Intent(SENDING_SMS_ID), 0);

    getActivity().registerReceiver(new BroadcastReceiver() {
        @Override
        public void onReceive(Context context, Intent intent) {
            switch (getResultCode()) {
            case Activity.RESULT_OK:
                callbackContext.sendPluginResult(new
PluginResult(Status.OK, "SMS message is sent successfully"));
                break;
            case SmsManager.RESULT_ERROR_NO_SERVICE:
                try {
                    JSONObject errorObject = new JSONObject();
```

```
                  errorObject.put("code", NO_SMS_SERVICE_AVAILABLE);
                  errorObject.put("message", "SMS is not sent
because no service is available");

                  callbackContext.sendPluginResult(new
PluginResult(Status.ERROR, errorObject));
               } catch (JSONException exception) {
                  exception.printStackTrace();
               }
               break;
          default:
             try {
                  JSONObject errorObject = new JSONObject();

                  errorObject.put("code", SMS_GENERAL_ERROR);
                  errorObject.put("message", "SMS general error");

                  callbackContext.sendPluginResult(new
PluginResult(Status.ERROR, errorObject));
               } catch (JSONException exception) {
                  exception.printStackTrace();
               }

             break;
          }
       }
    }, new IntentFilter(SENDING_SMS_ID));

    SmsManager sms = SmsManager.getDefault();

    sms.sendTextMessage(phoneNumber, null, message, sentPI, null);
}
```

In order to understand the sendSMS() method, let's look into the method's last two lines:

```
SmsManager sms = SmsManager.getDefault();
sms.sendTextMessage(phoneNumber, null, message, sentPI, null);
```

SmsManager is an Android class that provides an API to send text messages. Using SmsManager.getDefault() returns an object of SmsManager. In order to send a text-based message, a call to sms.sendTextMessage() should be performed.

The `sms.sendTextMessage (String destinationAddress, String scAddress, String text, PendingIntent sentIntent, PendingIntent deliveryIntent)` method has the following parameters:

- `destinationAddress`: This represents the address (phone number) to send the message to.

- `scAddress`: This represents the service center address. It can be set to `null` to use the current default SMS center.

- `text`: This represents the text message to be sent.

- `sentIntent`: This represents a `PendingIntent`, which broadcasts when the message is successfully sent or failed. It can be set to `null`.

- `deliveryIntent`: This represents a `PendingIntent`, which broadcasts when the message is delivered to the recipient. It can be set to `null`.

As shown in the preceding code snippet, we specified a destination address (`phoneNumber`), a text message (`message`), and finally, a pending intent (`sendPI`) in order to listen to the message-sending status.

If you return to the `sendSMS()` code and look at it from the beginning, you will notice that `sentPI` is initialized by calling `PendingIntent.getBroadcast()`, and in order to receive the SMS-sending broadcast, a `BroadcastReceiver` is registered.

When the SMS message is sent successfully or fails, the `onReceive()` method of `BroadcastReceiver` will be called, and the result code can be retrieved using `getResultCode()`. The result code can indicate:

- Success when `getResultCode()` is equal to `Activity.RESULT_OK`. In this case, a `PluginResult` object is constructed with `status = Status.OK` and `message = "SMS message is sent successfully"`, and it is sent to the client using `callbackContext.sendPluginResult()`.

- Failure when `getResultCode()` is not equal to `Activity.RESULT_OK`. In this case, a `PluginResult` object is constructed with `status = Status.ERROR` and `message = errorObject` (which contains the error code and error message), and it is sent to the client using `callbackContext.sendPluginResult()`.

These are the details of our SMS plugin implementation in Android platform. Now, let's move to the iOS implementation of our plugin.

Developing iOS code

As specified in our `plugin.xml` file's platform section for iOS, the implementation of our plugin in iOS is located at the `src/ios/Sms.h` and `src/ios/Sms.m` Objective-C files. The following code snippet shows the `Sms.h` file (the header file):

```
#import <Cordova/CDV.h>
#import <MessageUI/MFMessageComposeViewController.h>

@interface Sms : CDVPlugin <MFMessageComposeViewControllerDelegate> {
}

@property(strong) NSString* callbackID;
- (void)sendMessage:(CDVInvokedUrlCommand*)command;
@end
```

The preceding code declares an `Sms` class that extends `CDVPlugin`. It is important to note that in order to create a Cordova iOS plugin class, our Objective-C plugin class must extend the `CDVPlugin` class. In our `Sms` class declaration, there is a declared `callbackID` property of the `NSString` type and a declared `sendMessage` method, which returns `void` and takes `CDVInvokedUrlCommand` as a parameter. Now, let's move on to the `Sms` class implementation. The following code snippet shows the first part of the `Sms.m` file:

```
#import "Sms.h"

@implementation Sms

- (void)sendMessage:(CDVInvokedUrlCommand*)command
{
    CDVPluginResult* pluginResult = nil;
    NSString* phoneNumber = [command.arguments objectAtIndex:0];
    NSString* textMessage = [command.arguments objectAtIndex:1];

    self.callbackID = command.callbackId;

    if (![MFMessageComposeViewController canSendText]) {
        NSMutableDictionary* returnInfo = [NSMutableDictionary
dictionaryWithCapacity:2];

        [returnInfo setObject:@"SMS_FEATURE_NOT_SUPPORTED"
forKey:@"code"];
        [returnInfo setObject:@"SMS feature is not supported on
this device" forKey:@"message"];
```

```
        pluginResult = [CDVPluginResult
resultWithStatus:CDVCommandStatus_ERROR
messageAsDictionary:returnInfo];

        [self.commandDelegate sendPluginResult:pluginResult
callbackId:command.callbackId];

        return;
    }

    MFMessageComposeViewController *composeViewController =
[[MFMessageComposeViewController alloc] init];
    composeViewController.messageComposeDelegate = self;

    NSMutableArray *recipients = [[NSMutableArray alloc] init];

    [recipients addObject:phoneNumber];

    [composeViewController setBody:textMessage];
    [composeViewController setRecipients:recipients];

    [self.viewController presentViewController:composeViewController
animated:YES
completion:nil];
    }
    // Code is omitted from here for simplicity
@end
```

In our Sms class implementation, we have the Objective-C instance method,
- (void)sendMessage:(CDVInvokedUrlCommand*)command, which maps to
the action parameter in the cordova.exec() JavaScript API.

In the sendMessage() method of our Sms class, the phoneNumber and message
parameters are retrieved from the command.arguments parameter (phoneNumber is
located at index 0 and message is located at index 1).

The MFMessageComposeViewController class provides a standard system user
interface to compose text messages. Unlike Android, we cannot send SMS messages
directly in iOS devices from our plugin code without using the default device's
(iPhone or iPad) SMS application. In iOS, all we can do from our plugin code is use
the MFMessageComposeViewController class to launch the SMS application with
the SMS recipient and SMS message and listen for the user actions to know
if the user sent or, cancelled, or failed to send the message. However, before
interacting with the MFMessageComposeViewController class, we need to check
whether the current iOS device is capable of sending text messages. This can be
done using the canSendText method of MFMessageComposeViewController as
[MFMessageComposeViewController canSendText].

If the iOS device does not have the feature to send text messages (which means that `[MFMessageComposeViewController canSendText]` returns `NO`), we will create a `returnInfo` object (that is of the `NSMutableDictionary` type), which contains two entries: one for the error code and the other one for the error message that tells the plugin user that the SMS feature is not supported on this device. Our plugin tells the JavaScript caller that the operation failed by calling the `sendPluginResult` method (of `self.commandDelegate`), which has the following signature:

```
- (void) sendPluginResult: (CDVPluginResult*) result
callbackId: (NSString*) callbackId;
```

To this method, we pass a `CDVPluginResult` object (whose `status` is `CDVCommandStatus_ERROR`, and `message` is `returnInfo`) and `callbackId`, which is set to `command.callbackId`.

If your iOS device supports sending SMS messages, then a `composeViewController` object (of the `MFMessageComposeViewController` type) is created and initialized with `recipients` as the message recipients and `textMessage` as the message body. Then, we present `composeViewController` modally using the `presentModalViewController` method of `self.viewController`. It is important to highlight this line:

```
composeViewController.messageComposeDelegate = self;
```

This line tells `composeViewController` to send the message-related notifications to our `Sms` class. In order to receive these notifications, our `Sms` class needs to implement the `messageComposeViewController` method that has the following signature:

```
- (void) messageComposeViewController:
(MFMessageComposeViewController *) controller
didFinishWithResult: (MessageComposeResult) result
```

The `messageComposeViewController` class has the following parameters:

- `Controller`: This represents the message composition view controller that returns the result

- `Result`: This represents a result code that indicates how the user chose to complete the message composition (cancels or sends successfully or fails to send)

The following code snippet shows the implementation of messageComposeViewController in our Sms class:

```objectivec
- (void)messageComposeViewController:(MFMessageComposeViewController
*)controller didFinishWithResult:(MessageComposeResult)result {
    BOOL succeeded = NO;
    NSString* errorCode = @"";
    NSString* message = @"";

    switch(result) {
        case MessageComposeResultSent:
            succeeded = YES;
            message = @"Message sent";
            break;
        case MessageComposeResultCancelled:
            message = @"Message cancelled";
            errorCode = @"SMS_MESSAGE_CANCELLED";
            break;
        case MessageComposeResultFailed:
            message = @"Message Compose Result failed";
            errorCode = @"SMS_MESSAGE_COMPOSE_FAILED";
            break;
        default:
            message = @"Sms General error";
            errorCode = @"SMS_GENERAL_ERROR";
            break;
    }

    [self.viewController dismissViewControllerAnimated:YES
completion:nil];

    if (succeeded == YES) {
        [super writeJavascript:[[CDVPluginResult
resultWithStatus:CDVCommandStatus_OK messageAsString:message]
                            toSuccessCallbackString:self.
callbackID]];
    } else {
        NSMutableDictionary* returnInfo = [NSMutableDictionary
dictionaryWithCapacity:2];

        [returnInfo setObject:errorCode forKey:@"code"];
        [returnInfo setObject:message forKey:@"message"];
```

```
                [super writeJavascript:[[CDVPluginResult
    resultWithStatus:CDVCommandStatus_ERROR
    messageAsDictionary:returnInfo]
                                    toErrorCallbackString:self.
    callbackID]];
        }
    }
```

The `messageComposeViewController` method is called when the user taps on one of the buttons to dismiss the message composition interface. In the implementation of the `messageComposeViewController` method, the following two actions are performed:

- Dismiss the view controller by calling the `dismissViewControllerAnimated` method of `self.viewController`.

- Check whether the `result` parameter is equal to `MessageComposeResultSent` (which means that the user sent the message successfully) in order to send a `CDVPluginResult` with `status` = `CDVCommandStatus_OK` and `message` = `"Message sent"` to the plugin client. If the result is not equal to `MessageComposeResultSent`, then a `CDVPluginResult` is sent with `status` = `CDVCommandStatus_ERROR` and `message` = `returnInfo` (which contains two entries: one entry for the error code and the other one for the error message that contains the error details such as `"Message cancelled"` or `"Message Compose Result failed"`) to the plugin client.

These are the details of our SMS plugin implementation in iOS platform. Next, let's move to the Windows Phone 8 implementation of our plugin.

Developing Windows Phone 8 code

As specified in our `plugin.xml` file's platform section for Windows Phone 8 (wp8), the implementation of our plugin in wp8 is located at `src/wp8/Sms.cs`. The following code snippet shows `Sms.cs` code:

```
using System;
using Microsoft.Phone.Tasks;
using WPCordovaClassLib.Cordova;
using WPCordovaClassLib.Cordova.Commands;
using WPCordovaClassLib.Cordova.JSON;

namespace WPCordovaClassLib.Cordova.Commands
{
  public class Sms : BaseCommand
  {
```

```
public void sendMessage(string options)
{
    string[] optValues = JsonHelper.Deserialize<string[]>(options);
    String number = optValues[0];
    String message = optValues[1];

    SmsComposeTask sms = new SmsComposeTask();

    sms.To = number;
    sms.Body = message;

    sms.Show();

    /*Since there is no way to track SMS application events in
WP8, always send Ok status.*/
    DispatchCommandResult(new PluginResult(PluginResult.Status.OK,
"Success"));
    }
  }
}
```

In order to create our Cordova wp8 C# plugin class, our wp8 plugin C# class (Sms) must extend the BaseCommand class. In our Sms class, we have the C# method, public void sendMessage(string options), which maps to the action parameter in the cordova.exec() JavaScript API. The sendMessage() action method must follow these rules:

- The method must be public

- The method must return void

- Its argument is a string (not an array as you might expect as the cordova. exec() method's args parameter is originally an array)

In the `sendMessage()` method of our `Sms` class, in order to get the original arguments' array, we need to use the `JsonHelper.Deserialize()` method to deserialize the string parameter to an array. After performing this deserialization, the `number` and `message` parameters are retrieved from the result array (`optValues`).

After getting the `number` and `message` parameters, all we can do is create an `sms` object from `SmsComposeTask` and then set the (`To` and `Body`) attributes to the (`number` and `message`) parameters. After that, we call the `Show()` method of the `sms` object, which will show the wp8 SMS application.

Unfortunately in wp8, you cannot send an SMS message directly using the wp8 API. In order to send an SMS message in wp8, you have to use the default SMS application using `SmsComposeTask`, which does not give you any ability to know what the user did (this means that you will not know whether the user sent an SMS successfully or not or even whether the user cancels sending the SMS).

 The wp8 API is more restrictive than iOS API in SMS sending. In iOS, you cannot send an SMS directly using the iOS API, but the iOS API gives us the ability to know what the user did. This gives us the ability to send successful or failing plugin results to the plugin client in the case of our iOS implementation.

Finally, and because our plugin is now blind once the `Show()` method of `SmsComposeTask` is called, our plugin assumes that sending SMS is completed successfully and sends a `PluginResult` object, whose `status = PluginResult.Status.OK` and `message = "Success"`, to the plugin client in order to have a consistent behavior across the different platforms. Consistent behavior here means that when the users call our API from JavaScript in any supported platform, our API has to always respond to their calls with either successful or failed responses.

These are the details of our SMS plugin implementation on Windows Phone 8 platform. Now, let's publish our plugin to the Cordova Registry to be used by the Apache Cordova community.

Publishing our plugin to Cordova Registry

After completing our plugin implementation, we can publish our SMS plugin to the Apache Cordova Registry. Before publishing our custom SMS plugin, let's revise our final SMS plugin structure. The following screenshot shows the final structure of our custom SMS plugin:

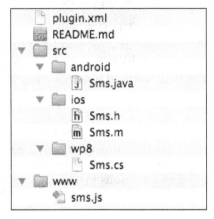

Hierarchy of our final plugin structure

As shown in the preceding screenshot, the final structure has the following main additions:

- A new wp8 directory under the src directory; it has our wp8 plugin implementation
- A markdown README.md file that explains the purpose of the plugin and an example of its usage

Now, after understanding the final structure of our custom SMS plugin, we can now publish our plugin to the Apache Cordova Registry. In order to do this, just execute the following plugman publish command specifying our SMS plugin directory:

```
> plugman publish sms
```

After executing this command successfully, you will be notified that our com.jsmobile.plugins.sms@0.0.1 plugin has been published successfully.

By uploading our custom plugin to the Apache Cordova Registry, the Apache Cordova community can now use our plugin by just using the normal Cordova CLI's `plugin add` command as follows:

```
> cordova plugin add com.jsmobile.plugins.sms
```

In order to make the source code of our plugin accessible, we published its source code on GitHub, and it can be downloaded from `https://github.com/hazems/cordova-sms-plugin`.

Publishing our custom plugin to GitHub gives our plugin consumers the ability to add our custom plugin to their projects by specifying the plugin GitHub URL as follows:

```
> cordova plugin add https://github.com/hazems/cordova-sms-plugin.git
```

In the next section, we will create our test Cordova application, which will test the functionality of our plugin across the different platforms (Android, iOS, and wp8).

Testing our Cordova plugin

Now, it is time to create our test Cordova application, `"SmsApp"`. In order to create our test Cordova application, we can execute the following `cordova create` command:

```
> cordova create smsApp com.jsmobile.sms.app SmsApp
```

Then, we can add Android, iOS, and wp8 from the application directory as follows:

```
> cordova platform add android
```

```
> cordova platform add ios
```

```
> cordova platform add wp8
```

The following code snippet shows the jQuery Mobile page (`index.html`), which allows the user to enter a phone number and message. The user can then click on the **Send** button to send an SMS.

```html
<html>
<head>
    <!-- meta data and jQuery mobile includes are omitted for
saving space -->
    <script src="jqueryMobile/jquery.validate.min.js"></script>
    <title>SMS App</title>
</head>
<body>
```

```
<div data-role="page" id="sms">
    <div data-role="header">
        <h1>Send SMS</h1>
    </div>
    <div data-role="content">
        <h1>Send SMS now</h1>
        <p>Enter mobile number and mobile message and click
"send" button.</p>

        <form id="smsForm">
            <div class="ui-field-contain">
                <label for="phoneNo">Phone Number</label>
                <input type="text" id="phoneNo"
name="phoneNo"></input>
            </div>
            <div class="ui-field-contain">
                <label for="textMessage">Message</label>
                <input type="text" id="textMessage"
name="textMessage"></input>
            </div>
            <input type="submit" id="sendSMS" data-icon="action"
value="Send"></input>
            <ul id="messageBox"></ul>
            <div id="result">
            </div>
        </form>
    </div>
</div>

<script type="text/javascript" src="cordova.js"></script>
<script type="text/javascript" src="js/sms.js"></script>
</body>
</html>
```

As shown in the preceding highlighted code, we are utilizing the jQuery validation plugin. This is why we included the `jquery.validate.min.js` file. The `"smsForm"` form element contains the following elements:

- `"phoneNo"`: It includes a label and an input text to enter phone number

- `"textMessage"`: It includes a label and an input text to enter text message.

- `"sendSMS"`: It is a button to send an SMS message

- `"messageBox"`: This is an unordered list used to display validation errors

- `"result"`: This div is used to display the SMS operation result

Finally, we included `sms.js`. The `sms.js` file includes the implementation for the event handlers of `"smsForm"`. The following code snippet shows the `sms.js` file's code:

```
(function() {
    $(document).on("pageinit", "#sms", function(e) {
        e.preventDefault();

        function onDeviceReady() {
            console.log("Apache Cordova is loaded ...");

            $("#sendSMS").on("tap", function(e) {
                e.preventDefault();

                if (! $("#smsForm").valid()) {
                    return;
                }

                var messageInfo = {
                    phoneNumber: $("#phoneNo").val(),
                    textMessage: $("#textMessage").val()
                };

                sms.sendMessage(messageInfo, function() {
                    $("#result").html("Message is sent successfully
...");
                }, function(error) {
                    $("#result").html("Error code: " + error.code +
", Error message: " + error.message);
                });
            });
        }

        document.addEventListener("deviceready", onDeviceReady,
false);
    });

    $(document).on("pageshow", "#sms", function(e) {
        e.preventDefault();

        $("#smsForm").validate({
            errorLabelContainer: "#messageBox",
            wrapper: "li",
            rules: {
                textMessage: "required",
```

```
                    phoneNo: {
                        required: true,
                        number: true
                    }
                },
                messages: {
                    textMessage: "Please specify text message",
                    phoneNo: {
                        required: "Please specify Phone number",
                        number: "Phone number is numeric only"
                    }
                }
            });
        });
    })();
```

As shown in the preceding code, in the `"pageinit"` event of the `"sms"` page, the `"tap"` event handler of the `"sendSMS"` button is registered after Apache Cordova is loaded. In the implementation of the `"sendSMS"` button's tap event handler:

- The `"smsForm"` is validated using `$("#smsForm").valid()`.

- If the form is valid, then, as shown in the preceding highlighted code, the `messageInfo` object is constructed using the `phoneNumber` and `textMessage` attributes. The `phoneNumber` and `textMessage` attributes are initialized with the `"phoneNo"` and `"textMessage"` input text values.

- A call to `sms.sendMessage(messageInfo, successCallback, errorCallback)` is performed with the following parameters in order:

    - The `messageInfo` object.
    - The `success` callback function that will be called when an SMS is successfully sent. The `success` callback function displays the `"Message is sent successfully ..."` message inside the `"result"` div.
    - The `error` callback function that will be called when sending SMS fails. The `failure` callback function displays both the error code and error message inside the `"result"` div.

In the `"pageshow"` event of the `"sms"` page, our form validation is specified as follows:

- `errorLabelContainer`: This is set to `"messageBox"` to display the validation errors inside

- `wrapper`: This is set to `"li"` to wrap the error messages in list items

- `rules`: This is set as follows:
    - `textMessage` is set to `required`
    - `phoneNumber` is set to `number` and `required`

- `messages`: This is set to `textMessage` and `phoneNumber` validation errors messages

Now, let's build and run our SMS app in order to observe how our custom SMS plugin will behave across the different platforms (Android, iOS, and Windows Phone 8). When the user enters a valid phone number and a text message and then clicks on the **Send** button, the following will happen:

- In Android, an SMS will be sent directly from our Android SMS app without any intervention from the platform's default SMS app.

- In iOS, the user will be forwarded to the default iOS SMS app initialized with the phone number and text message from our custom SMS plugin. Once the user clicks on the **Send** or even **Cancel** button, the user will get back to our SMS app with the correct result displayed.

- In Windows Phone 8, the user will be forwarded to the default Windows Phone 8 SMS app initialized with the phone number and text message from our custom SMS plugin. Unfortunately, due to wp8 API limitations, when the user clicks on the **Send** or even **Cancel** button, we will not be able to detect what happens. This is why when you click on your wp8 device's back button to get back to our SMS app, you will find our SMS application always displaying the success message, which is not always correct due to the current wp8 API limitations.

 The complete source code of `"SmsApp"` can be downloaded from the book's web page or from GitHub (`https://github.com/hazems/cordova-sms-plugin-test`).

Summary

This chapter showed you how to design and develop your own custom Apache Cordova plugin using JavaScript and Java for Android, Objective-C for iOS, and finally, C# for Windows Phone 8. In the next chapter, you will learn how to develop JavaScript tests for your Cordova app's logic using Jasmine. You will also learn how to automate the Jasmine tests that you will develop, using Karma and Jenkins CI.

7
Unit Testing the Cordova App's Logic

In this chapter, you will learn how to develop JavaScript unit tests for your Cordova app logic. In this chapter, you will:

- Learn the basics of the Jasmine JavaScript unit testing framework
- Use Jasmine in order to test both synchronous and asynchronous JavaScript code
- Utilize Karma as a powerful JavaScript test runner in order to automate the running of your developed Jasmine tests
- Generate test and code coverage reports from your developed tests
- Automate your JavaScript tests by integrating your developed tests with **Continuous Integration (CI)** tools

What is Jasmine

Jasmine is a powerful JavaScript unit testing framework. It provides a clean mechanism to test synchronous and asynchronous JavaScript code. It is a behavior-driven development framework that provides descriptive test cases, which focus on business value more than on technical details. As it is written in a simple, natural language, Jasmine tests can be read by nonprogrammers and provide a clear description when a single test succeeds or fails and the reason behind its failure.

Behavior-driven development (BDD) is an agile software development technique introduced by Dan North; it focuses on writing descriptive tests from a business perspective. BDD extends TDD by writing test cases that test the software behavior (requirements) in a natural language that anyone (does not necessarily have to be a programmer) can read and understand. The names of the unit tests are complete sentences that usually start with the word "should," and they are written in the order of their business value.

Configuring Jasmine

In order to configure Jasmine, the first step is to download the framework from `https://github.com/pivotal/jasmine/tree/master/dist`. In this download link, you will find the latest releases of the framework.

At the time of writing this book, the latest release is v2.0 that we will use in this chapter.

After unpacking `jasmine-standalone-2.0.0.zip`, you will find the following directories and files, as shown in the following screenshot:

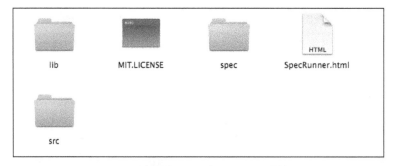

Jasmine Standalone 2.0 directories and files

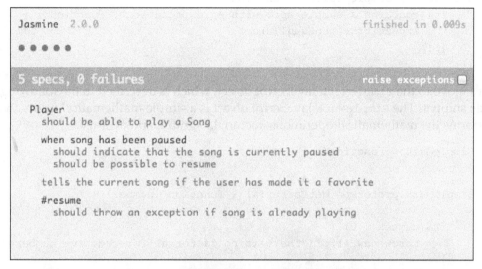

The `src` directory contains the JavaScript source files that you want to test. The `spec` directory contains the JavaScript test files, while the `SpecRunner.html` file is the test cases' runner HTML file. The `lib` directory contains the framework files.

In order to make sure that everything is running okay, click on the `SpecRunner.html` file; you should see specs passing, as shown in the following screenshot:

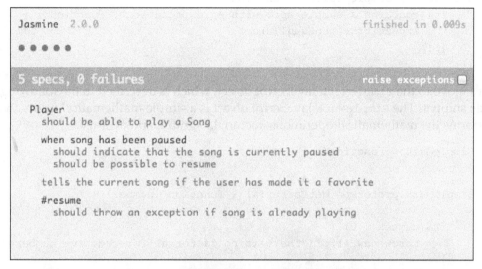

Jasmine specs passing

Note that this structure is not rigid; we can modify it to serve the organization of our app, as we will see in the *Jasmine in action – developing Cordova app tests* section.

Writing your first Jasmine test

Before writing our first Jasmine test, we need to understand the difference between a suite and a spec (test specification) in Jasmine. Jasmine suite is a group of test cases that can be used to test a specific behavior of the JavaScript code. In Jasmine, the test suite begins with a call to the `describe` Jasmine global function that has two parameters. The first parameter represents the title of the test suite, while the second parameter represents a function that implements the test suite.

A Jasmine spec represents a test case inside the test suite. In Jasmine, the test case begins with a call to the Jasmine global function `it` that has two parameters. The first parameter represents the title of the spec and the second parameter represents a function that implements the test case.

A Jasmine spec contains one or more expectations. Every expectation represents an assertion that can be either `true` or `false`. In order to pass the specs, all of the expectations inside the spec have to be `true`. If one or more expectations inside a spec is `false`, then the spec fails. The following code listing shows an example of a Jasmine test suite and a spec with an expectation:

```
describe("A sample suite", function() {
    it("contains a sample spec with an expectation", function() {
        expect(true).toEqual(true);
    });
});
```

Let's move to the `SimpleMath` JavaScript object, which is described in the following code snippet. The `SimpleMath` JavaScript object is a simple mathematical utility that performs the mathematical operations: factorial, Signum, and average:

```
SimpleMath = function() {
};

SimpleMath.prototype.getFactorial = function (number) {

    if (number < 0) {
        throw new Error("There is no factorial for negative numbers");
    }
    else if (number == 1 || number == 0) {

        // If number <= 1 then number! = 1.
        return 1;
    } else {

        // If number > 1 then number! = number * (number-1)!
        return number * this.getFactorial(number-1);
    }
}

SimpleMath.prototype.signum = function (number) {
    if (number > 0)   {
        return 1;
    } else if (number == 0) {
        return 0;
    } else {
        return -1;
    }
}
```

```
SimpleMath.prototype.average = function (number1, number2) {
    return (number1 + number2) / 2;
}
```

The `SimpleMath` object is used to calculate the factorial of numbers. In mathematics, the factorial of a non-negative integer n, denoted by $n!$, is the product of all the positive integers less than or equal to n, for example, $4! = 4 \times 3 \times 2 \times 1 = 24$.

The `SimpleMath` object calculates the factorial number using the `getFactorial` recursive function. It throws an error when the parameter passed to the `getFactorial` method is a negative number, because there is no factorial value for negative numbers.

Adding to calculating factorial, `SimpleMath` can get the Signum of any number using the `signum` method. In mathematics, the Signum function is a mathematical function that extracts the sign of a real number.

Finally, `SimpleMath` can calculate the average of two numbers using the average method. The average value of two numbers can be calculated by dividing the sum of the two numbers by 2.

Now, let's start writing the specs using Jasmine. First of all, in order to test the `getFactorial` method, let's look at the following three test scenarios. We will calculate the factorial of:

- A positive number
- Zero
- A negative number

The following code snippet shows how to calculate the factorial of a positive number 3, zero, and a negative number -10:

```
describe("SimpleMath", function() {
    var simpleMath;

    beforeEach(function() {
        simpleMath = new SimpleMath();
    });

    describe("when SimpleMath is used to find factorial",
function() {
        it("should be able to find factorial for positive number",
function() {
            expect(simpleMath.getFactorial(3)).toEqual(6);
        });
```

```
        it("should be able to find factorial for zero", function()
{
            expect(simpleMath.getFactorial(0)).toEqual(1);
        });

        it("should be able to throw an exception when the number
    is negative", function() {
            expect(
                function() {
                    simpleMath.getFactorial(-10)
                }).toThrow();
        });
    });
    //...
    });
```

The `describe` keyword declares a new test suite called `"SimpleMath"`. `beforeEach` is used for initialization of the specs inside the suite, that is, `beforeEach` is called once before the run of each spec in `describe`. `beforeEach`, `simpleMath` object is created using `new SimpleMath()`.

In Jasmine, it is also possible to execute the JavaScript code after running each spec in `describe` using the `afterEach` global function. Having `beforeEach` and `afterEach` in Jasmine allows the developer not to repeat the set up and finalization code for each spec.

After initializing the `simpleMath` object, you can either create a direct spec using the `"it"` keyword or create a child test suite using the `describe` keyword. For the purpose of organizing the example, we create a new `describe` function for each group of tests with similar functionalities. This is why we create an independent `"describe"` function to test the functionality of `getFactorial` provided by the `SimpleMath` object.

In the first test scenario of the `getFactorial` test suite, the spec title is `"should be able to find factorial for positive number"`, and the `expect()` function calls `simpleMath.getFactorial(3)` and expects it to be equal to 6. If `simpleMath.getFactorial(3)` returns a value other than 6, then the test fails.

We have many other options (matchers) to use instead of `toEqual`; we will show them in the *Jasmine Matchers* section.

In the second test scenario of the getFactorial test suite, the expect() function calls simpleMath.getFactorial(0) and expects it to be equal to 1. In the final test scenario of the getFactorial test suite, the expect() function calls simpleMath. getFactorial(-10) and expects it to throw an exception using the toThrow matcher. The toThrow matcher succeeds if the function of the expect() function throws an exception when executed.

After finalizing the getFactorial suite test, we come to a new test suite that tests the functionality of the signum method provided by the SimpleMath object, as shown in the following code snippet:

```
describe("when SimpleMath is used to find signum", function() {
    it("should be able to find the signum for a positive number",
function() {
        expect(simpleMath.signum(3)).toEqual(1);
    });

    it("should be able to find the signum for zero", function() {
        expect(simpleMath.signum(0)).toEqual(0);
    });

    it("should be able to find the signum for a negative number",
function() {
        expect(simpleMath.signum(-1000)).toEqual(-1);
    });
});
```

We have three test scenarios for the signum method. The first test scenario is getting the Signum of a positive number, the second test scenario is getting the Signum of zero, and the last test scenario is getting the Signum of a negative number. As validated by the specs, the signum method has to return 1 for a positive number (3), 0 for zero, and finally, -1 for a negative number (-1000). The following code snippet shows the average test suite:

```
describe("when SimpleMath is used to find the average of two
values", function() {
    it("should be able to find the average of two values",
function() {
        expect(simpleMath.average(3, 6)).toEqual(4.5);
    });
});
```

In the average spec, the test ensures that the average is calculated correctly by trying to calculate the average of two numbers, 3 and 6, and expecting the result to be 4.5.

Now, after writing the suites and specs, it is time to run our JavaScript tests. In order to run the tests, follow these steps:

1. Place the `simpleMath.js` file in the `src` folder.

2. Place the `simpleMathSpec.js` file in the `spec` folder.

3. Edit the `SpecRunner.html` file, as shown by the highlighted code in the following code snippet:

```html
<!DOCTYPE HTML>
<html>
    <head>
        <meta http-equiv="Content-Type" content="text/html;
charset=UTF-8">
        <title>Jasmine Spec Runner v2.0.0</title>

        <link rel="shortcut icon" type="image/png"
href="lib/jasmine-2.0.0/jasmine_favicon.png">
        <link rel="stylesheet" type="text/css"
href="lib/jasmine-2.0.0/jasmine.css">

        <script type="text/javascript" src="lib/jasmine-
2.0.0/jasmine.js"></script>
        <script type="text/javascript" src="lib/jasmine-
2.0.0/jasmine-html.js"></script>
        <script type="text/javascript" src="lib/jasmine-
2.0.0/boot.js"></script>

        <!-- include source files here... -->
        <script type="text/javascript" src="src/simpleMath.js"></
script>

        <!-- include spec files here... -->
        <script type="text/javascript" src="spec/simpleMathSpec.
js"></script>
    </head>
    <body>
    </body>
</html>
```

As shown in the highlighted lines, `<script type="text/javascript" src="spec/simpleMathSpec.js"></script>` is added under the `include spec files` omment , while `<script type="text/javascript" src="src/simpleMath.js"></script>` is added under the `include source files` comment. After clicking on the `SpecRunner.html` file, you will see our developed JavaScript tests succeed.

Jasmine Matchers

In the first Jasmine example, we used the `toEqual` and `toThrow` Jasmine Matchers. In the following table, some of the other built-in matchers provided by Jasmine are explained briefly:

Matcher	Description
`expect(x).toBe(y)`	The `toBe` matcher passes if x is of the same type and value of y. The `toBe` matcher uses `===` to perform this comparison.
`expect(x).toBeDefined()`	The `toBeDefined` matcher is used to ensure that x is defined.
`expect(x).toBeUndefined()`	The `toBeUndefined` matcher is used to ensure that x is undefined.
`expect(x).toBeNull()`	The `toBeNull` matcher is used to ensure that x is null.
`expect(x).toBeTruthy()`	The `toBeTruthy` matcher is used to ensure that x is *truthy*.
`expect(x).toBeFalsy()`	The `toBeFalsy` matcher is used to ensure that x is *falsy*.
`expect(x).toContain(y)`	The `toContain` matcher is used to check whether the x string or array value contains y. A valid y value can be a substring of x or an item of x.
`expect(x).toBeLessThan(y)`	The `toBeLessThan` matcher is used to ensure that x is less than y.
`expect(x).toBeGreaterThan(y)`	The `toBeGreaterThan` matcher is used to ensure that x is greater than y.
`expect(x).toMatch(y)`	The `toMatch` matcher is used to check whether x matches a string or regular expression (y).

Adding to built-in matchers, you can create your own Jasmine custom matcher. To create your own Jasmine custom matcher, check the Jasmine 2.0 custom matcher documentation page at `http://jasmine.github.io/2.0/custom_matcher.html`.

Jasmine in action – developing Cordova app tests

Now, let's see Jasmine in action. In the following sections, we will illustrate a Cordova mobile app (weather application), which we will develop its tests using Jasmine. We will see how to test both the synchronous and asynchronous JavaScript code of the app, automate running our developed Jasmine tests using Karma, run our tests on the mobile device browser, generate test and code coverage reports, and finally, fully automate our tests by integrating our developed tests with CI tools.

An overview of the weather application

The main purpose of the weather application is to allow its users to know the current weather information of a specified place. It has two main views; the first view represents **First Time login**, which appears to the users for their first login time, as shown in the following screenshot:

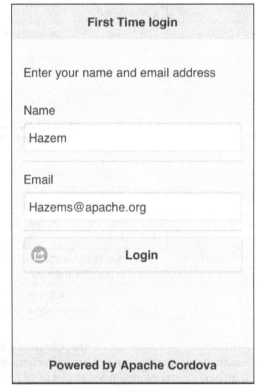

Weather application's first time login

After entering the valid information and clicking on the **Login** button, the user will be forwarded to the weather information page. On the weather information page, the user can enter the place information and then click on the **Weather Info** button to get the current weather information, as shown in the following screenshot:

Again, pretty obvious

After entering valid information on the **First Time login** page and clicking on the **Login** button, if the user exits the app and opens it again, the user will automatically be forwarded to the weather information page with his/her name displayed in the welcome message.

In order to create weather application from CLI, we run the following `cordova create` command:

```
> cordova create weather com.jsmobile.weather Weather
```

We run the usual `cordova platform add` commands from the `app` directory to add the platforms we want to support as follows:

```
> cd weather
> cordova platform add ios
```

Finally, we can build our app using the `cordova build` command as follows:

```
> cordova build
```

Now, let's examine the structure of our weather application code. The following screenshot shows our weather application hierarchy:

The www directory contains the following files and subdirectories:

- css: This directory contains the custom application's **Cascading Style Sheet (CSS)**.

- jqueryMobile: This directory contains the jQuery Mobile framework files.

- js: This directory contains all the application JavaScript code. It has two subdirectories:
  - api: This directory contains the app services.

- ○ vc: This directory contains the app view controllers, which register and implement the event handlers of every page and its user interface components. An event handler usually calls one or more app services in order to perform an action and optionally display the returned results on an app page.

- tests: This directory contains the tests of app services, which are implemented using Jasmine.

The js directory also includes common.js file, which includes the common app utilities. Under the www directory, the index.html file contains all of the app pages, and finally, the img directory can contain any app's custom images.

The index.html file contains the following pages:

- "landing": This page displays a loading message to the user in the app startup and forwards the user to either the **First Time login** page if the user has not logged in to the app before or to the weather information page if the user is already registered.

- "login": This page displays a form that includes the username and e-mail input fields and a **Login** button. The "login" page allows the users to enter their information while they are accessing the app for the first time. If the users enter valid information on the "login" page and clicks on the **Login** button, the users will not be introduced to this page during their next visit.

- "weather": This page allows the user to enter information about a place and then click on the **Weather Info** button to find out the current weather information of the place entered.

The following code snippet shows the "login" page:

```
<div data-role="page" id="login">
    <div data-role="header" data-position="fixed">
        <h1>First Time login</h1>
    </div>
    <div data-role="content">
        <p>Enter your name and email address</p>
        <form id="loginForm">
            <div class="ui-field-contain">
                <label for="userName">Name</label>
                <input type="text" id="userName"></input>
            </div>
            <div class="ui-field-contain">
                <label for="userEmail">Email</label>
```

```
                    <input type="text" id="userEmail"></input>
            </div>

            <input type="button" id="loginUser" data-icon="action"
    value="Login"/>

            <div id="loginFormMessages" class="error"></div>
        </form>
    </div>
    <div data-role="footer" data-position="fixed">
        <h1>Powered by Apache Cordova</h1>
    </div>
</div>
```

As shown in the preceding `"login"` page, it contains the following:

- A page header and page footer
- Page content that includes the following main elements:
    - `"userName"`: This input field is used to enter the username
    - `"userEmail"`: This input field is used to enter the user's e-mail
    - `"loginUser"`: This button is used to save the user information and then go to the weather information page
    - `"loginFormMessages"`: This div is used to display the error messages on the login page

The following code snippet shows the `"login"` page view controller JavaScript object that includes the event handlers of the page (`login.js`):

```
(function() {
    var userService = UserService.getInstance();

    $(document).on("pageinit", "#login", function(e) {
        e.preventDefault();

        $("#loginUser").on("tap", function(e) {
            e.preventDefault();

            try {
                userService.saveUser({
                    'name': $("#userName").val(),
                    'email': $("#userEmail").val(),
                });
```

```
                          $.mobile.changePage("#weather");
                  } catch (exception) {
                          $("#loginFormMessages").html(exception.message);
                  }
          });
      });
})();
```

The `"pageinit"` event handler that is called once in the initialization of the page registers the `"loginUser"` tap event handler, which:

- Saves the entered user information by calling the `saveUser()` method of the `userService` object, specifying the user object with the `name` and `email` attributes. The `name` and `email` attributes are populated with the `"userName"` and `"userEmail"` input field values, respectively.

- Forwards the user to the `"weather"` page.

If an exception occurs while saving the user information, the `"loginFormMessages"` div is populated with the exception message.

The following code snippet shows the `UserService` JavaScript object, which interacts with the Web Storage API to save and retrieve the user information (`UserService.js`):

```javascript
var UserValidationException = function(code, message) {
    this.code = code;
    this.message = message;
}


var UserService = (function () {
    var instance;
    var USER_KEY = "WEATHER_USER";

    function isValidEmail(email) {
        var regex = /^([a-zA-Z0-9_.+-])+\@(([a-zA-Z0-9-])+\.)+([a-zA-Z0-9]{2,4})+$/;

        return regex.test(email);
    }

    function createObject() {
        return {
            saveUser: function (user) {
```

```
                if (!user.name || !user.email || user.name.trim().
length == 0 || user.email.trim().length == 0) {
                    console.log("You need to specify both user name
and email!");

                    throw new UserValidationException("EMPTY_FIELDS",
"You need to specify both user name and email!");
                }

                if (user.name.trim().length > 6) {
                    console.log("User name must not exceed 6
characters!");

                    throw new UserValidationException("MAX_LENGTH_
EXCEEDED", "User name must not
exceed 6 characters!");
                }

                if (! isValidEmail(user.email)) {
                    console.log("Email is invalid!");

                    throw new UserValidationException("INVALID_
FORMAT", "Email is invalid!");
                }

                window.localStorage.setItem(USER_KEY,
JSON.stringify(user));
            },
            getUser:function() {
                var user = window.localStorage.getItem(USER_KEY);

                if (user) {
                    user = JSON.parse(user);
                }

                return user;
            }
        };
    };

    return {
        getInstance: function () {
            if (!instance) {
                instance = createObject();
            }
```

```
            return instance;
        }
    };
})();
```

As you can see, `UserService` is a singleton object that has two methods, as highlighted in the preceding code:

- `saveUser(user)`: This uses the `window.localStorage.setItem()` method to save the user information in the Local Storage:

    ○ `window.localStorage.setItem(USER_KEY, JSON.stringify(user))`: This has the two parameters in order: `USER_KEY`, which is a string that represents the Local Storage item name, and `JSON.stringify(user)`, which returns the user object JSON string. This parameter represents the Local Storage item value.

    ○ If any of the user object information is invalid, then an exception of the `UserValidationException` type is thrown.

- `getUser()`:This uses the `window.localStorage.getItem()` method to get the user information string from the Local Storage and then parses it as a JSON object using `JSON.parse()`.

We are now done with the `"login"` page; let's check out the `"weather"` page. The following code snippet shows the `"weather"` page:

```html
<div data-role="page" id="weather">
    <div data-role="header" data-position="fixed">
        <h1>Weather Info</h1>
    </div>
    <div data-role="content">
        <h2>Welcome <span id="user"></span>,</h2>
        <form id="weatherForm">
            <div class="ui-field-contain">
                <label for="location">Location</label>
                <input type="text" id="location"></input>
            </div>
            <input type="button" id="getWeatherInfo" data-
icon="action" value="Weather Info"/>

            <div id="weatherResult">
            </div>
        </form>
    </div>
</div>
```

As shown in the preceding `"weather"` page, it contains the following:

- A page header
- Page content that includes the following main elements:
    - `"user"`: This span is used to display the username
    - `"location"`: This input field is used to enter the location information
    - `"getWeatherInfo"`: This button is used to get the current weather information of the location entered in the `"location"` input field
    - `"weatherResult"`: This div is used to display the current weather information

The following code snippet shows the page view controller JavaScript object, which includes the event handlers of the page (`weather.js`):

```
(function() {
    var weatherService = WeatherService.getInstance();
    var userService = UserService.getInstance();

    $(document).on("pageinit", "#weather", function(e) {
        e.preventDefault();

        $("#getWeatherInfo").on("tap", function(e) {
            e.preventDefault();

            $("#location").blur(); //Hide keyboard

            $.mobile.loading('show');

            var successCallback = function(result) {
                $.mobile.loading('hide');
                $("#weatherResult").removeClass("error");

                var result = "<img class='center' src='" +
result.icon + "'><br/>"
                            + "Temperature: " + result.temperature
+ "<br/>"
                            + "Humidity: " + result.humidity +
"<br/>"
                            + "Description: " + result.description
+ "<br/>";

                $("#weatherResult").html(result);
            };
```

```
            var errorCallback = function(errorMessage) {
                $.mobile.loading('hide');
                $("#weatherResult").addClass("error");
                $("#weatherResult").html(errorMessage);
            };

            weatherService.getWeatherInfo($("#location").val(),
    successCallback, errorCallback);
            });
        });

    $(document).on("pageshow", "#weather", function(e) {
        $("#user").html(userService.getUser().name || "");
    });

})();
```

The `"pageinit"` event handler registers the `"getWeatherInfo"` tap event handler. The `"getWeatherInfo"` tap event handler gets the current weather information by calling the `getWeatherInfo()` method of the `weatherService` object with the following parameters in order:

- `$("#location").val()`: This is the user's location entered in the `"location"` input text

- `successCallback`: This is the successful callback that will be called if the weather information query operation succeeds

- `errorCallback`: This is the error callback that will be called if the weather information query operation fails

In `successCallback`, the `result` object, which holds the current weather information, is received as a parameter, and its main information is displayed in the `"weatherResult"` div.

In `errorCallback`, `errorMessage` is displayed in the `"weatherResult"` div.

 In our weather page, we use `$.mobile.loading` to show and hide the jQuery Mobile loading dialog. The jQuery Mobile loading dialog can be used to give the user the impression that there is an operation in progress.

The `"pageshow"` event handler displays the username (which is retrieved using `userService.getUser().name`) in the `"user"` span.

The following code snippet shows the `WeatherService` JavaScript object, which interacts with the weather API provided by `OpenWeatherMap` (`http://openweathermap.org`) to get the current weather information for a specified location (`WeatherService.js`):

```
var WeatherService = (function () {
    var instance;
    var BASE_ICON_URL = "http://openweathermap.org/img/w/";

    function createObject() {
        return {
            getWeatherInfo: function (locationText, successCallback,
errorCallback) {
                if (!location || locationText.trim().length == 0) {
                    errorCallback("You have to specify a location!");
                }

                $.ajax({
                    url: "http://api.openweathermap.org/data/2.5/
weather?q=" +
escape(locationText),
                    success: function(response) {
                        console.log(response);

                        // If response code != 200 then this is an
error
                        if (response.cod != 200) {
                            errorCallback(response.message);
                            return;
                        }

                        successCallback({
                            'temperature': (response.main.temp -
273.15).toFixed(1) + " °C",
                            'pressure': response.main.pressure,
                            'humidity': response.main.humidity + "%",
                            'description': (response.weather[0]) ?
(response.weather[0].description) : "NA",
                            'icon': (response.weather[0]) ?
BASE_ICON_URL+ (response.weather[0].icon) + ".png" : ""
                        });
                    }
                });
            }
        };
```

```
        };

        return {
            getInstance: function () {
                if (!instance) {
                    instance = createObject();
                }

                return instance;
            }
        };
    })();
```

As you can see, `WeatherService` is a singleton object that has a single method, as highlighted in the preceding code. The `getWeatherInfo(locationText, successCallback, errorCallback)` method which makes an Ajax call using `$.ajax` to `http://api.openweathermap.org/data/2.5/weather`, specifying `q` (the query parameter) with `locationText`. If the operation response code (`response.cod`) is not equal to `200` (this means that the operation was not performed successfully), then `errorCallback` is called with the response message specified by `response.message`. If the operation response code (`response.cod`) is equal to `200` (this means that the operation was performed successfully), then `successCallback` is called with a resulting JSON object that contains temperature, pressure, humidity, description, and icon information.

Finally, let's check the code of the `"landing"` page, which is used to decide the weather application initial page. The following code snippet shows the `"landing"` page HTML content:

```
<div id="landing" data-role="page">
    <div class="center-screen">Please wait ...</div>
</div>
```

The following code snippet shows the page view controller JavaScript object of the `"landing"` page, which is located in `landing.js`:

```
(function() {
    var userService = UserService.getInstance();

    $(document).on("pageinit", "#landing", function(e) {
        e.preventDefault();

        function onDeviceReady () {
            console.log("Apache Cordova is loaded");
```

```
            var home = '#login';

            if (userService.getUser()) {
                home = '#weather';
            }

            $.mobile.changePage(home);
        }

        document.addEventListener("deviceready", onDeviceReady,
    false);
        });
})();
```

The `"pageinit"` event handler of the landing page tries to get the user information using the `getUser()` method of `userService` once Cordova is loaded. If there is an object that is not returned as null from the `getUser()` method, then the initial page is chosen to be the `"weather"` page; else, the initial page is chosen to be the `"login"` page.

After exploring the weather application code, let's see how we can develop Jasmine tests for weather app services.

Developing synchronous code tests

It is the time to develop Jasmine tests for the synchronous JavaScript code (`UserService`) in our weather app services. First of all, in order to test the `UserService` object, let's basically consider the following four test scenarios:

- Test that `UserService` will not save a user with an empty user name
- Test that `UserService` will not save a user with an invalid e-mail
- Test that `UserService` will not save a user with a username of more than six characters
- Test that `UserService` will save a user with a valid username and e-mail, and load the saved user properly when requested

The following code snippet shows `UserServiceSpec.js`, which includes the test scenarios mentioned earlier:

```
describe("UserService", function() {
    var userService;

    beforeEach(function() {
        userService = UserService.getInstance();
```

```
    });

    it("should NOT be able to save a user with an empty user
name", function() {
        var user = {
            'name': ' ',
            'email': 'hazems@apache.org'
        };

        expect(function() {
            userService.saveUser(user);
        }).toThrow();
    });

    it("should NOT be able to save a user with invalid email",
function() {
        var user = {
            'name': 'Hazem',
            'email': 'Invalid_Email'
        };

        expect(function() {
            userService.saveUser(user);
        }).toThrow();
    });

    it("should NOT be able to save a user with a user name more
than 6 characters", function() {
        var user = {
            'name': 'LengthyUserName',
            'email': 'hazems@apache.org'
        };

        expect(function() {
            userService.saveUser(user);
        }).toThrow();
    });

    it("should be able to save and load a valid user", function()
{
        var originalUser = {
            'name': 'Hazem',
            'email': 'hazems@apache.org'
        };
```

```
        userService.saveUser(originalUser);

        var user = userService.getUser();

        expect(user).toEqual(originalUser);
    });
});
```

We have a test suite called "UserService", which has fours specs. In beforeEach, the userService object is created using UserService.getInstance().

In the first test scenario of the "UserService" test suite, the spec title is "should NOT be able to save a user with an empty user name". The spec creates a user object with an empty username and then passes the created user object to userService.saveUser(). Finally, the spec expects userService.saveUser() to throw an exception using the toThrow matcher.

In the second test scenario of the "UserService" test suite, the spec title is "should NOT be able to save a user with invalid email". The spec creates a user object specifying an invalid e-mail ('Invalid_Email') and then passes the created user object to userService.saveUser(). Finally, the spec expects userService.saveUser() to throw an exception using the toThrow matcher.

In the third test scenario of the "UserService" test suite, the spec title is "should NOT be able to save a user with a user name more than 6 characters". The spec creates a user object specifying a username whose length is more than six characters ('LengthyUserName') and then passes the created user object to userService.saveUser(). Finally, the spec expects userService.saveUser() to throw an exception using the toThrow matcher.

In the final test scenario of the "UserService" test suite, the spec title is "should be able to save and load a valid user". The spec creates a user object (originalUser) with a valid username and e-mail. The spec then passes the originalUser object to userService.saveUser() to save the user. After saving originalUser, the spec then retrieves the saved user object by calling userService.getUser(). Finally, the spec makes sure that the retrieved user object is identical to originalUser using the toEqual matcher.

Developing asynchronous code tests

Before developing Jasmine tests for the asynchronous JavaScript code in our weather app services, you need to understand how we can test asynchronous operations in Jasmine.

Since Jasmine 2.0, testing asynchronous JavaScript code in Jasmine is a very simple task. In order to develop asynchronous operation Jasmine tests, you need to know that:

- Jasmine provides an optional single parameter (usually named done) for specs (and also for beforeEach and afterEach).

- A spec will not complete until done is called. This means that if done is included as a parameter of a spec, then done has to be called when the asynchronous operation completes in all cases (whether the operation succeeds or fails). Note that if done is included as a parameter in beforeEach, then the spec after beforeEach will not start until done is called in beforeEach.

- If done is not called for 5 seconds by default, then the test will fail; however, you can change this default timeout interval by setting the jasmine.DEFAULT_TIMEOUT_INTERVAL variable.

Now, let's develop Jasmine tests for the asynchronous JavaScript code (WeatherService) in our weather application services to see how to develop Jasmine tests for asynchronous JavaScript code in action. In order to test the WeatherService object, let's basically consider the following two test scenarios:

- Test that WeatherService will be able to get the weather information for a valid place

- Test that WeatherService will not be able to get the weather information for an invalid place

The following code snippet shows WeatherServiceSpec.js, which covers the test scenarios mentioned earlier:

```
describe("WeatherService", function() {
    var weatherService;
    var originalTimeout;

    beforeEach(function() {
        weatherService = WeatherService.getInstance();
        originalTimeout = jasmine.DEFAULT_TIMEOUT_INTERVAL;
        jasmine.DEFAULT_TIMEOUT_INTERVAL = 8000;
    });

    it("should be able to get weather information for a valid place",
function(done) {
        var successCallback = function(result) {
            expect(result.temperature).not.toBeNull();
            done();
        };
```

```
        var errorCallback = function() {
            expect(true).toBe(false); // force failing test manually
            done();
        };

        weatherService.getWeatherInfo("Paris, France",
    successCallback, errorCallback);
    });

    it("should NOT be able to get weather information for an invalid
place", function(done) {
        var successCallback = function(result) {
            expect(true).toBe(false); // force failing test manually
            done();
        };

        var errorCallback = function(message) {
            expect(message).not.toBeNull();
            done();
        };

        weatherService.getWeatherInfo("Invalid Place",
    successCallback, errorCallback);
    });

    afterEach(function() {
        jasmine.DEFAULT_TIMEOUT_INTERVAL = originalTimeout;
    });
});
```

We have a test suite called `"WeatherService"`, which has two specs. In `beforeEach`, the `weatherService` object is created using `WeatherService.getInstance()`, and `jasmine.DEFAULT_TIMEOUT_INTERVAL` is set to 8000 to change the default timeout interval to 8 seconds instead of 5 seconds. In `afterEach`, the `jasmine.DEFAULT_TIMEOUT_INTERVAL` is set to its default timeout value again.

As shown in the preceding highlighted code, in the first test scenario of the `"WeatherService"` test suite, the spec title is `"should be able to get weather information for a valid place"`. The spec calls the `weatherService.getWeatherInfo(locationText, successCallback, errorCallback)` method, specifying the following parameters in order:

*   `locationText`: This is set to a valid place, that is, `"Paris, France"`.

- successCallback: This is set to a successful callback function that takes result as a parameter. In successCallback(result), the result returned is validated to have a valid temperature value, and finally, the done parameter is called.

- errorCallback: This is set to an error callback function. In errorCallback(), the test is forced to fail as this callback should never be called if weatherService.getWeatherInfo executes successfully. Finally, the done parameter is called.

In the second test scenario of the "WeatherService" test suite, the spec title is "should NOT be able to get weather information for an invalid place". The spec calls the weatherService.getWeatherInfo(locationText, successCallback, errorCallback) method, specifying the following parameters in order:

- locationText: This is set to an invalid place, that is, "Invalid Place".

- successCallback: This is set to a successful callback function that takes result as a parameter. In successCallback(result), the test is forced to fail. This is because this successful callback should never be called if weatherService.getWeatherInfo behaves correctly, as it does not make sense to get the weather information successfully for an invalid place. Finally, the done parameter is called.

- errorCallback: This is set to an error callback function that takes message as a parameter. In errorCallback(message), the returned message is validated to be a non-null value, which means that weatherService.getWeatherInfo behaves correctly, as it produces an error message when asked to get the weather information for an invalid place. Finally, the (done) parameter is called.

It is important to note that JavaScript unit testing can be implemented using many frameworks and has many details that cannot be covered completely by a single small chapter. To get more information about Jasmine (such as mocking asynchronous operations using Spies and loading HTML fixtures using jasmine-jquery) and other popular JavaScript Unit testing frameworks such as YUI Test and QUnit, we recommend that you read *JavaScript Unit Testing, Hazem Saleh, Packt Publishing*.

Manually executing tests

After developing Jasmine tests for both the weather application's synchronous and asynchronous JavaScript code, it is the time to run the developed Jasmine tests from the `SpecRunner.html` file. The following code snippet shows the important contents of the `SpecRunner.html` file:

```html
<!DOCTYPE HTML>
<html>
    <head>
        <meta http-equiv="Content-Type" content="text/html;
charset=UTF-8">
        <title>Jasmine Spec Runner v2.0.0</title>

        <script src="../jqueryMobile/jquery-1.10.2.min.js"></script>

        <!-- ... Jasmine files are included here .. -->

        <!-- include source files here... -->
        <script type="text/javascript" src="../js/api/UserService.
js"></script>
        <script type="text/javascript" src="../js/api/WeatherService.
js"></script>

        <!-- include spec files here... -->
        <script type="text/javascript" src="spec/UserServiceSpec.
js"></script>
        <script type="text/javascript" src="spec/WeatherServiceSpec.
js"></script>
    </head>

    <body>
    </body>
</html>
```

As shown in the preceding highlighted code, besides the Jasmine framework files, `SpecRunner.html` also includes the following files:

- `jquery-1.10.2.min.js`, as it is required by `WeatherService`
- JavaScript source files (`UserService.js` and `WeatherService.js`)
- JavaScript test files (`UserServiceSpec.js` and `WeatherServiceSpec.js`)

We can check the results of our developed tests by clicking on the `SpecRunner.html` file, and then we will see the tests passing.

Automating tests using Karma

Running Jasmine tests manually by running `SpecRunner.html` on every browser can be a time-consuming process; this is why automating Jasmine tests is important. In order to automate Jasmine tests, we can use Karma (`http://karma-runner.github.io`).

Karma is one of the best modern JavaScript test runners that can be used to automate JavaScript tests. Karma is based on Node.js and is distributed as a node package. Karma provides an easy-to-use command-line interface that we will illustrate in detail in the following sections.

Karma includes a web server that can capture one or more browser(s), execute JavaScript tests on the captured browsers, and finally, report the test results of every browser in the command-line interface. In order to capture a browser in Karma, you can execute one of the following two methods:

- Make the browser(s) that you want to capture visiting Karma server URL (usually, it is `http://${karma_server_ip}:9876/`).
- In the configuration file, you can specify the browser(s) to launch automatically when the Karma server starts (check the *Karma Configuration* section). Doing this configuration will save a lot of time spent on executing your JavaScript tests manually on the different browsers.

The following sections will show you how we will use Karma with Jasmine in detail.

Installing Karma

In order to work with Karma, you need to make sure that you have Node.js installed in your operating system. In order to install Node.js in Windows and Mac, you can download their installers from `http://nodejs.org/download/`; for Linux, you can use the **Node Version Manager** (**NVM**) from `https://github.com/creationix/nvm`. Currently, Karma works perfectly with the latest stable versions of Node.js (0.8.x and 0.10.x).

It is recommended that you install Karma and all of its plugins that our project needs in the `project` directory. In order to install Karma in our project, execute the following command directly under the www directory of our weather project:

```
> npm install karma --save-dev
```

Then, we can install karma-Jasmine 2.0 (to run the Jasmine 2.0 code over Karma) and karma-chrome-launcher (to launch the Chrome browser automatically when requested by the Karma configuration) plugins from the command-line interface as follows:

```
> npm install karma-jasmine@2_0  karma-chrome-launcher --save-dev
```

In order to avoid typing the full path of Karma every time you execute a karma command, it is recommended that you install Karma CLI globally by executing the following command:

```
> npm install -g karma-cli
```

Karma configuration

We can generate the initial Karma configuration using CLI by executing the following command and answering the Karma configuration questions:

```
> karma init config.js
Which testing framework do you want to use?
Press tab to list possible options. Enter to move to the next
question.
> jasmine

Do you want to use Require.js?
This will add Require.js plugin.
Press tab to list possible options. Enter to move to the next
question.
> no

Do you want to capture any browsers automatically?
Press tab to list possible options. Enter empty string to move to the
next question.
> Chrome
>

What is the location of your source and test files?
You can use glob patterns, eg. "js/*.js" or "test/**/*Spec.js".
Enter empty string to move to the next question.
>jqueryMobile/jquery-1.10.2.min.js
>js/api/*.js
> tests/spec/*.js
>
```

```
Should any of the files included by the previous patterns be excluded
?
You can use glob patterns, eg. "**/*.swp".
Enter empty string to move to the next question.
>


Do you want Karma to watch all the files and run the tests on change ?
Press tab to list possible options.
> yes
Config file generated at "${somePath}/config.js".
```

The following code snippet shows the generated Karma `config.js` file:

```javascript
module.exports = function(config) {
    config.set({
        basePath: '',
        frameworks: ['jasmine'],
        files: [
            'jqueryMobile/jquery-1.10.2.min.js',
            'js/api/*.js',
            'tests/spec/*.js'
        ],
        exclude: [
        ],
        preprocessors: {
        },
        reporters: ['progress'],
        port: 9876,
        colors: true,
        logLevel: config.LOG_INFO,
        autoWatch: true,
        browsers: ['Chrome'],
        singleRun: false
    });
};
```

The following table explains the meaning of the generated configuration attributes briefly:

Attribute	Description
basePath	This specifies the base path that will be used to resolve all patterns in files, exclude attributes. In our case, we specified ' ', which means that the current configuration file path is the base path.
frameworks	This specifies the frameworks to use. You can use many frameworks, other than Jasmine, with Karma, such as QUnit and mocha. In our case, we specified 'jasmine'.
files	This specifies the list of files (or file patterns) to load in the browser. In our case, we specified the jQuery JavaScript file, 'jqueryMobile/jquery-1.10.2.min.js' (as a dependency needed by the source files), the source files, 'js/api/*.js', and finally, the test files, 'tests/spec/*.js'.
exclude	This specifies the list of files to exclude.
preprocessors	This specifies the files that should be preprocessed before serving them to the browser. We will use this attribute in the code coverage section.
reporters	This specifies the test result reporter to use. In our case, we specified the 'progress' reporter to show the detailed test progress (in every browser) in the console. You can specify the 'dots' reporter to ignore these details and replace them with dots for simplification.
port	This specifies the Karma server port.
colors	This specifies whether to enable or disable colors in the output.
logLevel	This specifies the level of logging. It can have one of the possible values: config.LOG_DISABLE, config.LOG_ERROR, config.LOG_WARN, config.LOG_INFO, and config.LOG_DEBUG. In our case, we specified config.LOG_INFO.
autoWatch	If this attribute is set to true, then Karma will watch the files and execute tests whenever any file changes.
browsers	This specifies the browser(s) to launch and capture when the Karma server starts. In our case, we specify 'Chrome'; we can also specify the Safari, Firefox, Opera, PhantomJS, and IE browsers.
singleRun	Setting this attribute to true means that Karma will start the specified browser(s), run the tests, and finally exit. Setting this attribute to true is suitable for a Continuous Integration mode (check the *Integrating tests with Build and CI tools* section). In our case, we set it to false to declare that it is not a single run.

Running tests (on mobile devices)

In order to start running our developed Jasmine test using Karma, we can start the Karma server specifying our configuration file as a parameter as follows:

```
> karma start config.js
```

This will automatically start a Chrome browser instance and execute our developed Jasmine tests on it. Finally, you will find output results like the following in the console:

```
INFO [karma]: Karma v0.12.19 server started at http://localhost:9876/
INFO [launcher]: Starting browser Chrome
INFO [Chrome 36.0.1985 (Mac OS X 10.9.2)]: Connected on socket
PF71hJWBohNMJqOlUdnP with id 78567722
... Some test results information here...
Executed 6 of 6 SUCCESS (1.575 secs / 1.57 secs)
```

If we want Karma to test our Jasmine code on more browsers, we can simply:

- Specify more browsers in the `browsers` attribute of the configuration file
- Install the browser launcher plugin in our `app` directory

For example, if we want to test our Jasmine code in Firefox, we will do the following:

1. In the `config.js` file, add `'Firefox'` to the browser's attribute as follows:

    ```
    browsers: ['Chrome', 'Firefox']
    ```

2. Install the Firefox launcher plugin in our `app` directory as follows:

    ```
    > npm install karma-firefox-launcher --save-dev
    ```

3. Run the `karma start config.js` command again to see the test results in the CLI for both Chrome and Firefox.

In order to run our tests on a mobile browser, we can make the mobile browser visit the URL of the Karma server. The following screenshot shows the tests run on an Android mobile browser.

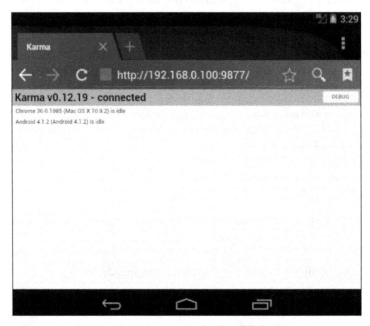

Running the tests on an Android mobile browser

The following are the test results in the Android browser that are displayed in the console:

```
INFO [Android 4.1.2 (Android 4.1.2)]: Connected on socket
Rv85bR0dfNpt5S8ecBnc with id manual-7523
... Some test results information here ...
Android 4.1.2 (Android 4.1.2): Executed 6 of 6 SUCCESS (1.094 secs /
1.02 secs)
```

Generating XML JUnit and code coverage reports

Karma, by default, outputs test results in the console. In order to output the test results in an XML JUnit report, we need to use the Karma JUnit reporter plugin (`https://github.com/karma-runner/karma-junit-reporter`).

In order to install Karma JUnit reporter plugin, execute the following command:

```
> npm install karma-junit-reporter --save-dev
```

Then, we need to add the plugin configuration in our `config.js` file, as highlighted in the following code snippet:

```
module.exports = function(config) {
    config.set({
        reporters: ['progress', 'junit'],

        // The default configuration
        junitReporter: {
            outputFile: 'test-results.xml',
            suite: ''
        }
    });
};
```

This means that the JUnit reporter will output the test results in the `'test-results.xml'` file. In order to see the XML JUnit report, execute `karma start config.js` again, and you will find the XML JUnit report, as shown in the following code:

```
<?xml version="1.0"?>
<testsuites>
    ...
    <testsuite name="Chrome 36.0.1985 (Mac OS X 10.9.2)" package=""
timestamp="2014-08-11T10:42:53" id="0" hostname="IBMs-
MacBook-Pro-2.local" tests="6" errors="0" failures="0" time="1.017">
        <properties>
            <property name="browser.fullName" value="Mozilla/5.0
(Macintosh; Intel Mac OS X 10_9_2) AppleWebKit/537.36 (KHTML, like
Gecko) Chrome/36.0.1985.125 Safari/537.36"/>
        </properties>
        <testcase name="should NOT be able to save a user with an
empty user name" time="0.004" classname="Chrome 36.0.1985 (Mac OS
X 10.9.2).UserService"/>
        <testcase name="should NOT be able to save a user with
invalid email" time="0.001" classname="Chrome 36.0.1985 (Mac OS X
10.9.2).UserService"/>
        <testcase name="should NOT be able to save a user with a
user name more than 6 characters" time="0" classname="Chrome
36.0.1985 (Mac OS X 10.9.2).UserService"/>
```

```
        <testcase name="should be able to save and load a valid
user" time="0.002" classname="Chrome 36.0.1985 (Mac OS X
10.9.2).UserService"/>
        <testcase name="should be able to get weather information
for a valid place" time="0.419" classname="Chrome 36.0.1985 (Mac
OS X 10.9.2).WeatherService"/>
        <testcase name="should NOT be able to get weather
information for an invalid place" time="0.591" classname="Chrome
36.0.1985 (Mac OS X 10.9.2).WeatherService"/>
        <system-out> ... </system-out>
        <system-err/>
    </testsuite>
</testsuites>
```

Adding to JUnit XML reports, Karma can generate code coverage reports. In order to generate code coverage using Karma, we can use the Karma coverage plugin (https://github.com/karma-runner/karma-coverage).

In order to install the Karma coverage plugin, execute the following command:

```
> npm install karma-coverage --save-dev
```

Then, we need to add the plugin configuration in our config.js file, as highlighted in the following code snippet:

```
module.exports = function(config) {
    config.set({
        // ...
        reporters: ['progress', 'coverage'],
        preprocessors: {
            'js/api/*.js': ['coverage']
        },
        coverageReporter: {
            type : 'html',
            dir : 'coverage/'
        }
    });
};
```

This previous configuration means that the Karma code coverage plugin will generate code coverage report(s) for our JavaScript source files, 'js/api/*.js', and output the code coverage results under the 'coverage' directory in an HTML format. Note that every browser will have its own directory under the 'coverage' directory, including its code coverage report. The following screenshot shows the code coverage report for the Chrome browser:

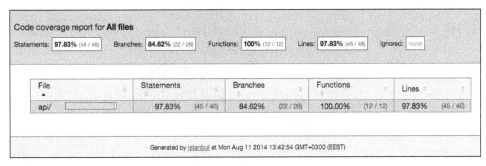

Code coverage report

As shown in the preceding screenshot, the code coverage is generated for code statements, branches, and functions.

Integrating tests with the CI tools

Having the ability to execute Karma tests from the command-line interface allows us to fully automate running Karma tests using CI tools. In order to integrate Karma tests with Jenkins (a popular CI tool), we need to perform the following steps in the Jenkins project configuration:

1. Select **Execute Shell** from **Add build step** (or **Execute Windows batch command** if you are using Windows), then specify the location of the shell file that starts the Karma server and run the tests. The shell file can have the following commands:

   ```bash
   #!/bin/bash
   cd weather/www
   export PATH=$PATH:/usr/local/bin

   karma start config.js --single-run --browsers PhantomJS
   ```

   The previous shell script code starts the Karma server in a single run mode and specifies PhantomJS (http://phantomjs.org) as the browser that will execute JS tests. PhantomJS is a very light-weight, headless browser that can be a good choice for CI environments. In order to work with PhantomJS in Karma, we have to install its launcher plugin from CLI as follows:

   ```
   > npm install karma-phantomjs-launcher --save-dev
   ```

2. Select **Publish JUnit test result report** from **Post-build Actions**, and in **test report XML**, specify the path of the XML JUnit report, `'weather/www/test-results.xml'`. Jenkins fortunately recognizes the JUnit XML format, which we generate in our JavaScript tests.

After making these main changes and building the Jenkins CI project, we will find the JavaScript test results shown in the project dashboard after some builds have been done, as shown in the following screenshot:

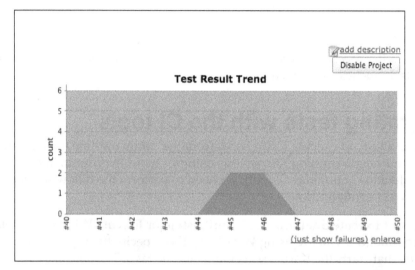

JavaScript test results in the Jenkins project dashboard

 You can get the complete source code of the weather application with its JavaScript tests from the book page or from GitHub using `https://github.com/hazems/cordova-js-unit-testing`.

Summary

In this chapter, you understood how to develop JavaScript tests for both synchronous and asynchronous JavaScript code of your Cordova app logic using Jasmine. You learned how to utilize Karma in order to automate running your JavaScript tests. You know how to generate test and code coverage reports from your JavaScript tests. Finally, you learned how to fully automate your JavaScript tests by integrating your tests with Jenkins as an example of the CI tools. In the next chapter, you will learn how to design and develop a complete app (Mega App) using Apache Cordova and the jQuery Mobile API on the three popular mobile platforms (Android, iOS, and Windows Phone 8).

8

Applying it All – the Mega App

In this chapter, you will learn how to design and develop a complete app (the Mega App) using Apache Cordova and jQuery Mobile APIs. Mega App is a memo utility that allows users to create, save, and view audible and visual memos on the three most popular mobile platforms (Android, iOS, and Windows Phone 8). In order to create this utility, Mega App uses jQuery Mobile to build the user interface and Apache Cordova to access the device information, camera, audio (microphone and speaker), and filesystem. In this chapter, you will learn how to create a portable app that respects the philosophy differences between Android, iOS, and Windows Phone 8.

Mega App specification/wireframes

Mega App is a Cordova App that uses some of the Cordova plugins and jQuery Mobile in order to build a memo utility. It allows you to create your audible memos (such as talks, lectures, reminders, business meetings, and kids' voices) and also visual memos using an easy-to-use and responsive user interface. It also allows you to manage all your memos from a single unified listing. Mega App works on the Android, iOS, and Windows Phone 8 platforms. The following screenshot shows the home page of Mega App; it displays a list of the user's audio and visual memos:

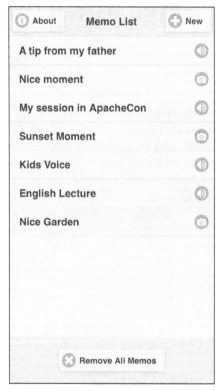

Mega App home page

In order to create a new memo, click on the **New** button on the page header, and you can select to create either **"Voice memo"** or **"Photo memo"**. When you select creating a new **"Voice memo"**, you will be introduced to the voice memo page in which you can enter the voice memo details in the **Title** and **Details** fields and click on the **Record** button to start recording audio, as shown in the following screenshot:

Creating a new voice memo

Once you are done, click on the **Stop Recording** button to finish recording. You can then listen to the recorded voice by clicking on the **Playback** button. After entering all the voice-recording information, you can finally click on the **Save Memo** button to save your voice memo. After clicking on the **Save Memo** button, you will be forwarded to the app's home page to view your saved voice memo in the memo list (a voice memo is marked with an audio icon at the end of the voice memo item).

In order to create a new photo memo, click on the **New** button on the page header and then select the **Photo Memo** option; you will be introduced to the photo memo page in which you can enter the photo memo details in the **Title** and **Details** fields and click on the **Get Photo** button to get a photo either by capturing it using the camera or by getting it from the device's gallery.

If you choose to get a photo from **Gallery**, you will be forwarded to the device's gallery to pick a picture from there, and if you choose to get a photo from **Camera**, then the device's camera app will be launched to allow you to capture a photo. Once you are done with getting the photo, you can view the photo in the photo memo page, as shown in the following screenshot:

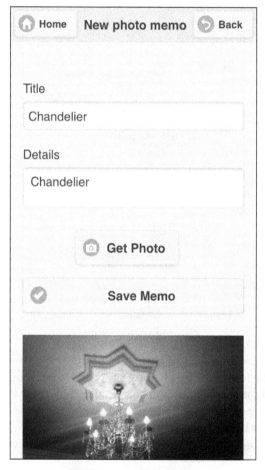

Creating a new photo memo

After entering all the photo memo information, you can click on the **Save Memo** button to save your photo memo. After clicking on the **Save Memo** button, you will be forwarded to the app's home page to view your saved photo memo in the memo list (a photo memo is marked with a camera icon at the end of the photo memo item).

It is important to note that at any point in time, you can click on any listing item (in the app's home page listing), which represents either a voice or a photo memo, to get its details. The following screenshot shows a detailed saved voice memo:

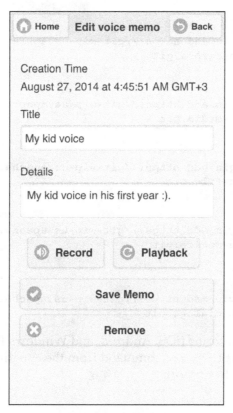

Editing voice memo details

In the memo details page, you can view and edit the memo information and can also delete the created memo by clicking on the **Remove** button.

Finally, in the home page, you have the option to delete all of the created memos by clicking on the **Remove All Memos** button and confirming the deletion of memo items.

Preparing for the Mega App

In order to create our Mega App's initial files from the Cordova CLI, we run the `cordova create` command as follows:

```
> cordova create megaapp com.jsmobile.megaapp MegaApp
```

Then, we will add the following Cordova plugins to our project using the `cordova plugin add` command:

- Camera plugin:

  ```
  > cordova plugin add https://git-wip-us.apache.org/repos/asf/
  cordova-plugin-camera.git
  ```

- Media plugin:

  ```
  > cordova plugin add https://git-wip-us.apache.org/repos/asf/
  cordova-plugin-media.git
  ```

- File plugin:

  ```
  > cordova plugin add https://git-wip-us.apache.org/repos/asf/
  cordova-plugin-file.git
  ```

- Device plugin:

  ```
  > cordova plugin add https://git-wip-us.apache.org/repos/asf/
  cordova-plugin-device.git
  ```

- Dialogs plugin:

  ```
  > cordova plugin add https://git-wip-us.apache.org/repos/asf/
  cordova-plugin-dialogs.git
  ```

As we support three platforms (iOS, Android, and Windows Phone 8), we run the following `cordova platform add` command from the app directory to add the platforms that we want to support:

```
> cd megaapp
> cordova platform add ios
> cordova platform add android
> cordova platform add wp8
```

Finally, we can build our app on all the platforms using the following `cordova build` command:

```
> cordova build
```

Do not forget to apply the general Cordova 3.4 app fixes for iOS 7 and Windows Phone 8, which were illustrated in detail in *Chapter 3, Apache Cordova Development Tools*.

The Mega App architecture

As Mega App needs to store audio and image files in the device's storage so that users can access them later, we need to be aware of the nature of every platform's filesystem to properly store our app's audio and image files.

In Android, we do not have any restrictions on storing our app files under the device's SD card root if the SD card is available, so we can save our audio and picture files in our app's directory under the device's SD card root without any issues.

 As a matter of fact, not all Android devices have SD cards. This is why if your Android device does not have an SD card, then the Mega App's audio files will be stored under the app's private data directory, /data/data/[app_directory].

At the time of writing this book, storing app files outside the app directory is not possible in iOS. iOS places each app (including its preferences and data) in a Sandbox at the time of installation for security reasons. As part of the Sandboxing process, the system installs each app in its own Sandbox directory, which acts as the home for the app and its data. The following screenshot shows the subdirectories for an iOS app's Sandbox directory:

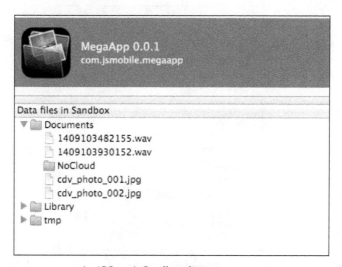

An iOS app's Sandbox directory content

As shown in the preceding screenshot, an iOS app's Sandbox directory mainly contains the following subdirectories:

- `Documents`: This directory can be used to store the user's documents and app's data files.
- `Library`: This is a directory for the files that are not user data files.
- `tmp`: This directory can be used to store temporary files that you don't need to persist between launches of your app. Note that iOS might purge files from this directory when your app is not running.

We will store our app's voice and picture files under the `Documents` directory of our iOS app's Sandbox directory.

 Besides the shown Sandbox directory content, an iOS app's Sandbox directory also includes `<<AppName>>.app`, which represents the bundle directory that contains the app.

Finally, in Windows Phone 8, we will save our audio and picture files under the app local directory. Note that using the native Windows Phone 8 API (`Window.Storage`), you can read and write files in an SD card with some restrictions, check: `http://msdn.microsoft.com/en-us/library/windows/apps/xaml/dn611857.aspx`. However, at this moment, you cannot do this using Apache Cordova; hopefully, this capability will be supported soon by Cordova.

Now, let's check the Mega App structure. The following screenshot shows the structure of our Mega App:

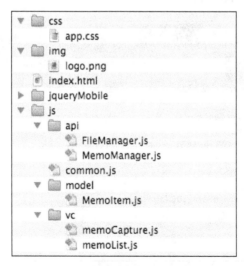

Mega App structure

The www directory contains the following files and subdirectories:

- css: This directory contains the custom app's Cascading Style Sheets.
- jqueryMobile: This directory contains the jQuery Mobile framework files.
- js: This directory contains all the app JavaScript code. It has three subdirectories:
    - api: This directory contains the app's services (managers).
    - model: This directory contains the app's model.
    - vc: This directory contains the app's view controllers, which register and implement the event handlers of every page and its user interface elements. An event handler usually calls one or more of the app's services (specifying a model object or more if needed) in order to perform an action and optionally display the returned results on an app page.

This js directory also includes common.js file, which includes the common app utilities. Under the www directory, the index.html file contains all the app pages, and finally, the img directory can contain any app custom images.

The details of the most important app files will be illustrated in the next sections of the chapter.

The Mega App model and API

The Mega App model contains only one JavaScript object that represents the voice and photo memo data, as shown in the following code snippet:

```
var MemoItem = function(memoItem) {
    this.id = memoItem.id || "Memo_" + (new Date()).getTime();
    this.title = memoItem.title || "";
    this.desc = memoItem.desc || "";
    this.type = memoItem.type || "voice";
    this.location = memoItem.location || "";
    this.mtime = memoItem.mtime || "";
};
```

The MemoItem object contains the following attributes:

- id: This represents the memo ID (its default value is unique as it includes a numeric value of the current time in milliseconds)
- title: This represents the memo title

- desc: This represents the memo description
- type: This represents the memo type, and it can be "voice" or "photo" (its default value is "voice")
- location: This represents the location of the media (audio or photo) file in the device's filesystem
- mtime: This represents the time when the memo was created

We mainly have one service (MemoManager) that is used by the app view controllers. The MemoManager object contains the API needed to:

- Save a memo
- Update a memo
- Remove a memo
- Remove all memos
- Get memo details
- Get all memos
- Record and play a voice
- Get a photo from the camera or gallery

The MemoManager object uses FileManager in order to perform the required file operations, which will be illustrated later.

The following code snippet shows the first part of the MemoManager object:

```
var MemoManager = (function () {
    var instance;

    function createObject() {
        var MEMOS_KEY = "memos";
        var APP_BASE_DIRECTORY = "Mega";
        var audioMedia;
        var recordingMedia;
        var mediaFileName;

        return {
            getMemos: function () {
                var items = window.localStorage.getItem(MEMOS_KEY);

                if (items) {
```

```
                    memoMap = JSON.parse(items);
                } else {
                    memoMap = {};
                }

                return memoMap;
            },
            getMemoDetails: function (memoID) {
                var memoMap = this.getMemos();

                return memoMap[memoID];
            },
            saveMemo: function (memoItem) {
                var memoMap = this.getMemos();

                memoMap[memoItem.id] = memoItem;

                window.localStorage.setItem(MEMOS_KEY, JSON.
stringify(memoMap));
            },
            removeMemo: function(memoID) {
                var memoMap = this.getMemos();

                if (memoMap[memoID]) {
                    delete memoMap[memoID];
                }

                window.localStorage.setItem(MEMOS_KEY, JSON.
stringify(memoMap));
            },
            removeAllMemos: function() {
                window.localStorage.removeItem(MEMOS_KEY);
            }

            // code is omitted for simplicity ...
        };
    };

    return {
        getInstance: function () {
            if (!instance) {
                instance = createObject();
            }
```

```
                return instance;
            }
        };
    })();
```

As shown in the preceding code, the first part of `MemoManager` is straightforward. It has the following methods, which are used to save, update, delete, and retrieve memos:

- `saveMemo(memoItem)`: This uses the `window.localStorage.setItem()` method to save or update a memo item in the device's Local Storage by adding (updating) it to the `memoMap` object. The `memoMap` object is a JSON map whose key represents the memo item ID and value represents the memo item object.

- `removeMemo(memoID)`: This removes the memo, whose ID is `memoID`, from `memoMap` and finally saves the updated `memoMap` object in the device's local storage using the `window.localStorage.setItem()` method.

- `removeAllMemos()`: This uses the `window.localStorage.removeItem()` method to remove `memoMap` from the device's local storage.

- `getMemoDetails(memoID)`: This gets the memo details from `memoMap` using `memoID`.

- `getMemos()`: This gets all the app's memos by returning the stored `memoMap` object. The stored `memoMap` object is retrieved from the device's local storage using the `window.localStorage.getItem()` method.

The following code snippet shows the voice recording and playback parts of `MemoManager`:

```
startRecordingVoice: function (recordingCallback) {
    var recordVoice = function(dirPath) {
        var basePath = "";

        if (dirPath) {
            basePath = dirPath;
        }

        mediaFileName = (new Date()).getTime() + ".wav";

        var mediaFilePath = basePath + mediaFileName;

        var recordingSuccess = function() {
            recordingCallback.recordSuccess(mediaFilePath);
        };
```

```
        recordingMedia = new Media(mediaFilePath, recordingSuccess,
recordingCallback.recordError);

        // Record audio
        recordingMedia.startRecord();
    };

    if (device.platform === "Android") {

        // For Android, store the recording in the app directory
under the SD Card root if available ...
        var callback = {};

        callback.requestSuccess = recordVoice;
        callback.requestError = recordingCallback.recordError;

        fileManager.requestDirectory(APP_BASE_DIRECTORY, callback);
    } else if (device.platform === "iOS") {

        // For iOS, store recording in app documents directory ...
        recordVoice("documents://");
    } else {

        // Else for Windows Phone 8, store recording under the app
directory
        recordVoice();
    }
},
stopRecordingVoice: function () {
    recordingMedia.stopRecord();
    recordingMedia.release();
},
playVoice: function (filePath, playCallback) {
    if (filePath) {
        this.cleanUpResources();

        audioMedia = new Media(filePath, playCallback.playSuccess,
playCallback.playError);

        // Play audio
        audioMedia.play();
    }
},
```

```
cleanUpResources: function() {
    if (audioMedia) {
        audioMedia.stop();
        audioMedia.release();
        audioMedia = null;
    }

    if (recordingMedia) {
        recordingMedia.stop();
        recordingMedia.release();
        recordingMedia = null;
    }
}
```

The `startRecordingVoice(recordingCallback)` method, starts the voice recording action, checks the current device's platform in order to save the audio file properly:

- If the current platform is Android, then it requests the `app` directory path (**"Mega"**) in order to save the recorded media file under it. In order to do this, a call to `fileManager.requestDirectory(APP_BASE_DIRECTORY, callback)` is performed in order to get the `app` directory path and optionally create it if it does not exist under the device's SD card root using the Apache Cordova file API (or create it under the app's private data directory, (`/data/data/[app_directory]`, if the SD card is not available). If the `app` directory request operation succeeds, then `recordVoice(dirPath)` will be called, in this case, and the `app` directory path (`dirPath`) will be passed as a parameter. The `recordVoice()` function starts recording the voice using the `Media` object's `startRecord()` method. In order to create a `Media` object, the following parameters are specified in the `Media` object constructor:
    - The complete path of the media file (`mediaFilePath`).
    - `recordingSuccess` which refers to the callback that will be invoked if the media operation succeeds. `recordingSuccess` calls the original `recordingCallback.recordSuccess` method specifying `mediaFilePath` as a parameter.
    - `recordingCallback.recordError` which refers to the callback that will be invoked if the media operation fails.

- In iOS, `recordVoice()` is called with `"documents://"` as the directory path (`dirPath`) in order to save our app's media audio file under the `Documents` directory of the app's Sandbox directory.

> In iOS, if we just specify the audio filename without any path in the `Media` object constructor:
>
> ```
> var recordingMedia = new Media("test.wav" ...);
> ```
>
> Then `"test.wav"` will be saved under the `tmp` directory of our iOS app's Sandbox directory (if you do this, then your app users will be surprised to find, maybe after a while, that their saved audio files have been deleted as the `tmp` directory can be cleaned automatically by iOS, so be aware of this).
>
> Specifying the `"documents://"` prefix before the media filename in the `Media` object constructor will enforce the `Media` object to save the `"test.wav"` file under the app's `Documents` directory:
>
> ```
> var recordingMedia = new Media("documents://test.wav"
>     ...);
> ```

- In the final `else` block that represents the Windows Phone 8 case, `recordVoice()` is called without specifying any parameters that tell the `Media` object to save the audio file under the `app` local directory.

As you can see, we have to respect the nature of every supported platform in order to get the expected results.

The `stopRecordingVoice()` method simply stops recording the voice by calling the `stopRecord()` method of the `Media` object and finally releases the used media resource by calling the `release()` method of the `Media` object.

The `playVoice(filePath, playCallback)` method creates a `Media` object that points to the file specified in `filePath`, and then plays the file using the `play()` method of the `Media` object. The `cleanUpResources()` method makes sure that all of the used media resources are cleaned up.

The following code snippet shows the photo capturing and picking part of `MemoManager`:

```
getPhoto: function (capturingCallback, fromGallery) {
    var source = Camera.PictureSourceType.CAMERA;

    if (fromGallery) {
        source = Camera.PictureSourceType.PHOTOLIBRARY;
    }

    var captureSuccess = function(filePath) {
```

```
                    //Copy the captured image from tmp to app directory ...
                    var fileCallback = {};

                    fileCallback.copySuccess = function(newFilePath) {
                        capturingCallback.captureSuccess(newFilePath);
                    };

                    fileCallback.copyError = capturingCallback.captureError;

                    if (device.platform === "Android") {

                        //If it is Android then copy image file to App
          directory under SD Card root if available ...
                        fileManager.copyFileToDirectory(APP_BASE_DIRECTORY,
          filePath, true, fileCallback);
                    } else if (device.platform === "iOS") {

                        //If it is iOS then copy image file to Documents
          directory of the iOS app.
                        fileManager.copyFileToDirectory("", filePath, true,
          fileCallback);
                    } else {

                        //Else for Windows Phone 8, store the image file in
          the application's isolated store ...
                        capturingCallback.captureSuccess(filePath);
                    }
                };
            navigator.camera.getPicture(captureSuccess,
                capturingCallback.captureError,
                {
                    quality: 30,
                    destinationType: Camera.DestinationType.FILE_URI,
                    sourceType: source,
                    correctOrientation: true
                });
    }
```

The getPhoto(capturingCallback, fromGallery) method, is used to get the
photo by picking it from the device's gallery or by capturing it using the device's
camera, it checks the fromGallery parameter and if it is set to true, then the picture
source type is set to Camera.PictureSourceType.PHOTOLIBRARY, and if it is set to
false, the picture source type will be Camera.PictureSourceType.CAMERA.

A photo is obtained by calling the `navigator.camera.getPicture()` method specifying the following parameters in order:

- `captureSuccess`: This refers to the callback that will be invoked if the `getPicture()` operation succeeds

- `capturingCallback.captureError`: This refers to the callback that will be invoked if the `getPicture()` operation fails

- In the last parameter, the camera options are set (`destinationType` is set to `Camera.DestinationType.FILE_URI` to get the image file URI, `sourceType` is set to the picture source type, quality is set to `30`, and finally, `correctOrientation` is set to `true`)

`captureSuccess` checks the current device's platform to properly save the picture file:

- If the current platform is Android, then it copies the picture file to the `app` directory. In order to do this, a call to the `fileManager.copyFileToDirectory(APP_BASE_DIRECTORY, filePath, true, fileCallback)` method is performed. The `fileManager.copyFileToDirectory(dirPath, filePath, enforceUniqueName, fileCallback)` method has the following parameters placed in order:

    ◦ `dirPath`: This represents the full path of the destination directory to which the file will be copied.

    ◦ `filePath`: This represents the full path of the file to be copied.

    ◦ `enforceUniqueName`: If this parameter is set to `true`, this will enforce the copied file to have a new name in the destination directory.

    ◦ `fileCallback`: This represents a callback object that includes the two callback attributes (`copySuccess`, which will be called if the copy file operation succeeds, and `copyError`, which will be called if the copy file operation fails).

    If the file-copy operation succeeds, then `fileCallback.copySuccess` will be called. In this case, `fileCallback.copySuccess` calls `capturingCallback.captureSuccess(newFilePath)`, specifying the new copied file path (`newFilePath`) as a parameter.

- In iOS, the image file is copied to the app's `Documents` directory. In order to do this, a call to `fileManager.copyFileToDirectory("", filePath, true, fileCallback)` is performed.

In iOS, when any photo is captured using the device camera or picked from the device gallery using `navigator.camera.getPicture()`, it is placed under the `tmp` directory of the iOS app's Sandbox directory. If you want to access the captured image later, make sure to copy or move the captured image to the app's `Documents` directory as shown earlier.

- Finally, in the final `else` block that represents the Windows Phone 8 case, there is no need to do any file copy, as the image file (captured using the camera or picked from the device gallery) is automatically placed under the `app` local directory.

`FileManager` is very similar to the `FileManager` object discussed in *Chapter 5, Diving Deeper into the Cordova API* (refer to this chapter if you feel uncomfortable with the highlighted code in the following code snippet):

```
var FileManager = (function () {
    var instance;

    function createObject() {
        var FILE_BASE = "file:///";

        return {
            copyFileToDirectory: function (dirPath, filePath,
enforceUniqueName, fileCallback) {
                var directoryReady = function (dirEntry) {
                    if (filePath.indexOf(FILE_BASE) != 0) {
                        filePath = filePath.replace("file:/", FILE_
BASE);
                    }

                    window.resolveLocalFileSystemURL(filePath,
function(file) {
                        var filename = filePath.replace(/^.*[\\\/]/,
'');

                        if (enforceUniqueName) {
                            console.log("file name before: " +
filename);
                            filename = (new Date()).getTime() +
filename;
                            console.log("file name after: " +
filename);
                        }
```

```
                            file.copyTo(dirEntry, filename,
function(fileEntry) {
                                fileCallback.copySuccess(dirEntry.toURL()
+ filename);
                            }, fileCallback.copyError);
                    }, fileCallback.copyError);
                };

                var fileSystemReady = function(fileSystem) {
                    fileSystem.root.getDirectory(dirPath, {create:
true}, directoryReady);
                };

                window.requestFileSystem(LocalFileSystem.PERSISTENT,
0, fileSystemReady, fileCallback.copyError);
            },
            requestDirectory: function (dirPath, callback) {
                var directoryReady = function (dirEntry) {
                    callback.requestSuccess(dirEntry.toURL());
                };

                var fileSystemReady = function(fileSystem) {
                    fileSystem.root.getDirectory(dirPath, {create:
true}, directoryReady);
                };

                window.requestFileSystem(LocalFileSystem.PERSISTENT,
0, fileSystemReady, callback.requestError);
            }
        };
    };

    return {
        getInstance: function () {
            if (!instance) {
                instance = createObject();
            }

            return instance;
        }
    };
})();
```

Now that we are done with the model and API code of our Mega App, the next section will illustrate the Mega App's pages and view controllers.

The Mega App user interface

In Mega App, we have three main pages:

- "memoList": This page is the app's home page. It displays the different types of the user memos

- "memoCapture": This page is used to create, view, and edit a memo

- "about": This page is a simple app about page

The following code snippet shows the "memoList" page:

```
<div data-role="page" id="memoList">
    <div data-role="header" data-position="fixed" data-tap-
toggle="false">
        <a href="#about" data-role="button" data-icon="info" data-
mini="true">About</a>
        <h1>Memo List</h1>
        <a id="newMemo" data-role="button" data-
icon="plus">New</a>
    </div>
    <div data-role="content">
        <ul data-role="listview" id="memoListView">
        </ul>
        <div data-role="popup" id="memoTypeSelection">
            <ul data-role="listview" data-inset="true"
class="selectionMenu">
                <li data-role="divider">Memo Type</li>
                <li><a href="#memoCapture?newMemo=voice">Voice
Memo</a></li>
                <li><a href="#memoCapture?newMemo=photo">Photo
Memo</a></li>
            </ul>
        </div>
    </div>
    <div data-role="footer" data-position="fixed" data-tap-
toggle="false">
        <h1>
            <a href="#" data-role="button" data-icon="delete"
id="removeAllMemos">Remove All Memos</a>
        </h1>
    </div>
</div>
```

As shown in the preceding code, the `"memoList"` page contains the following:

- A page header that includes two buttons: the `"newMemo"` button to create a new memo and the `"About"` button to display the about page.

- Page content that includes:

  - `"memoListView"`: This is used to display the different user's saved memos.

  - `"memoTypeSelection"`: This pop up contains a list view that allows the user to select the memo type that the user wants to create. You might notice that every selection item in the list view forwards to the `"memoCapture"` page with a `newMemo` parameter that specifies whether the new memo's type is `"voice"` or `"photo"`.

- A page footer that includes:

  - `"removeAllMemos"`: This button is used to remove all the memos.

The following code snippet shows the `"memoList"` page's view controller in `memoList.js`:

```
(function() {
    var memoManager = MemoManager.getInstance();

    $(document).on("pageinit", "#memoList", function(e) {
        $("#removeAllMemos").on("tap", function(e) {
            e.preventDefault();
            memoManager.showConfirmationMessage("Are you sure you
want to remove all the memos?", deleteAllMemos);
        });

        $("#newMemo").on("tap", function(e) {
            e.preventDefault();
            $("#memoTypeSelection").popup("open");
        });

    });

    $(document).on("pageshow", "#memoList", function(e) {
        e.preventDefault();
        updateMemoList();
    });
```

```
function deleteAllMemos() {
    memoManager.removeAllMemos();
    updateMemoList();
}


function updateMemoList() {
    var memos = memoManager.getMemos(), memo;
    var type = "";

    $("#memoListView").empty();

    if (jQuery.isEmptyObject(memos)) {
        $("<li>No Memos Available</li>").
appendTo("#memoListView");
    } else {
        for (memo in memos) {
            if (memos[memo].type == "voice") {
                type = "audio";
            } else if (memos[memo].type == "photo") {
                type = "camera";
            }

            $("<li data-icon='" + type + "'><a
href='#memoCapture?memoID=" + memos[memo].id + "'>" +
                memos[memo].title + "</a></li>").
appendTo("#memoListView");
        }
    }

    $("#memoListView").listview('refresh');
}
})();
```

As shown in the preceding highlighted code snippet, the "pageinit" event handler registers the "tap" event handlers of the "removeAllMemos" and "newMemo" buttons.

In the "tap" event handler of the "removeAllMemos" button, a confirmation message is shown to the user, and if the user confirms, then a call to the deleteAllMemos() function is performed. The deleteAllMemos() function calls the removeAllMemos() method of MemoManager in order to remove all the app memos, and then, it calls the updateMemoList() method, which updates the memo list view with the saved memos.

The `updateMemoList()` method simply gets all the saved memos by calling the `memoManager.getMemos()` method and then renders every memo item as a list view item. Every list view item has an icon that is rendered based on its associated memo's type (`"voice"` or `"photo"`). When any list view item is clicked, it forwards to the `"memoCapture"` page, passing a `memoID` parameter in order to allow us to view and update the current memo details in the `"memoCapture"` page.

In the `"tap"` event handler of the `"newMemo"` button, the `"memoTypeSelection"` pop up is opened for the user to select either creating a voice memo or a photo memo. When a selection item of the `"memoTypeSelection"` list view is clicked, it forwards to the `"memoCapture"` page, passing a `newMemo` parameter in order to tell the `"memoCapture"` page whether the new memo's type is `"voice"` or `"photo"`.

In the `"pageshow"` event handler, `updateMemoList()` is called in order to display all of the saved memos in the page list view.

The following code snippet shows the `"memoCapture"` page:

```html
<div data-role="page" id="memoCapture">
    <div data-role="header">
        <a href="#memoList" data-role="button" data-icon="home">Home</a>
        <h1 id="memoCaptureTitle">Your Memo</h1>
        <a href="#" data-role="button" data-rel="back" data-icon="back">Back</a>
    </div>
    <div data-role="content">
        <input type="hidden" id="mid"/>
        <input type="hidden" id="mtype"/>
        <input type="hidden" id="location"/>

        <div data-role="ui-field-contain">
            <label for="mtime" id="mtime_label">Creation Time</label>
            <div name="mtime" id="mtime"></div>
        </div>

        <div data-role="ui-field-contain">
            <label for="title">Title</label>
            <input type="text" name="title" id="title"></input>
        </div>

        <div data-role="ui-field-contain">
            <label for="desc">Details</label>
```

```
            <textarea name="desc" id="desc"></textarea>
        </div>

        <div class="center-wrapper">
            <input type="button" id="getPhoto" data-icon="camera"
value="Get Photo" class="center-button" data-inline="true"/>
            <input type="button" id="recordVoice" data-
icon="audio" value="Record" class="center-button" data-
inline="true"/>
            <input type="button" id="playVoice" data-
icon="refresh" value="Playback" class="center-button" data-
inline="true"/><br/>
        </div>

        <input type="button" value="Save Memo" data-icon="check"
id="saveMemo"/>
        <input type="button" id="removeMemo" data-icon="delete"
value="Remove"/> <br/>

        <div class="memoPhoto">
            <img id="imageView" class="memoPhoto"></img>
        </div>

        <div data-role="popup" id="photoTypeSelection">
            <ul data-role="listview" data-inset="true"
class="selectionMenu">
                <li data-role="divider">Get Photo From</li>
                <li><a id="photoFromGallery" href="#">Gallery</a></li>
                <li><a id="photoFromCamera" href="#">Camera</a></li>
            </ul>
        </div>

        <div data-role="popup" id="recordVoiceDialog" data-
dismissible="false" class="recordVoicePopup">
            <div data-role="header">
                <h1>Recording</h1>
            </div>

            <div data-role="content">
                <div class="center-wrapper">
                    <div id="voiceDuration"></div>
                    <input type="button" id="stopRecordingVoice"
value="Stop Recording" class="center-button" data-inline="true"/>
                </div>
            </div>
```

```
            </div>
        </div>
    </div>
```

As shown in the preceding code, the `"memoCapture"` page contains the following:

- A page header.
- Page content that mainly includes:
    - `"title"`: This is the input field to enter the memo title (it should be empty when the user creates a new memo and should display the current memo title when the user opens an existing memo to view or update it).
    - `"desc"`: This is the text area field to enter the memo description (it should be empty when the user creates a new memo and should display the current memo description when the user opens an existing memo to view or update it).
    - `"mtime"`: This is the div that displays the time when the memo was created; this field will be displayed only when the user opens an existing memo to view or update it.
    - `"mid"`: This is the hidden field to store the memo ID.
    - `"mtype"`: This is the hidden field to store the memo type.
    - `"location"`: This is the hidden field to store the memo location.
    - `"getPhoto"`: This button is displayed if the memo type is `"photo"`, and it opens a `"photoTypeSelection"` pop up to allow the user to select a photo source.
    - `"photoTypeSelection"`: This pop up includes a list view to allow the user to select a photo source (`"Camera"` or `"Gallery"`). The `"photoTypeSelection"` pop up includes two list item links: `"photoFromGallery"`, which opens the device's gallery for the user to pick a photo from, and `"photoFromCamera"`, which launches the camera app for the user to capture a photo.
    - `"imageView"`: This image displays the captured camera image or the picked gallery image. `"imageView"` is displayed only if the memo type is `"photo"` and there is an available captured or picked image.
    - `"recordVoice"`: This button is displayed if the memo type is `"voice"`, and it opens the `"recordVoiceDialog"` dialog to allow the user to record a voice.

- ○ `"recordVoiceDialog"`: This dialog includes a `"voiceDuration"` div to display the voice-recording duration progress and a `"stopRecordingVoice"` button to stop recording the voice.

- ○ `"playVoice"`: This button plays a voice; it is displayed if the memo type is `"voice"` and there is a recorded voice to play.

- ○ `"saveMemo"`: This button saves or updates the voice or photo memo.

- ○ `"removeMemo"`: This button removes a saved memo. Note that this button will be shown only if the user opens an existing memo to view or update it.

The following code snippet shows the first part of the `"memoCapture"` page's view controller in `memoCapture.js`:

```
(function() {

    var memoManager = MemoManager.getInstance();
    var recInterval;

    $(document).on("pageinit", "#memoCapture", function(e) {
        e.preventDefault();

        $("#saveMemo").on("tap", function(e) {
            e.preventDefault();

            var memoItem = new MemoItem({
                "type": $("#mtype").val(),
                "title": $("#title").val() || "Untitled",
                "desc": $("#desc").val() || "",
                "location": $("#location").val() || "",
                "mtime":  $("#mtime").html() || new Date().
    toLocaleString(),
                "id": $("#mid").val() || null
            });

            memoManager.saveMemo(memoItem);

            $.mobile.changePage("#memoList");
        });

        $("#removeMemo").on("tap", function(e) {
            e.preventDefault();
```

```
        memoManager.showConfirmationMessage("Are you sure you
want to remove this memo?", removeCurrentMemo);
    });

    $("#recordVoice").on("tap", function(e) {
        e.preventDefault();

        var recordingCallback = {};

        recordingCallback.recordSuccess = handleRecordSuccess;
        recordingCallback.recordError = handleRecordError;

        memoManager.startRecordingVoice(recordingCallback);

        var recTime = 0;

        $("#voiceDuration").html("Duration: " + recTime + "
seconds");

        $("#recordVoiceDialog").popup("open");

        recInterval = setInterval(function() {
                                    recTime = recTime + 1;
                                    $("#voiceDuration").
html("Duration: " + recTime + " seconds");
                                }, 1000);
    });

    $("#recordVoiceDialog").on("popupafterclose", function(event,
ui) {
        clearInterval(recInterval);
        memoManager.stopRecordingVoice();
    });

    $("#stopRecordingVoice").on("tap", function(e) {
        e.preventDefault();
        $("#recordVoiceDialog").popup("close");
    });

    $("#playVoice").on("tap", function(e) {
        e.preventDefault();

        var playCallback = {};
```

```
            playCallback.playSuccess = handlePlaySuccess;
            playCallback.playError = handlePlayError;

            memoManager.playVoice($("#location").val(),
    playCallback);
        });

        $("#getPhoto").on("tap", function(e) {
            e.preventDefault();
            $("#photoTypeSelection").popup("open");
        });

        $("#photoFromGallery").on("tap", function(e) {
            e.preventDefault();
            $("#photoTypeSelection").popup("close");

            getPhoto(true);
        });

        $("#photoFromCamera").on("tap", function(e) {
            e.preventDefault();
            $("#photoTypeSelection").popup("close");

            getPhoto(false);
        });
    });

    function removeCurrentMemo() {
        memoManager.removeMemo($("#mid").val());
        $.mobile.changePage("#memoList");
    }

    function handleRecordSuccess(currentFilePath) {
        $("#location").val(currentFilePath);
        $("#playVoice").closest('.ui-btn').show();
    }
```

```
    function handleRecordError(error) {
        //log error in the console ...
    }

    function handlePlaySuccess() {
        console.log("Voice file is played successfully ...");
    }

    function handlePlayError(error) {
        //log error in the console ...
    }

    function getPhoto(fromGallery) {
        var capturingCallback = {};

        capturingCallback.captureSuccess = handleCaptureSuccess;
        capturingCallback.captureError = handleCaptureError;

        memoManager.getPhoto(capturingCallback, fromGallery);
    }

    function handleCaptureSuccess(currentFilePath) {
        $("#imageView").attr("src", currentFilePath);
        $("#imageView").show();
        $("#location").val(currentFilePath);
    }

    function handleCaptureError(message) {
        //log error in the console ...
    }

    // code is omitted for simplicity ...
})();
```

As shown in the preceding highlighted code snippet, the `"pageinit"` event handler registers the `"tap"` event handlers of `"saveMemo"`, `"removeMemo"`, `"recordVoice"`, `"stopRecordingVoice"`, `"playVoice"`, `"getPhoto"`, `"photoFromGallery"`, and `"photoFromCamera"`. It also registers the `"popupafterclose"` event handler of `"recordVoiceDialog"`.

The following table illustrates the "tap" event handlers of all of the previous mentioned UI elements:

UI element	Tap event handler description
The "saveMemo" button	1. An object of the MemoItem type is created and initialized with the UI input values of "mtype", "title", "desc", "location", "mtime", and "mid". 2. A call to memoManager.saveMemo() is performed; specifying memoItem as a parameter to save the memo. 3. The user is forwarded to the "memoList" page.
The "removeMemo" button	1. A confirmation message pops up for the user to confirm whether the memo needs to be removed. 2. If the user confirms, removeCurrentMemo() is called. 3. In removeCurrentMemo(), a call to memoManager.removeMemo() is performed; specifying $("#mid").val() as a parameter that represents the memo ID to be deleted. 4. The user is forwarded to the "memoList" page.

UI element	Tap event handler description
The "recordVoice" button	1. In order to start recording a voice, a call to memoManager.startRecordingVoice() is performed; specifying recordingCallback as a parameter. The recordingCallback parameter is an object that has a successful callback and error callback attributes (recordSuccess, which is set to handleRecordSuccess, and recordError, which is set to handleRecordError, respectively).
	2. The "recordVoiceDialog" pop up is opened and updated with the recording duration in seconds using a timer.
	3. When memoManager.startRecordingVoice() succeeds, handleRecordSuccess is called with the currentFilePath parameter (which represents the path of the audio file). In handleRecordSuccess, currentFilePath is saved in the "location" hidden field, and the "playVoice" button is shown.
	4. When memoManager.startRecordingVoice() fails, handleRecordError is called with an error parameter (which represents the operation error object). In handleRecordError, the error is simply logged.

UI element	Tap event handler description
The "stopRecordingVoice" button	This closes the "recordVoiceDialog" pop up. Closing the "recordVoiceDialog" pop up triggers the "popupafterclose" event of "recordVoiceDialog". This will execute the "popupafterclose" event handler of "recordVoiceDialog", which does the following: • Clears the recording duration timer. • Calls memoManager.stopRecordingVoice() to stop recording the audio.

The "playVoice" button	1. In order to play a recorded voice, a call to memoManager.playVoice() is performed; specifying the following parameters:
	
	   ○ $("#location").val(): This function call gets the location of the audio file to be played.
	
	   ○ playCallback: This is an object that has a success callback and error callback attributes (playSuccess, which is set to handlePlaySuccess, and playError, which is set to handlePlayError, respectively).
	
	2. In handlePlaySuccess and handlePlayError, the operations are simply logged in the console.

The "getPhoto" button	This opens the "photoTypeSelection" pop up to allow the user to choose the picture source: "Camera" or "Gallery".

UI element	Tap event handler description

The "photoFromGallery" and "photoFromCamera" anchors	1. This calls getPhoto() specifying the fromGallery parameter with true in case of "photoFromGallery" and with false in case of "photoFromCamera".
	
	2. In order to get a photo using a camera or from the device gallery, a call to memoManager.getPhoto() is performed; specifying the following parameters in order:
	
	   ° capturingCallback: This is an object that has a success callback and error callback attributes (captureSuccess, which is set to handleCaptureSuccess, and captureError, which is set to handleCaptureError, respectively).
	
	   ° fromGallery: This determines whether to get the photo from gallery (if it is set to true) or using camera (if it is set to false).
	
	3. When memoManager.getPhoto() succeeds, handleCaptureSuccess is called with the currentFilePath parameter (which represents the path of the photo file). In handleCaptureSuccess, currentFilePath is saved in the "location" hidden field, and "imageView" shows the current photo file.
	
	4. When memoManager.getPhoto() fails, handleCaptureError is called with a message error parameter. In handleCaptureError, the error is simply logged.

The following code snippet shows the second part of the "`memoCapture`" page view controller:

```
(function() {
    var memoManager = MemoManager.getInstance();

    // ...

    $(document).on("pageshow", "#memoCapture", function(e) {
        e.preventDefault();

        var memoID = ($.mobile.pageData && $.mobile.pageData.memoID)
? $.mobile.pageData.memoID : null;
        var memoType = ($.mobile.pageData && $.mobile.pageData.
newMemo) ? $.mobile.pageData.newMemo : null;
        var memoItem = null;
        var isNew = true;

        if (memoID) {

            //Update Memo
            memoItem = memoManager.getMemoDetails(memoID);
            isNew = false;

            //Change title
            $("#memoCaptureTitle").html("Edit " + (memoItem.type ?
memoItem.type : "") + " memo");
        } else {

            //Create a new Memo
            memoItem = new MemoItem({"type": memoType});

            //Change title
            $("#memoCaptureTitle").html("New " + (memoType ? memoType
: "") + " memo");
        }

        initFields(memoItem, isNew);
    });

    $(document).on("pagebeforehide", "#memoCapture", function(e) {
        memoManager.cleanUpResources();
    });
```

```javascript
function initFields(memoItem, isNew) {
    $("#mid").val(memoItem.id);
    $("#mtype").val(memoItem.type);
    $("#title").val(memoItem.title);
    $("#desc").val(memoItem.desc);
    $("#location").val(memoItem.location);
    $("#mtime").html(memoItem.mtime);

    $("#recordVoice").closest('.ui-btn').hide();
    $("#getPhoto").closest('.ui-btn').hide();
    $("#playVoice").closest('.ui-btn').hide();
    $("#removeMemo").closest('.ui-btn').hide();
    $("#imageView").hide();
    $("#imageView").attr("src", "");

    if (! isNew) {
        $("#removeMemo").closest('.ui-btn').show();
        $("#mtime").show();
        $("#mtime_label").show();
    } else {
        $("#mtime").hide();
        $("#mtime_label").hide();
    }

    if (memoItem.type == "voice") {
        $("#recordVoice").closest('.ui-btn').show();

        if (memoItem.location && memoItem.location.length > 0)
{
            $("#playVoice").closest('.ui-btn').show();
        }
    } else if (memoItem.type == "photo") {
        $("#getPhoto").closest('.ui-btn').show();

        if (memoItem.location && memoItem.location.length > 0)
{
            $("#imageView").show();
            $("#imageView").attr("src", memoItem.location);
        }
    }
}

// ...
})();
```

It is important to know that the `"memoCapture"` page works in the following two modes:

- **Creating a new memo mode**: In this case, a `newMemo` parameter is sent to the page from the caller. The `newMemo` parameter holds the type of new memo that the caller wants to create.

- **Editing an existing memo mode**: In this case, a `memoID` parameter is sent to the page from the caller. The `memoID` parameter refers to the existing memo identifier.

As shown in the preceding highlighted code snippet, in the `"pageshow"` event handler, both `memoID` and `memoType` are retrieved, thanks to the jQuery Mobile page parameters plugin (for more information about this plugin, refer to *Chapter 4, Cordova API in Action*).

If `memoID` is available, this means that the `"memoCapture"` page is required to work in the edit mode, which implies that `"memoCapture"` needs to:

- Get the existing memo details by calling `memoManager.getMemoDetails(memoID)`

- Change the page title to `"Edit xxx"` (for example, `"Edit photo memo"`)

If `memoID` is not available, this means that the `"memoCapture"` page is in the **create new memo** mode, which implies that `"memoCapture"` needs to:

- Create a new `MemoItem` object by setting the type to `memoType` (`"voice"` or `"photo"`)

- Change the page title to `"New xxx"` (for example, `"New voice memo"`)

The fields are then populated with data and are shown based on the current page mode using the `initFields()` method.

Finally, the `"pagebeforehide"` event handler ensures that all the media resources are cleaned up (before transitioning away from the `"memoCapture"` page) by calling `memoManager.cleanUpResources()`.

Finalizing Mega App

The last part that we need to check in Mega App is `index.html`; the following code snippet shows the most important part of the `index.html` page:

```html
<html>
    <head>
        <meta charset="utf-8" />
        <meta name="format-detection" content="telephone=no" />
```

```
        <meta name="viewport" content="user-scalable=no, initial-
scale=1, maximum-scale=1, minimum-scale=1, width=device-width,
height=device-height, target-densitydpi=device-dpi" />
        <link rel="stylesheet" type="text/css" href="css/app.css"
/>
        <link rel="stylesheet" href="jqueryMobile/jquery.mobile-
1.4.0.min.css">

        <script src="jqueryMobile/jquery-1.10.2.min.js"></script>

    <script>
        var deviceReadyDeferred = $.Deferred();
        var jqmReadyDeferred = $.Deferred();

        $(document).ready(function() {
            document.addEventListener("deviceready", function() {
                deviceReadyDeferred.resolve();
            }, false);
        });

        $(document).on("mobileinit", function () {
            jqmReadyDeferred.resolve();
        });

        $.when(deviceReadyDeferred, jqmReadyDeferred).
then(function () {

            //Now everything loads fine, you can safely go to the
app home ...
            $.mobile.changePage("#memoList");
        });
    </script>

        <script src="jqueryMobile/jquery.mobile-1.4.0.min.js"></
script>
        <script src="jqueryMobile/jqm.page.params.js"></script>

        <title>Mega</title>
    </head>
    <body>
        <div id="loading" data-role="page">
            <div class="center-screen">Please wait ...</div>
        </div>
```

```
            <!-- App pages omitted here for simplicity ... --->

            <script type="text/javascript" src="cordova.js"></script>

            <!-- Application JS files -->
            <script type="text/javascript" src="js/common.js"></script>
            <script type="text/javascript" src="js/api/FileManager.js"></
    script>
            <script type="text/javascript" src="js/api/MemoManager.js"></
    script>

            <script type="text/javascript" src="js/model/MemoItem.js"></
    script>

            <script type="text/javascript" src="js/vc/memoList.js"></
    script>
            <script type="text/javascript" src="js/vc/memoCapture.js"></
    script>
        </body>
</html>
```

As shown in the preceding code, `index.html` includes the following:

- App custom CSS file (`app.css`)
- jQuery Mobile library files
- A jQuery Mobile page params plugin file (`jqm.page.params.js`)
- A CommonJS (`common.js`) file, app managers, and app view controllers'
  JS files

The preceding highlighted code makes sure that Apache Cordova and jQuery Mobile
are loaded correctly (using the jQuery `Deferred` object) before proceeding to the
app pages. If Apache Cordova and jQuery Mobile are loaded correctly, then the
user will leave the `"loading"` page and be forwarded to the app's home page (the
`"memoList"` page) to start using the app.

As you know from *Chapter 5, Diving Deeper into the Cordova API*, in order to boost the
performance of jQuery Mobile 1.4 with Cordova, it is recommended that you disable
the transition effects. The `common.js` file applies this tip in Mega App, as shown in
the following code snippet:

```
$.mobile.defaultPageTransition   = 'none';
$.mobile.defaultDialogTransition = 'none';
$.mobile.buttonMarkup.hoverDelay = 0;
```

In order to exit the application when the user presses the back button (which exists on Android and Windows Phone 8 devices) on the app's home page, common.js also implements this behavior. It uses the same technique used in the *Finalizing the Cordova Exhibition app* section in *Chapter 5, Diving Deeper into the Cordova API.*

Deploying and running Mega App

Now, we can deploy our Mega App to our Android, iOS, and Windows Phone 8 devices to see the app in action. All of the screenshots that illustrated the Mega App functionality in the *Mega App specification/wireframes* section were captured from a real iPhone 5 device.

The following screenshot shows the deployed Mega App on a real Android Samsung Galaxy Tab 3 device:

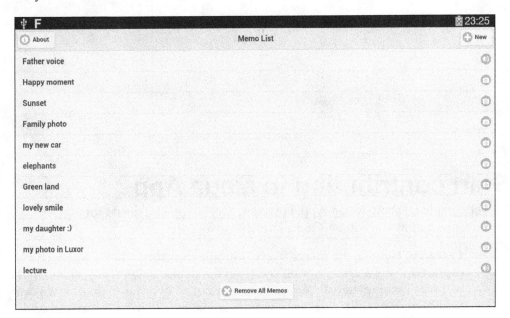

The following screenshot shows the deployed Mega App on a real Windows Phone 8 device:

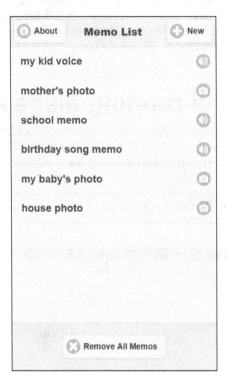

Start contributing to Mega App

This chapter is all about Mega App; however, Mega App still needs some improvements that you can add to it. They are as follows:

- Instead of copying the image files to our `app` directory when a photo is captured using a camera or picked from the device gallery, we can move the picture file completely to avoid file redundancy. In order to do this, we can simply replace `file.copyTo()` with `file.moveTo()` in `FileManager` and change the method name to `moveFileToDirectory`.

- Instead of only deleting the file reference in the Local Storage when removing a memo (or memos) as requested by the `removeMemo()` or `removeAllMemos()` methods of `MemoManager`, we can delete the physical files as well using the `remove()` method of the `FileEntry` Cordova object and adding this to a new method (`deleteFile`) of `FileManager`. The `deleteFile()` method will be called by the `removeMemo()` and `removeAllMemos()` methods to make sure that the memo files are completely removed from the device's filesystem.

This is a good chance for you to improve Mega App by making these updates. Let's go and download the App source code from GitHub at `https://github.com/hazems/cordova-mega-app` and start playing with it. You can also download the source code of this chapter from the book page on the Packt Publishing website.

Summary

This chapter showed you how to utilize Apache Cordova and jQuery Mobile in order to design and develop a useful mobile app that respects the nature of different mobile platforms (iOS, Android, and Windows Phone 8).

Index

Thank you for buying
JavaScript Mobile Application Development

About Packt Publishing

Packt, pronounced 'packed', published its first book "*Mastering phpMyAdmin for Effective MySQL Management*" in April 2004 and subsequently continued to specialize in publishing highly focused books on specific technologies and solutions.

Our books and publications share the experiences of your fellow IT professionals in adapting and customizing today's systems, applications, and frameworks. Our solution based books give you the knowledge and power to customize the software and technologies you're using to get the job done. Packt books are more specific and less general than the IT books you have seen in the past. Our unique business model allows us to bring you more focused information, giving you more of what you need to know, and less of what you don't.

Packt is a modern, yet unique publishing company, which focuses on producing quality, cutting-edge books for communities of developers, administrators, and newbies alike. For more information, please visit our website: www.packtpub.com.

About Packt Open Source

In 2010, Packt launched two new brands, Packt Open Source and Packt Enterprise, in order to continue its focus on specialization. This book is part of the Packt Open Source brand, home to books published on software built around Open Source licenses, and offering information to anybody from advanced developers to budding web designers. The Open Source brand also runs Packt's Open Source Royalty Scheme, by which Packt gives a royalty to each Open Source project about whose software a book is sold.

Writing for Packt

We welcome all inquiries from people who are interested in authoring. Book proposals should be sent to author@packtpub.com. If your book idea is still at an early stage and you would like to discuss it first before writing a formal book proposal, contact us; one of our commissioning editors will get in touch with you.

We're not just looking for published authors; if you have strong technical skills but no writing experience, our experienced editors can help you develop a writing career, or simply get some additional reward for your expertise.

Creating Mobile Apps with jQuery Mobile

ISBN: 978-1-78216-006-9   Paperback: 254 pages

Learn to make practical, unique, real-world sites that span a variety of industries and technologies with the world's most popular mobile development library

1. Write less, do more: learn to apply the jQuery motto to quickly craft creative sites that work on any smartphone and even not-so-smart phones.

2. Learn to leverage HTML5 audio and video, geolocation, Twitter, Flickr, blogs, Reddit, Google maps, content management system, and much more.

3. All examples are either in use in the real world or were used as examples to win business across several industries.

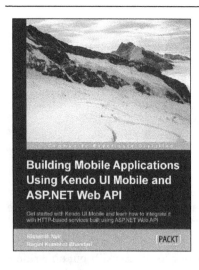

Building Mobile Applications Using Kendo UI Mobile and ASP.NET Web API

ISBN: 978-1-78216-092-2   Paperback: 256 pages

Get started with Kendo UI Mobile and learn how to integrate it with HTTP-based services built using ASP.NET Web API

1. Learn the basics of developing mobile applications using HTML5 and create an end-to-end mobile application from scratch.

2. Discover all about Kendo UI Mobile, ASP.NET Web API, and how to integrate them.

3. Get your hands dirty in a jiffy with 50+ jsFiddle examples.

Please check **www.PacktPub.com** for information on our titles

jQuery Mobile First Look

ISBN: 978-1-84951-590-0 Paperback: 216 pages

Discover the endless possibilities offered by jQuery Mobile for rapid mobile web development

1. Easily create your mobile web applications from scratch with jQuery Mobile.

2. Learn the important elements of the framework and mobile web development best practices.

3. Customize elements and widgets to match your desired style.

jQuery Mobile Web Development Essentials

Second Edition

ISBN: 978-1-78216-789-1 Paperback: 242 pages

Build mobile-optimized websites using the simple, practical, and powerful jQuery-based framework

1. Create websites that work beautifully on a wide range of mobile devices.

2. Develop your own jQuery Mobile project with the help of three sample applications.

3. Packed with easy-to-follow examples and clear explanations of how to easily build mobile-optimized websites.

Please check **www.PacktPub.com** for information on our titles